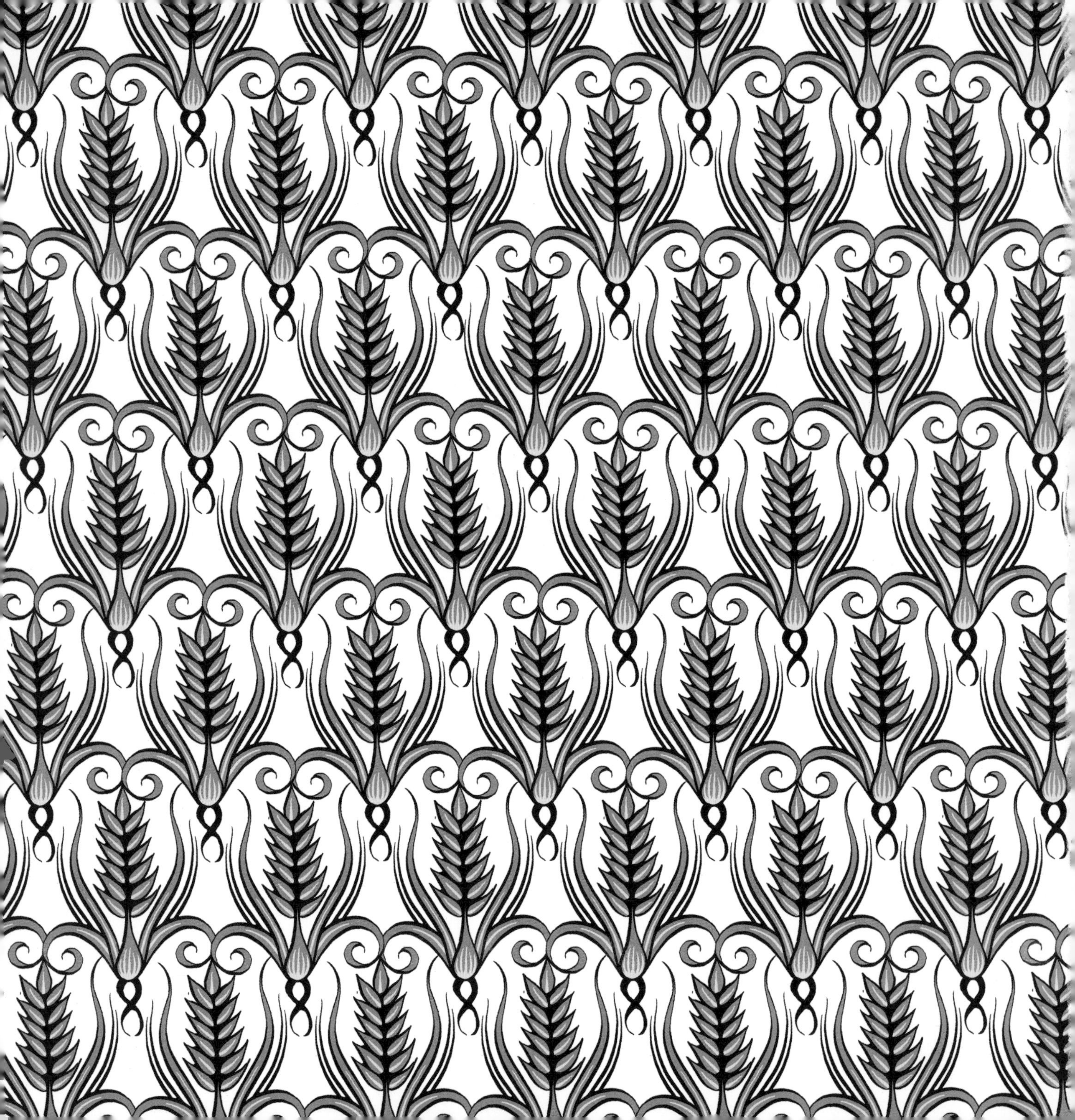

WOODY GUTHRIE

AND THE DUST BOWL BALLADS

THE RIME OF THE
MODERN
MARINER

WOODY GUTHRIE
AND THE DUST BOWL BALLADS

by nick hayes

Abrams ComicArts · New York

Library of Congress Control Number: 2015946818

ISBN: 978-1-4197-1945-5

Printed and bound in China
10 9 8 7 6 5 4 3 2 1

THE ART OF BOOKS SINCE 1949
115 West 18th Street
New York, NY 10011
www.abramsbooks.com

for
Benedict & Katherine

"What is this you call property? It cannot be the earth. For the land is our mother, nourishing all her children, beasts, birds, fish, and all men. The woods, the streams, everything on it belongs to everybody and is for the use of all. How can one man say it belongs to him only?"

—Massasoit

PIKKITTTYTIKKITYT

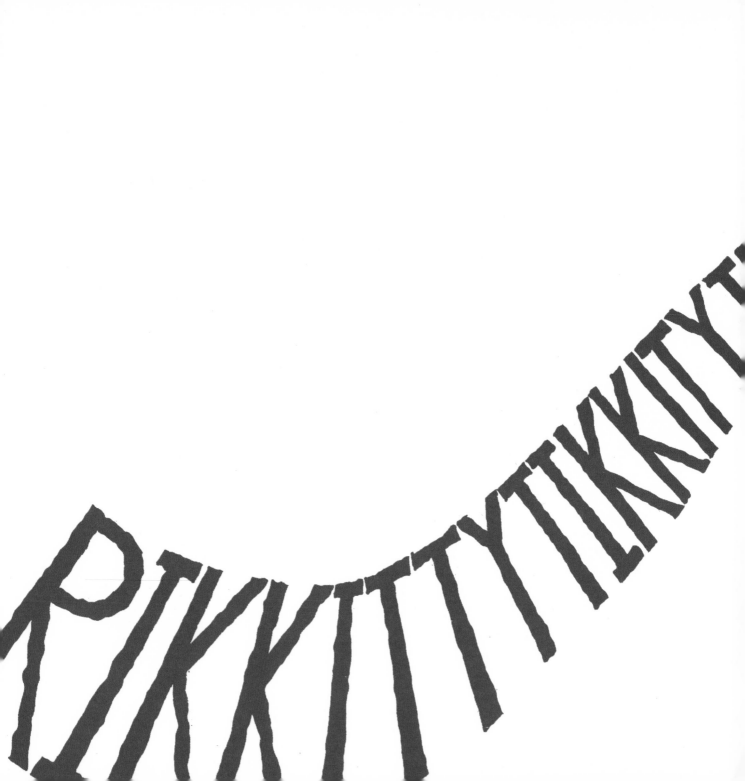

CHAPTER 1

So Pa upped our sticks, and sent us on the move 'n' go agin, and we followed that boom up the highway...and we got ourselves here.

Well, y' cain't be in our gang—we got more new fellers than a corner of spider's eggs—school's crammed, gang's rammed, there's more boom than room in this ol' town...

What IS that noise?

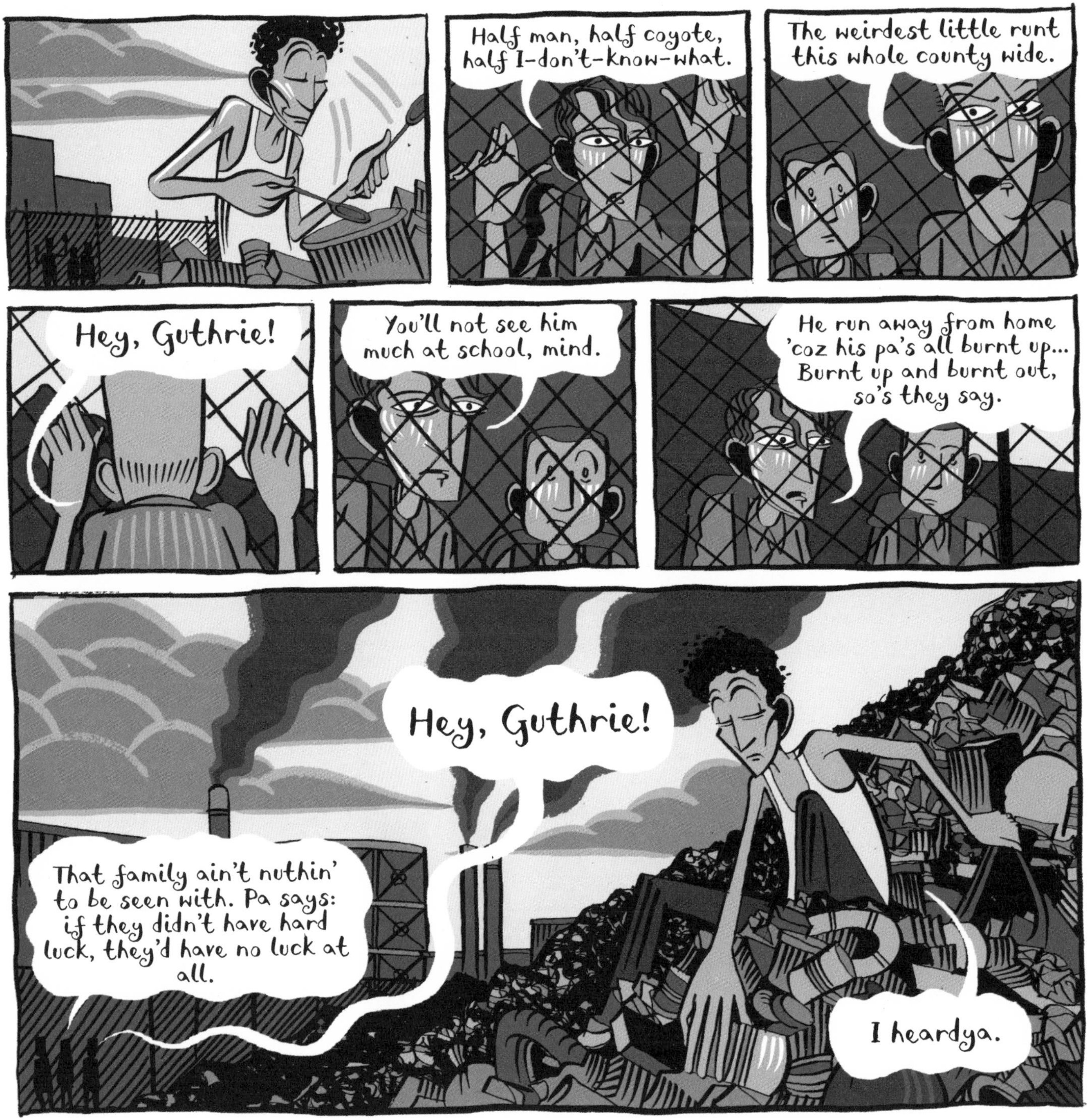
Half man, half coyote, half I-don't-know-what.
The weirdest little runt this whole county wide.
Hey, Guthrie!
You'll not see him much at school, mind.
He run away from home 'coz his pa's all burnt up... Burnt up and burnt out, so's they say.
Hey, Guthrie!
That family ain't nuthin' to be seen with. Pa says: if they didn't have hard luck, they'd have no luck at all.
I heardya.

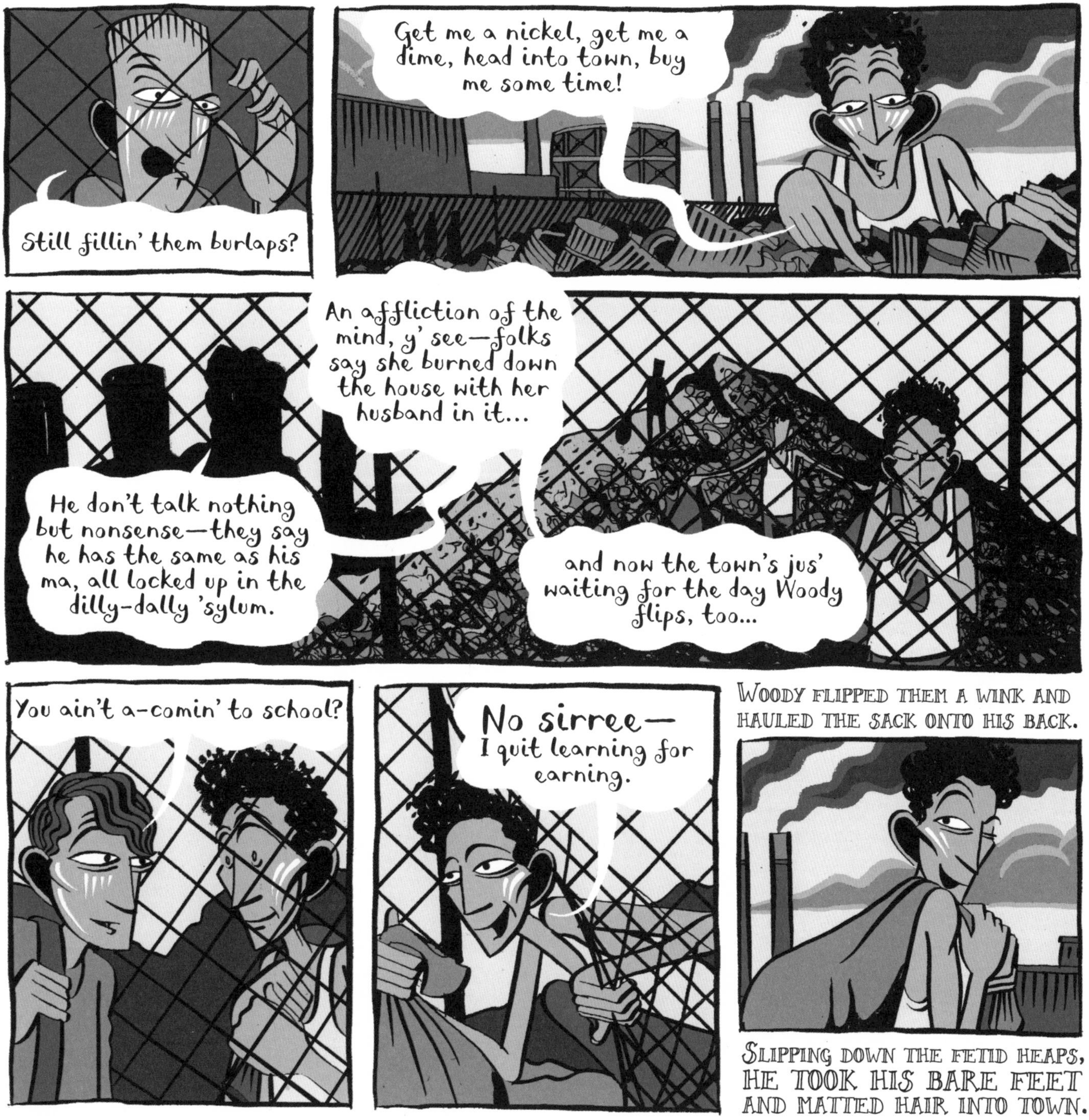

Still fillin' them burlaps?
Get me a nickel, get me a dime, head into town, buy me some time!
He don't talk nothing but nonsense—they say he has the same as his ma, all locked up in the dilly-dally 'sylum.
An affliction of the mind, y' see—folks say she burned down the house with her husband in it...
and now the town's jus' waiting for the day Woody flips, too...
You ain't a-comin' to school?
No sirree— I quit learning for earning.
WOODY FLIPPED THEM A WINK AND HAULED THE SACK ONTO HIS BACK.
SLIPPING DOWN THE FETID HEAPS, HE TOOK HIS BARE FEET AND MATTED HAIR INTO TOWN.

EVEN AT THAT TIME IN THE MORNING, THE WHOLE TOWN WAS A MILLING MORASS OF ROUGHNECKS AND ROUSTABOUTS—WORKERS FROM THE FOUR CORNERS OF AMERICA WHO HAD FLOCKED TO THIS PROMISE OF A HASTY BUCK.

A WHILE BACK, THEY'D STRUCK OIL.

AND SUDDENLY THE TOWN WAS ANOTHER GASOLINE LAMP LIGHTING UP THE LAND...

ATTRACTING ALL MANNER OF CREATURES TO BUZZ, WHIR, AND FLITTER AROUND ITS GLOW...

TILL THE FUEL RAN OUT.

FIRST CAME THE MONEYMEN—THE PROSPECTORS—WITH THEIR WAIST-COATS, POCKET WATCHES, AND GREASE-TIPPED MUSTACHES. THEY DRILLED BORES INTO THE GROUND, TESTED ITS WORTH, PREDICTED ITS VALUE, AND DISAPPEARED TO SIGN CHECKS UP NORTH.

THEY BOUGHT IT ALL.

THEN CAME THE TOOL PUSHERS, THE DRILLERS, THE GINZELS, DERRICK-HANDS, MOTORMEN, AND LEAD HANDS OF THE OIL TRADE,

THE GRIT-GRAINED, GREASE-STAINED, CREASED FACES OF THE LUMBERMEN AND TRUCKERS SETTING UP SHOP, IMPORTING THE SUPPLIES,

AND PUTTING MEN ON THE CORNER, DISTRIBUTING HANDBILLS, PROMISING WORK:

A notice to all the men of this purty town! A new boom is now! Its rig builders! Its carpenters! Its nail drivers, screw-drivers, mule drivers, and truck drivers! We need your manly strength, your broad shoulders, and your big, broad smiles. Let's get this oil field built—write your name and win your fame!

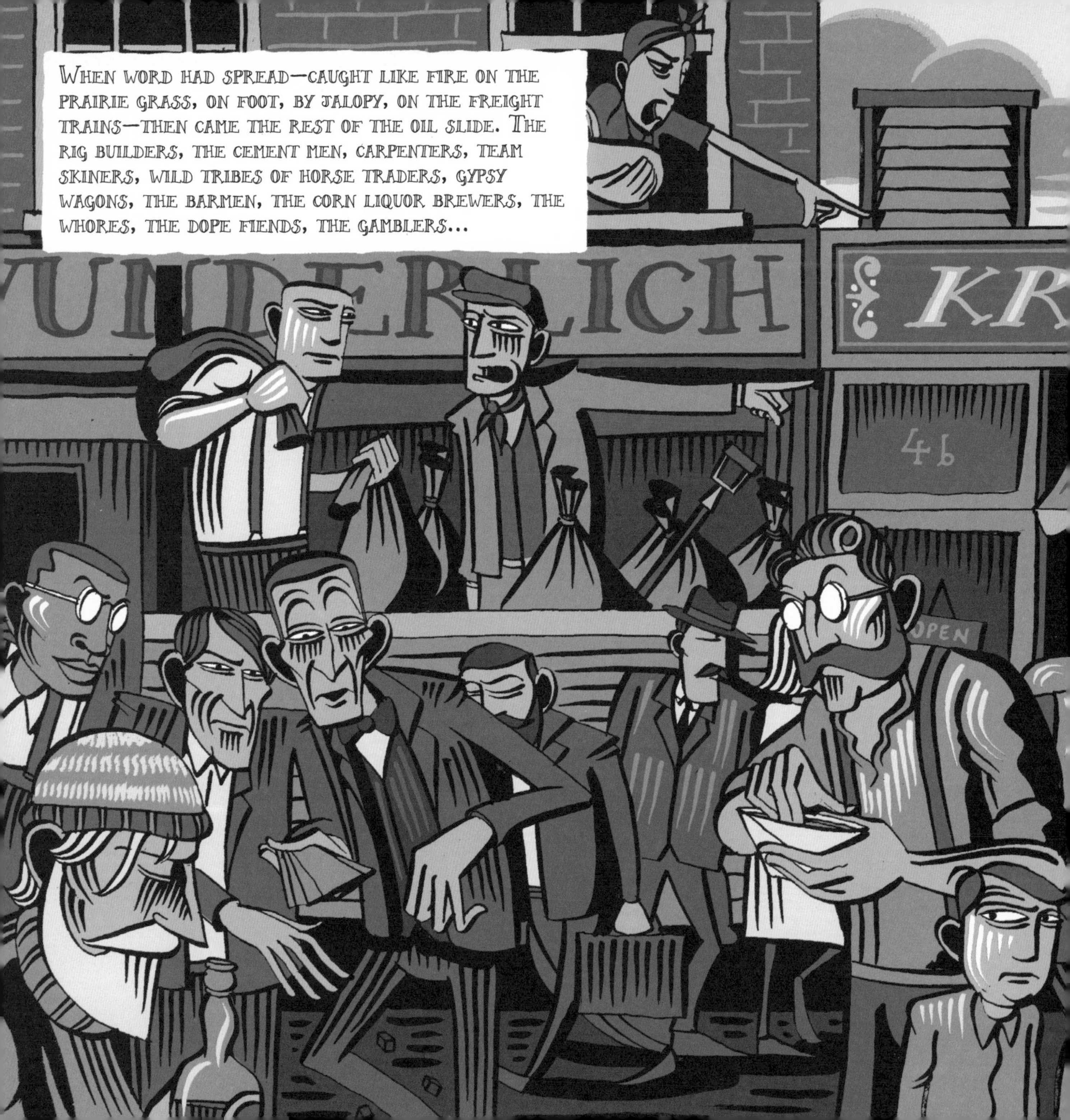
WHEN WORD HAD SPREAD—CAUGHT LIKE FIRE ON THE PRAIRIE GRASS, ON FOOT, BY JALOPY, ON THE FREIGHT TRAINS—THEN CAME THE REST OF THE OIL SLIDE. THE RIG BUILDERS, THE CEMENT MEN, CARPENTERS, TEAM SKINERS, WILD TRIBES OF HORSE TRADERS, GYPSY WAGONS, THE BARMEN, THE CORN LIQUOR BREWERS, THE WHORES, THE DOPE FIENDS, THE GAMBLERS...
WUNDERLICH
& KR
46
OPEN

THEY ALL FLOODED THROUGH THE TOWN, TEETH GRITTED INTO SMILES OR SNARLS, FOR THIS WAS THEIR MOMENT—THIS NOW, AT LAST, WAS THEIR TIME:

THEY WOULD MAKE THEIR FORTUNES WITH THIS BOOM, STRIKE IT LUCKY, AND RETIRE ON FARMS IN THE LUSH HILLS OF CALIFORNIA, SOME TWENTY YEARS HENCE, HAVING MADE SOMETHING OF THEMSELVES.

TODAY ON THE HIGH STREET, THE SWELTER AND FERVOR OF THIS CAPITALIST CARNIVAL WAS IN FULL SWING, AND THERE WAS SUCH A FRENZY OF ACTIVITY, SUCH A RUBBING OF SHOULDERS AND ELBOWS, THAT IT SEEMED TO HEAT THE AIR ITSELF, AND DRIVE THE SUN HIGH INTO THE SKY JUST FOR IT TO CATCH A BREEZE.

WOODY SCUTTLED THROUGH THIS TWISTED MUSCLE OF COMMERCE,

DEPOSITED HIS SACK FULL OF TIN AND COPPER PIPES,

AND MADE HIS NICKEL.

A SACK OF METAL FOR A COIN.

WANDERING AROUND THE BACK ALLEYS, BELLY GRUMBLING, HE WONDERED ON HIS OLD MAN, CHARLEY GUTHRIE, OUT IN PAMPA.

WORD WAS, HE WAS BACK ON HIS FEET.

AND IT WAS THEN THAT WOODY HEARD IT.

A LOW SUCK OF AIR THAT RANG HIS EARS RAW, AND LEFT THEM RINGING.

LIKE A FREIGHT-TRAIN WHISTLE, BUT LOWER,

LIKE A SEPIA PHOTO OF THE WHISTLE'S BLARE.

AND THEN IT CAME AGAIN, A LOW BENT SUCK OF AIR, THIS TIME FOLLOWED BY A CHUKKA-CHUKKA RHYTHM, LIKE A CARRIAGE OF WHEELS ON A STEEL RAIL, THE FLATWHEEL HAMMERING ON AND OFF, SYNCOPATED, JERKY.

MESMERIZED, AN ELECTRIC SHIVER RUNNING FROM HIS SPINE TO THE TIPS OF HIS FINGERS, HE TURNED THE CORNER OF THE BARBERSHOP, AND THERE, SITTING ON THE GROUND, WAS A BAREFOOT, STRINGY SHOE-SHINER, SUCKING ON A HARMONICA.

MISTER!

That there is undoubtedly the lonesomest line of music that I ever run into my whole life.

WHERE in the WORLD did you learn it?

Hell! There ain't no learning to it. This 'ere is ear music. I just lay here and listen to the railroad whistle, and whatever it say, I say it, too.

AND WITH THAT, WOODY WAS HOOKED. NO LESSONS, NO RULES, NO RIGHTS OR WRONGS, NO GETTING IT STRAIGHT OR CLEANING IT UP, JUST LISTENING AND REPEATING, HEARING AND SAYING.

AND AS THE DAYS PASSED, AND THE WEEKS ROLLED WITH THEM, WOODY WOULD RETURN TO THAT SPOT, HELPING THE SHOE-SHINER POLISH THE DUSTY SHOES OF OKEMAH.

HE WOULD HOLD THAT OLD HARMONICA, KNOCK THE SPIT FROM IT ON HIS THIGH, AND TRY HIS TONGUE AT THAT TRAIN RHYTHM.

There in't no theory in the world that can get you closer to sucking a bend in those holes. You just gotta try it, and try agin. Try it twice more and then you'll have it.

AND SO HE SUCKED AND HE BLEW, AND HE SUCKED AND HE BLEW, AND HE GOT CLOSER AND CLOSER TO IT.

WOODY HAD NEVER SAVED FOR ANYTHING IN HIS LIFE BEFORE, AND RARELY WOULD AGAIN, BUT FOR THE NEXT MONTH OR SO, EVERY NICKEL HE EARNED FROM THE SCRAP HEAPS WENT INTO HIS CIGAR BOX UNDER THE FLOORBOARDS OF MRS. ATKINS'S SHACK, WHERE HE'D BEEN HIDING OUT THE LAST SIX MONTHS.

HE KEPT A CLOSE EYE ON THE PAWNSHOP, WHICH WAS THE BUSIEST STORE IN TOWN,

AND WHEN EVERY DAY THOSE TRAINS RATTLED BY, HIS TONGUE AND LUNGS FOUND THE RHYTHM, AND WHEN THAT WHISTLE SOUNDED, ITS PITCH PULLED DOWN BY THE BEND IN THE RAILS AS THEY TOOK THE TRAIN OUT OF OKEMAH, HE SUCKED IT FAREWELL. AND FINALLY HE HAD IT.

CRAMMED WITH PEOPLE'S BELONGINGS AS THEY HEADED OUT FOR A NEW BOOM, AND THRONGING WITH THOSE NEW IN TOWN

WHO FANCIED THAT THIS, RIGHT NOW, WAS THEIR TIME.

AND ONE DAY,

IT WAS THERE.

A HARMONICA IN THE KEY OF G, WOOD SLATS AND A TIN COVER, TWO LOOSE SCREWS HOLDING IT ON EITHER SIDE, EMBOSSED WITH A STEAM PADDLE BOAT, GLEAMING IN THE WINDOW. AND WITH THE MOUTH HARP IN HIS HAND, HE TORE BACK TO THE SHACK ON THE EDGE OF TOWN, SUCKING AND BLOWING IT ALL THE WAY. MRS. ATKINS HAD BEEN ONE OF THOSE TOWN CRONIES, THE WITCHES OF OLD, SOMEONE THEY WOULD HAVE BURNED TWO HUNDRED YEARS EARLIER.

NO ONE QUITE UNDERSTOOD HER, THEY CALLED HER HALFWAY BETWEEN CUCKOO AND KOOKY, AND THEY LEFT HER WELL ALONE. AND FOR THIS, WOODY HAD ALWAYS ADMIRED HER.

THE WAY SHE WORE HER SUNDAY BEST TO GET THE GROCERIES,

THE WAY SHE TOOK HER WALKS LATE AT NIGHT,

THE WAY SHE DID AS SHE PLEASED AND DIDN'T GIVE TWO COYOTE HOOTS ABOUT WHAT THE REST OF THE TOWN THOUGHT.

THIS APPEALED TO WOODY. THIS CHIMED.

AND SO, SHORTLY AFTER WOODY'S FATHER HAD GONE TO PAMPA TO RECUPERATE, SHORTLY AFTER HIS MOTHER HAD BEEN ADMITTED TO THE HOSPITAL,

WHEN MRS. ATKINS HAD ONE DAY SUDDENLY DISAPPEARED FROM TOWN,

WOODY HAD MOVED INTO HER SHACK, AS IF IT WERE FAMILIAR WITH OUTCASTS, AS IF IT KNEW WHAT TO DO WITH THE SNIPING COMMENTS THAT FOLLOWED HIM UP THE HILL.

AND HE SAT THERE NOW, AS DUSK SOFTENED THE DAY, WATCHING THE FLUMES OF SMOKE PUMP FROM THE OIL DERRICKS, AND HEARD THE DISTANT CLATTER AND CONVERSATION OF ANOTHER WORKING DAY COMING TO ITS CLOSE.

OKEMAH WAS SURROUNDED BY DRILLING STATIONS, EACH THUMPING AND PUMPING AWAY AT THE BEDROCK, POUNDING THE EARTH FOR ALL IT WAS WORTH. IT WAS AS IF THEY HAD ARMORED THE LAND, CASED IT IN STEEL, PIERCED IT AND DRAINED IT OF ITS BLACK BLOOD.

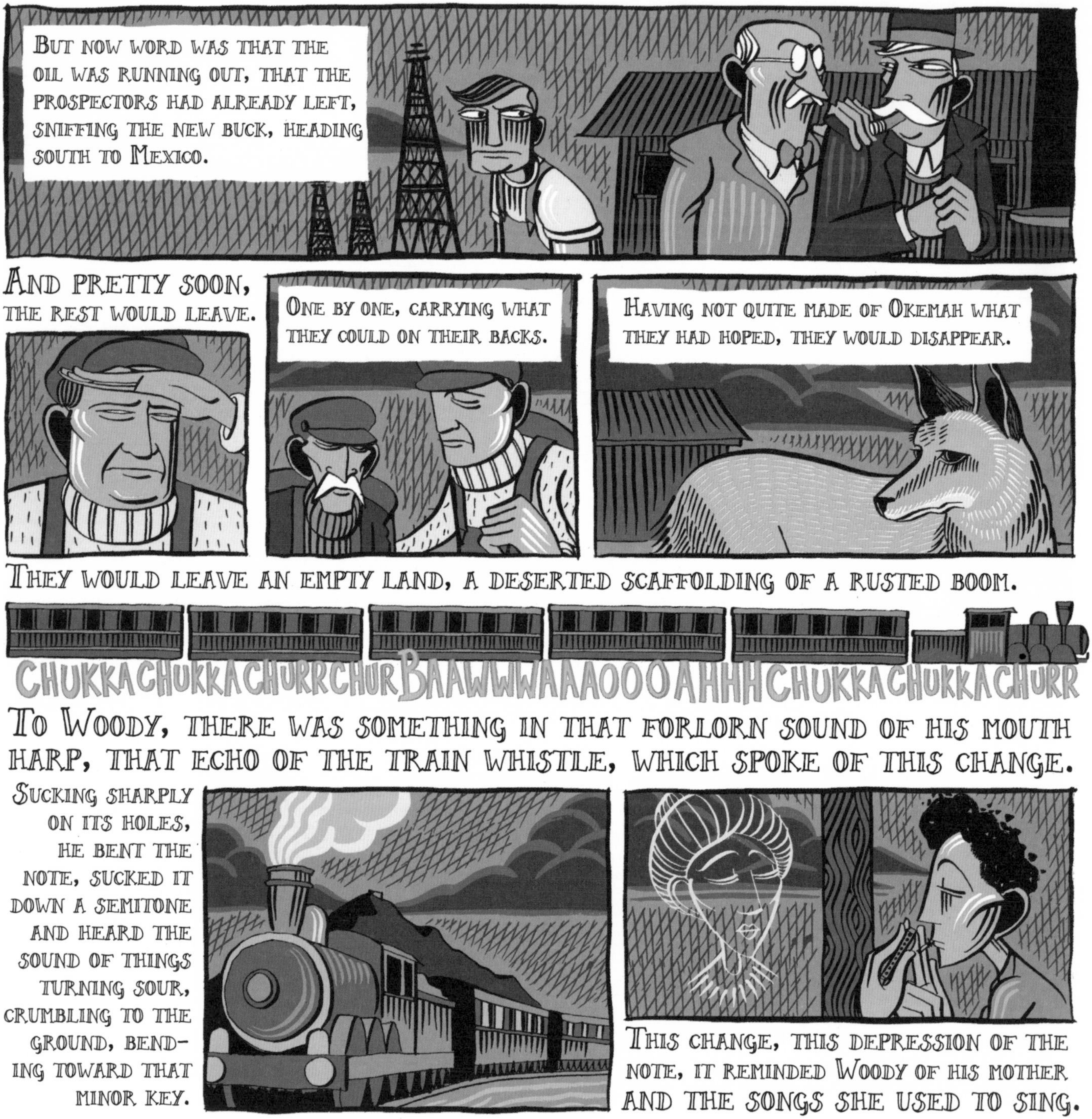
BUT NOW WORD WAS THAT THE OIL WAS RUNNING OUT, THAT THE PROSPECTORS HAD ALREADY LEFT, SNIFFING THE NEW BUCK, HEADING SOUTH TO MEXICO.
AND PRETTY SOON, THE REST WOULD LEAVE.
ONE BY ONE, CARRYING WHAT THEY COULD ON THEIR BACKS.
HAVING NOT QUITE MADE OF OKEMAH WHAT THEY HAD HOPED, THEY WOULD DISAPPEAR.
THEY WOULD LEAVE AN EMPTY LAND, A DESERTED SCAFFOLDING OF A RUSTED BOOM.
CHUKKACHUKKACHURRCHURBAAWWWAAAOOOAHHHCHUKKACHUKKACHURR
TO WOODY, THERE WAS SOMETHING IN THAT FORLORN SOUND OF HIS MOUTH HARP, THAT ECHO OF THE TRAIN WHISTLE, WHICH SPOKE OF THIS CHANGE.
SUCKING SHARPLY ON ITS HOLES, HE BENT THE NOTE, SUCKED IT DOWN A SEMITONE AND HEARD THE SOUND OF THINGS TURNING SOUR, CRUMBLING TO THE GROUND, BENDING TOWARD THAT MINOR KEY.
THIS CHANGE, THIS DEPRESSION OF THE NOTE, IT REMINDED WOODY OF HIS MOTHER AND THE SONGS SHE USED TO SING.

CHAPTER 2

A LETTER ARRIVED FOR WOODY AT THE POST OFFICE.

FROM THE DECORATIVE HANDWRITING ON THE ENVELOPE...

HE KNEW IT WAS FROM HIS FATHER.

THE NEWS WAS GOOD:

CHARLEY WAS BACK ON THE LADDER.

HE HAD BEEN MADE MANAGER OF SOME ROUGHNECK FLOPHOUSE ON THE NEW SIDE OF TOWN, AND THERE WAS AN OPPORTUNITY FOR WOODY TO BE A GENERAL HANDYMAN AROUND THE PLACE.

THERE WAS NO DISCUSSION:

CHARLEY WANTED HIS FAMILY BACK TOGETHER AGAIN.

AND SO, A WEEK LATER, HE ARRIVED TO PICK UP HIS SON.

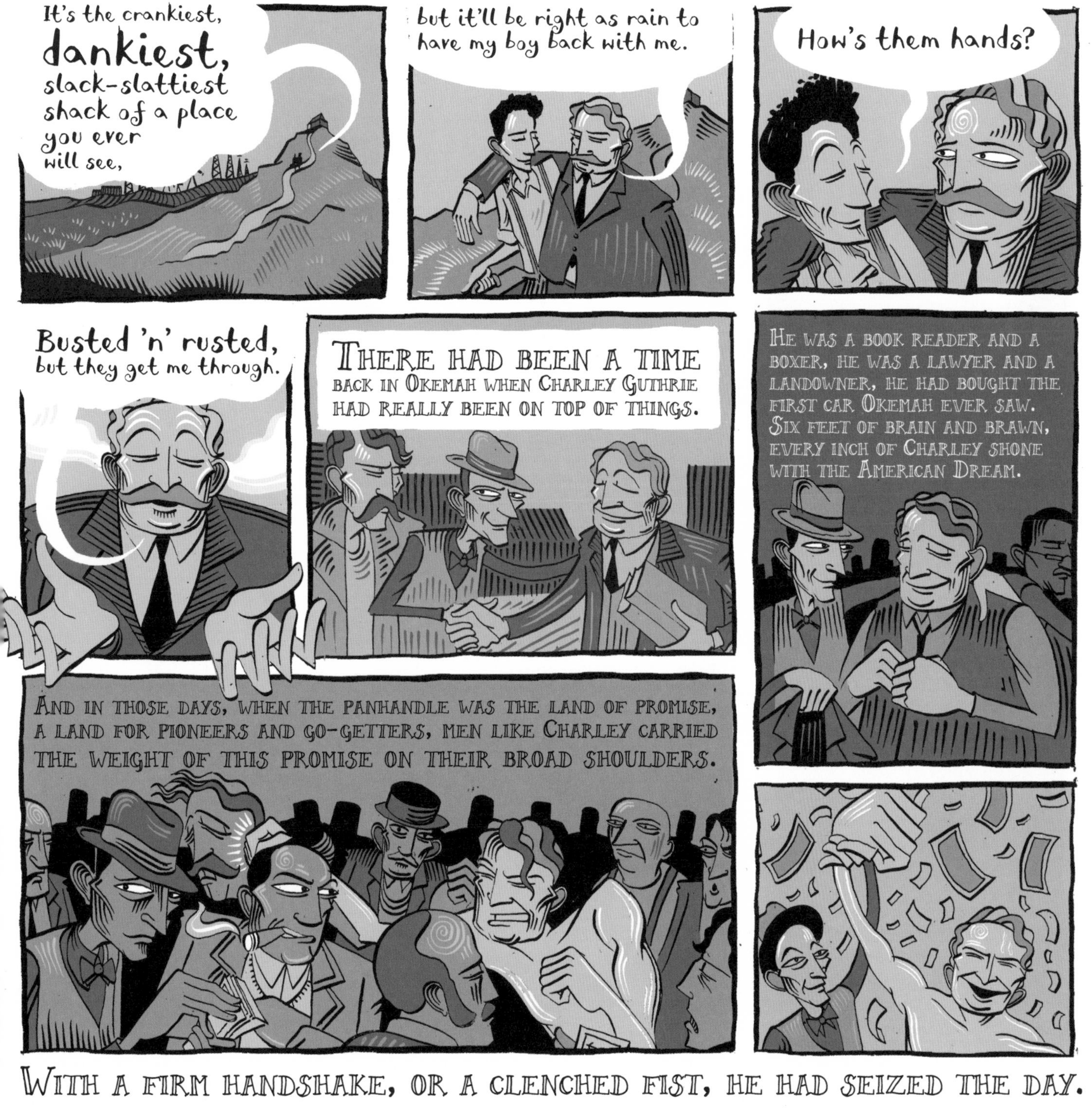
It's the crankiest, dankiest, slack-slattiest shack of a place you ever will see,
but it'll be right as rain to have my boy back with me.
How's them hands?
Busted 'n' rusted, but they get me through.
THERE HAD BEEN A TIME BACK IN OKEMAH WHEN CHARLEY GUTHRIE HAD REALLY BEEN ON TOP OF THINGS.
HE WAS A BOOK READER AND A BOXER, HE WAS A LAWYER AND A LANDOWNER, HE HAD BOUGHT THE FIRST CAR OKEMAH EVER SAW. SIX FEET OF BRAIN AND BRAWN, EVERY INCH OF CHARLEY SHONE WITH THE AMERICAN DREAM.
AND IN THOSE DAYS, WHEN THE PANHANDLE WAS THE LAND OF PROMISE, A LAND FOR PIONEERS AND GO-GETTERS, MEN LIKE CHARLEY CARRIED THE WEIGHT OF THIS PROMISE ON THEIR BROAD SHOULDERS.
WITH A FIRM HANDSHAKE, OR A CLENCHED FIST, HE HAD SEIZED THE DAY.

BUT AS THE YEARS PASSED, AS HIS FARMS WERE SOLD OFF, AS THE FANFARE OF PROSPERITY SUCKED SLOWLY TO THAT MINOR KEY, HIS HANDS HAD TIGHTENED WITH ARTHRITIS.

THE TENDONS, SNAPPED AND GNARLED FROM HIS YEARS OF HAMMERING OUT DEALS, HAD CONTRACTED AND PULLED HIS FINGERS INTO A LUMPY CLAW.

AND WHEN FINALLY HIS WIFE'S NERVES WERE CRACKING AND EXPLODING IN VICIOUS SNARLS, THAT'S WHEN CHARLEY GOT BURNED.

LYING ON THE COUCH ONE DAY, JUST HIM AND NORA IN THE HOUSE, HE AWOKE TO FIND BURNING COAL OIL ON HIS LAP.

HE HAD NEVER TOLD THE TRUTH ABOUT THAT DAY, AND KEPT IT TO HIS GRAVE, BUT WORDLESSLY, ALL THE GUTHRIES HAD KNOWN.

AND QUICKLY, LIKE A DAM BREAKING, THE FAMILY DISINTEGRATED. CHARLEY WAS CARRIED OUT OF THE HOUSE ON A STRETCHER, NEVER TO RETURN.

FROM HIS HOSPITAL BED, HE ORGANIZED THAT THE YOUNGER TWO CHILDREN, GEORGE AND MARY JO, BE SHIPPED OFF TO HIS SISTER'S QUIET FARM IN THE TEXAS PANHANDLE. HE FOLLOWED THEM THERE A FEW WEEKS LATER, LIFTED THROUGH THE WINDOW OF THE TRAIN ON HIS STRETCHER.

EARLY ONE MORNING, NORA WAS DISCREETLY REMOVED FROM HER HOUSE BY THE AUTHORITIES, AND TAKEN TO THE OKLAHOMA STATE HOSPITAL FOR THE INSANE.

WOODY'S OLDER BROTHER, ROY, MADE ARRANGEMENTS TO SELL THE HOUSE.

HE FOUND LODGING WITH A RESPECTED FAMILY IN TOWN, AND TOOK A JOB AS A GROCER'S CLERK, AS IF A SHIRT AND TIE COULD BEGIN TO COVER HIS SHAME.

WOODY, HOWEVER, WENT FERAL.

LIKE A WOUNDED ANIMAL, HE SLOPED OFF TO MRS. ATKINS'S SHACK.

CARRYING HIS MOTHER'S FEATURES ON HIS FACE, IT WAS IMPOSSIBLE TO HIDE HIS HERITAGE. SO HE PLAYED UP TO IT.

My first trip up the Saginaw River,

HE FORGOT HIS SHOES SOMEWHERE, LET HIS TIGHT-CURLED HAIR BRISTLE WILD UPON HIS HEAD, WANDERED THE STREETS DAY AND NIGHT SINGING BAWDY SALOON SONGS

My first trip to the Canada shore,

There I met sweet Rosie O'Grady,

Better known as the Winnipeg Whore.

...DOING HIS UTMOST TO COURT THE OUTRAGE OF THE GOOD FOLK OF OKEMAH.

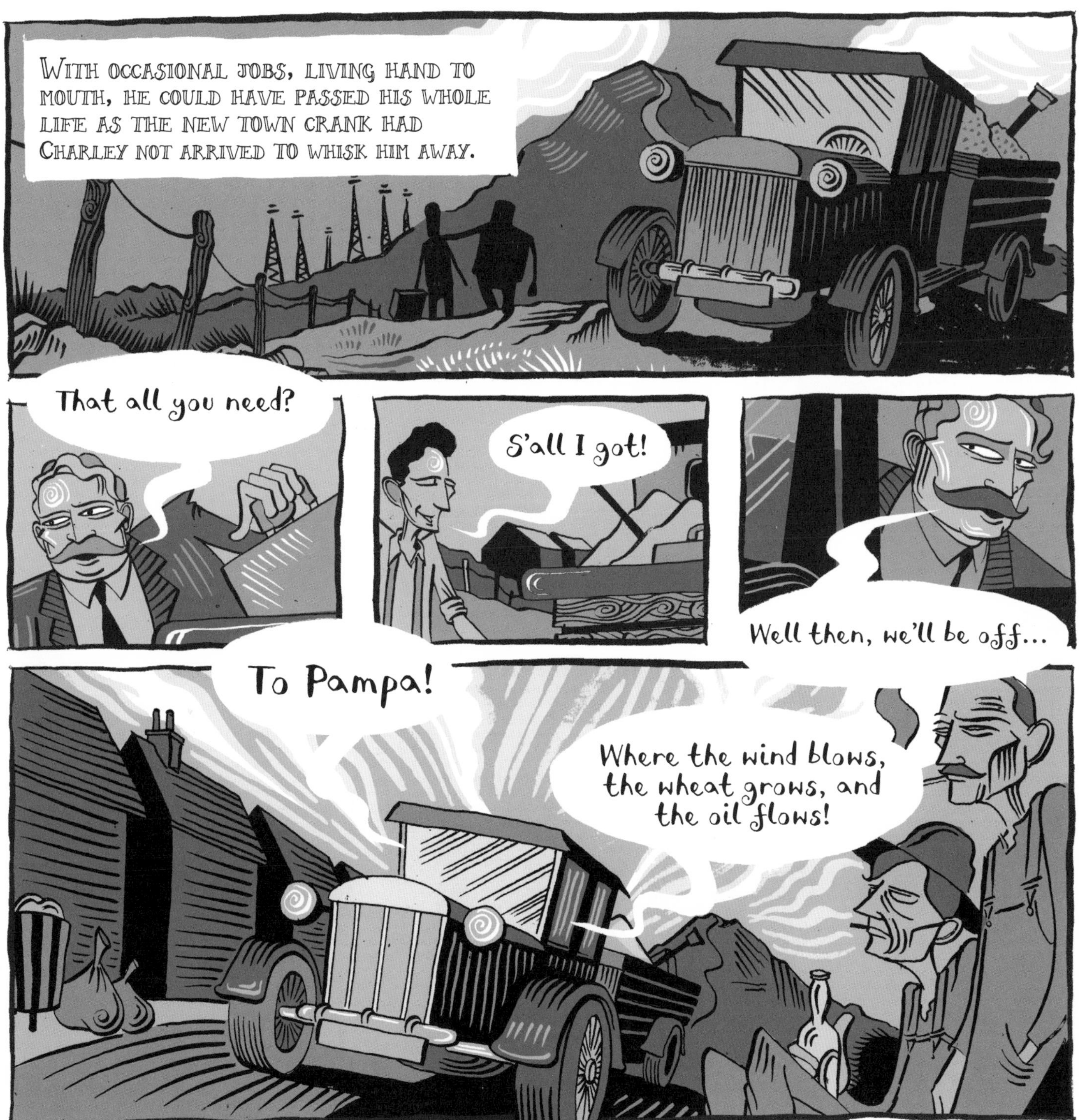

WITH OCCASIONAL JOBS, LIVING HAND TO MOUTH, HE COULD HAVE PASSED HIS WHOLE LIFE AS THE NEW TOWN CRANK HAD CHARLEY NOT ARRIVED TO WHISK HIM AWAY.
That all you need?
S'all I got!
Well then, we'll be off...
To Pampa!
Where the wind blows, the wheat grows, and the oil flows!

THE TOWN SEEMED TO BUCKLE AS THEY LEFT,

THE HIGH STREET COLLAPSING INTO ISOLATED SHACKS,

THE ROADS CRUMBLING TO DUST,

FOR HERE, IN THE VAST SPACE BETWEEN SETTLEMENTS, THE SKY BIT DEEP INTO THE EARTH, GREEDY FOR DOMINION.

IT WAS LOUD, BLARING, DAZZLING, AND SANG THROUGHOUT THE DAY LIKE THE PARPING BLAST OF A DIXIE BRASS BAND.

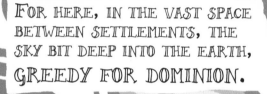

Welcome TO OKEMAH

AND IN NO TIME AT ALL, THEIR EYES WERE FILLED WITH SKY.

TO MANY, THIS WAS DANGEROUS COUNTRY.

To look up at the sky too long, you felt giddy, like gravity had turned on its heels, as if you might suddenly fall upward into the blue and be lost forever.

Beneath this eternal emptiness, the land itself was disorienting. The early pioneers, accustomed to the hills of Germany or the craggy mountains of Scotland, had suffered bouts of prairie malady, a delirium of isolation in a sea of unending flatness.

Without a tree or a hill to fix a gaze upon, with no start or end point in sight,

The land confronted people with a dizzy sense of eternity.

IN TEXAS, THEY SAID, YOU DON'T HAVE TO DIE TO GO TO HEAVEN.

AND THE SAME WAS SAID OF HELL.

Gold! Gold! Gold! All around us, boy!

Seems the sun itself is shining from the ground— you can barely look at it.

Looks like them Spanishers was right after all: the panhandle, paved with gold. I ever write you about that expedition? 'Bout that Cibola there, that old myth of them seven cities of gold.

BOYEEEE!!!! They told tales for years 'bout a glorious city, seen from afar, that was clear made of gold. So, one day, they figure they'd best go check on it, and send their man, Mister Francisco Vázquez de Coronado.

And BOYEEE! Do they see it, shining like redemption in the distance. This is it, this is SURELY it, says Don Francisco.

So they goes on in. And what do they find? What do they find??!! HA!! Mud! Mud and dirt and soil and dust. That city weren't made up of nothing but dirt. Houses built of red clay, baked into bricks in the sun. And inside that dirt, hundreds and thousands of little splinters of mica.

BOY! Wheat never looked so good. Sheez! A fortunate feller could make a clear fortune here.
Off he goes, from Mehiko right up to the road we on now, and far past it, up to Kansas. They find an Injun thar, and he tells 'em, "Oooh, yessar! Yessirree, sir! They got them cities of pure gold all right, I seen 'em with my own two eyes. They got more riches than they can handle, they'll be mighty happy to let you offload 'em of their burden."
So they go, thirty men on horseback, a coupla boys 'round their feet, and right at the end of two weeks on the plains, that's when they see it...
And it was the mica that played in the light and played in their eyes, and it was the mica that sent them back empty-handed.
That ol' dirt bin playing tricks on man since the day they landed on it.

THEY WERE, BY THIS TIME, ON THE EDGE OF TEXAS,

AND AS THEY TRAVELED WEST TO PAMPA, THEY SAW GREAT MOUNTAINS OF GRAIN PILED UP ON THE EDGES OF THE TOWNS, HEAPED AROUND THE SILOS, ROTTING FROM THEIR DAMP CORES TO THEIR HEAT-WITHERED HUSKS.

KEEP OUT

Now, of course, it's a different kinda gold rush. Greatest wheat-growing country in the whole of Americee. There's so much gold steaming out o' them combines that they don't know what t' do with it.

They just leave 'em there to spoil?

Yessir...

And if folks is hungry?

They cain't go nowhere near it. You produce so much wheat, the danger is the price'll fall. Fact is, prices been fallin' since the end of the war. So they keep it fenced off to drive the prices up. Farmers producing too much.

That's crazy.

No son, that's economics.

WHEN THEY REACHED PAMPA, THE STREETS WERE TEEMING WITH A THOUSAND PEOPLE, AND THE NOISE AND THE CLATTER COULD HAVE RAISED THE ROOFS OFF ALL THE HOUSES.

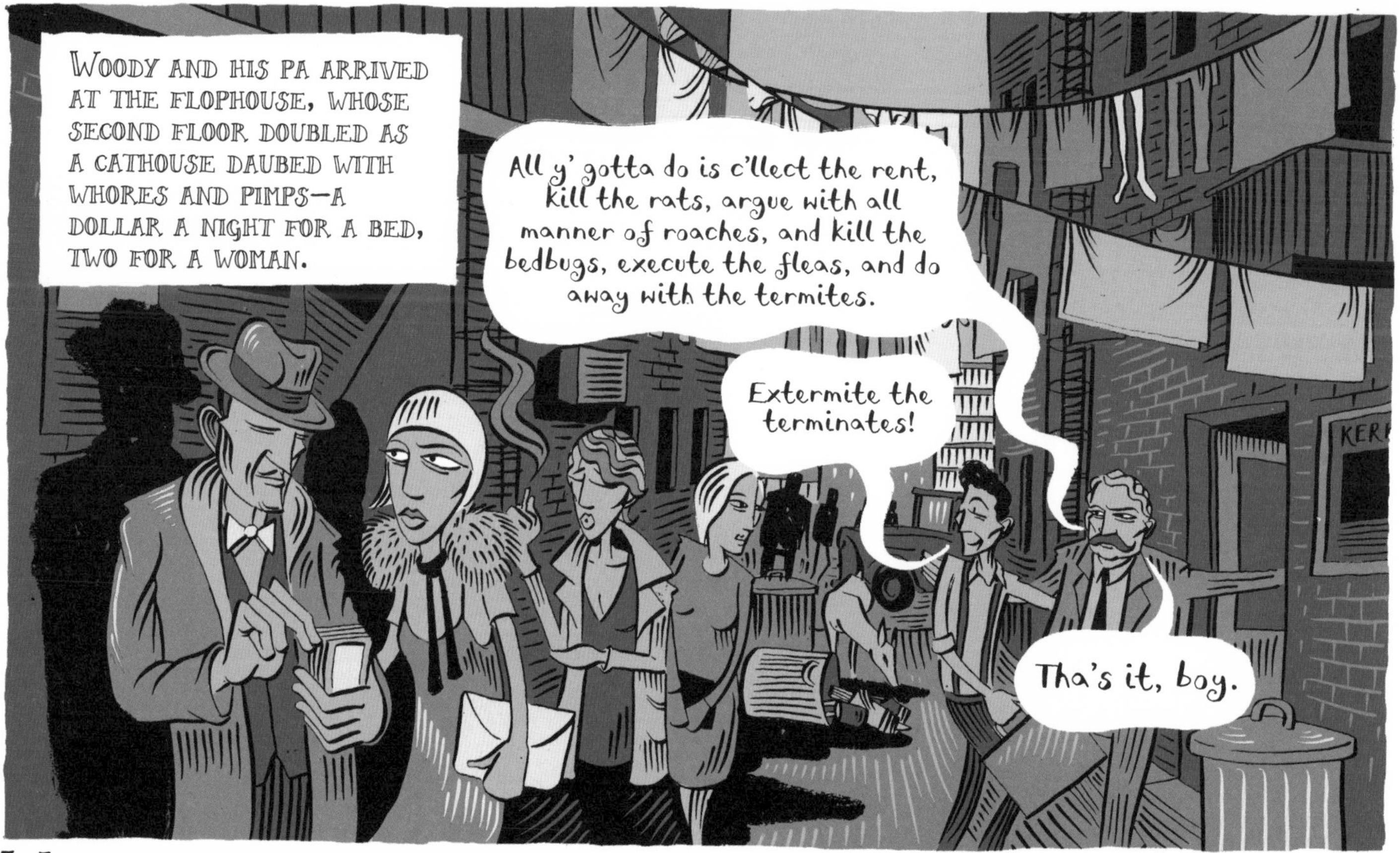
WOODY AND HIS PA ARRIVED AT THE FLOPHOUSE, WHOSE SECOND FLOOR DOUBLED AS A CATHOUSE DAUBED WITH WHORES AND PIMPS—A DOLLAR A NIGHT FOR A BED, TWO FOR A WOMAN.
All y' gotta do is c'llect the rent, kill the rats, argue with all manner of roaches, and kill the bedbugs, execute the fleas, and do away with the termites.
Extermite the terminates!
Tha's it, boy.
KER

WOODY SOON FOUND HIS PLACE IN THIS HONKING PIT OF PAMPA.

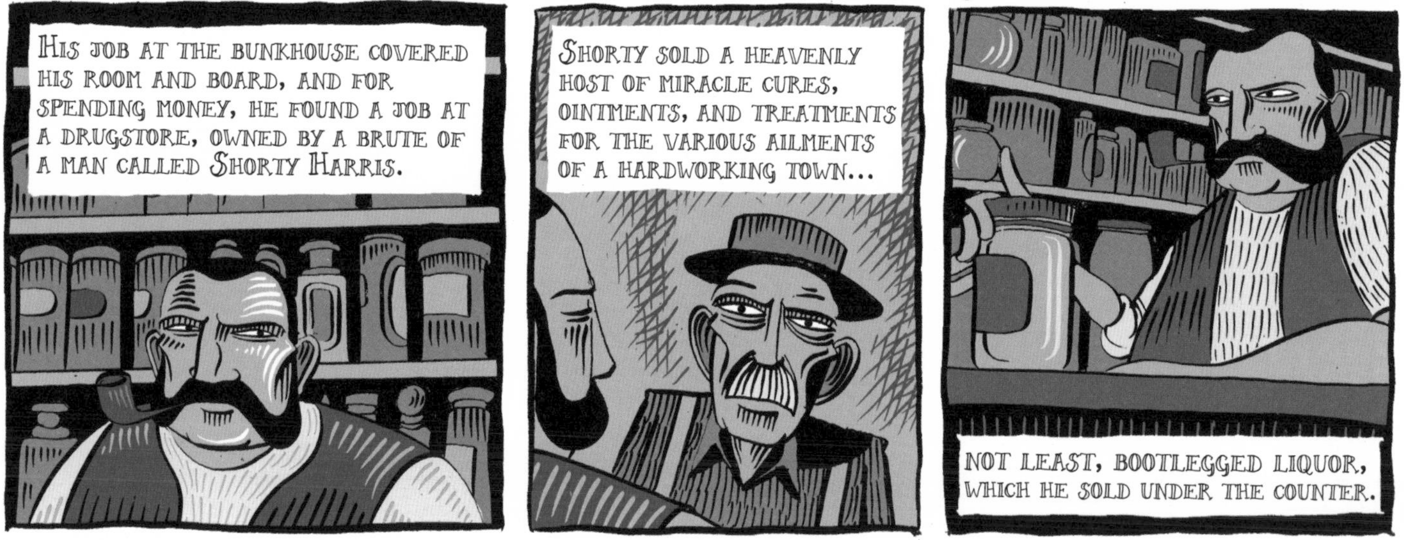
HIS JOB AT THE BUNKHOUSE COVERED HIS ROOM AND BOARD, AND FOR SPENDING MONEY, HE FOUND A JOB AT A DRUGSTORE, OWNED BY A BRUTE OF A MAN CALLED SHORTY HARRIS.
SHORTY SOLD A HEAVENLY HOST OF MIRACLE CURES, OINTMENTS, AND TREATMENTS FOR THE VARIOUS AILMENTS OF A HARDWORKING TOWN...
NOT LEAST, BOOTLEGGED LIQUOR, WHICH HE SOLD UNDER THE COUNTER.

He served hooch, a concoction of boiled-down vegetable slurry and a handful of yeast left to boil on a stove.

He sold canned heat, a jellied mix of ethanol and methanol, which could be strained through a sock into fruit juice to create a cocktail called jungle juice.

And most popular of all, he served Jake, an extract of Jamaican gingerroot and denatured alcohol, which was sold as a medicine. Diluted into a glass of Coke, it would fizz like a furious rainstorm and wipe the mind like a chalkboard.

Cowhands, circus folk, construction workers, drillers, pipeliners, wheat raisers, cattle grazers—the entire parade of Pampa's boom chasers—walked through Shorty's door...

And crawled out again, seeing double and seeking trouble.

WOODY HAD FOUND A BATTERED, STRINGLESS GUITAR IN THE BACK OF SHORTY'S STORE...

AND IT DIDN'T TAKE HIM LONG TO GET IT BACK TO CHARLEY'S BROTHER, UNCLE JEFF, WHO LIVED JUST UP FROM THE FLOPHOUSE, WHERE WOODY HAD THE GUITAR RESTRUNG AND SET ABOUT LEARNING THE FIRST BASIC CHORDS THAT WOULD SEE HIM THROUGH HIS LIFE.

JEFF WAS THE FAMILY'S MUSICIAN, A FIDDLE VIRTUOSO WITH THE ROSETTES TO PROVE IT. HIS WIFE, ALLYNE, PLAYED MELODEON, AND THEY WOULD OFTEN PERFORM AT FAMILY GET-TOGETHERS OR AT NEIGHBORHOOD SQUARE DANCES.

This here ain't no concert-hall piano fortissimay...

this here is the gittar, and any old fool can play it.

It's just ear music, son. Copy what I do, then do it howsoever, whichsoever way you damn please. Ain't no right or wrong way.

AND SO, IN THIS CYCLONE OF PAMPAN COMMERCE...

WOODY FOUND HIS OWN STILL CENTER.

AS CUSTOMERS CAME AND WENT, SUCKING FIERY GELATIN THROUGH SOCKS, STRETCHING THEIR PUPILS AND SLURRING THEIR WORDS,

HE PLAYED THOSE SAME THREE CHORDS 'ROUND AND 'ROUND, AGAIN AND AGAIN, OVER AND OVER.

AND SHORTY DIDN'T MIND,

AND HIS CUSTOMERS DIDN'T MIND.

SOMEHOW, THAT CYCLE OF CHORDS SUITED THE RHYTHM OF THEIR DAYS...

THAT REPETITION OF HEAVY SHUNTING AND HARD GRUNTING THAT THEY COULD NEVER SEEM TO SHAKE.

But those black pupils of Shorty's customers held an emptiness that scared Woody, and reminded him of his pa. They streamed to Shorty's soda store for a fountain not of hope, but of paralysis. For while some were there for a stiff pick-me-up, others, the most of them, sought oblivion.

THEY RAILED AND MOANED AND CUSSED ABOUT THE PLUMMETING PRICE OF WHEAT, ABOUT THE MORTGAGES THEY OWED ON THEIR LAND, ABOUT THE LEASES THSEY STILL HAD TO PAY OFF FOR THOSE NEW COMBINE MACHINES THEY'D BOUGHT SEVERAL YEARS BACK. IN THE SQUALL OF PAMPA'S PROSPERITY, IN THE COMMERCE THAT FLOODED THE STREETS, THESE MEN WERE DROWNING.

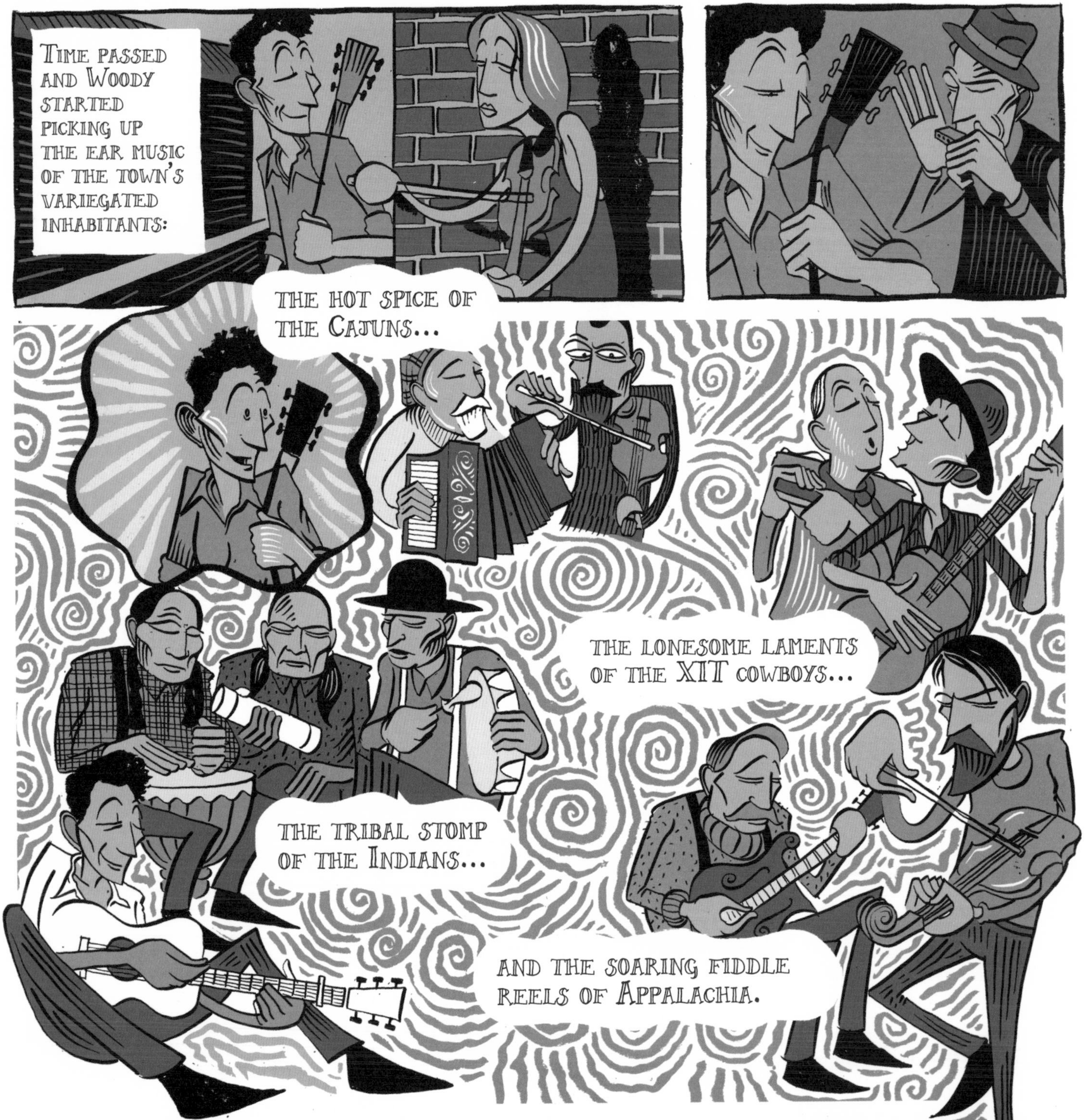

Time passed and Woody started picking up the ear music of the town's variegated inhabitants:
The hot spice of the Cajuns...
The lonesome laments of the XIT cowboys...
The tribal stomp of the Indians...
And the soaring fiddle reels of Appalachia.

Every now and then, the medicine shows would pass through town, peddling snake oil and other miracle elixirs that promised to smooth wrinkles, remove stains, cure the whooping cough, and prolong life—some all in one pot.

To attract more customers, these teams of traveling barrows and wagons would put on carnival acts, flea circuses, freak shows, magic tricks, and of course, an assortment of musical attractions.

And the people would gather, Woody among them, to purchase the ointments that eased their ailments,

AND TO HEAR THE MUSIC THAT SOOTHED THEIR SOULS.

CHAPTER 3

FOR WOODY, THESE WERE THE GOOD TIMES.

ON WEEKENDS, THE LOCAL FAMILIES WOULD MEET WITH THEIR FRIENDS FOR HOMEMADE FOOD, DRINK, AND MUSIC.

AND WITH EACH FAMILY, CAME A DIFFERENT DISH FROM THEIR HERITAGE.

THEY PILED THE TABLES WITH A SMORGASBORD OF THE CULTURES THAT HAD MIGRATED TO AMERICA.

THERE WERE GREAT BOWLS OF
JAMBALAYA AND GUMBO,
CAJUN DISHES FROM SPAIN AND
FRANCE AND THE CARIBBEAN.

THERE WERE RASPBERRY
AND PEACH COBBLERS,
RECIPES BROUGHT OVER BY
THE BRITISH PILGRIMS...

THERE WERE CONCH CHOWDERS FROM THE
BAHAMAS AND CORN DODGERS FROM FRANCE.

LIKE THE SONGS THE PEOPLE BROUGHT WITH THEM, THESE OLD RECIPES HAD BEEN PASSED DOWN THROUGH THE GENERATIONS, PASSED ON FROM MOUTH TO MOUTH. EACH HAD A HUNDRED VARIATIONS, AND EACH HAD ADAPTED TO THE VERNACULAR OF THE LAND AROUND IT.

THEY WOULD ALL SIT OUT AT NIGHT, BENEATH THE LOCUST TREES, EXCHANGING FOOD AND SONGS...

AND THE SKY WOULD FILL WITH THE SMELLS AND SOUNDS OF THEIR ANCESTRY— RECIPES AND STORIES THAT TIED THEM TO ONE ANOTHER, AND TO THEIR PAST.

BUT FOR THE REST OF THE COUNTRY, THE CITIES ESPECIALLY, THINGS WERE STARTING TO SLIDE.

THE TWENTIES HAD SEEN THE BIGGEST SPENDING SPREE IN AMERICA'S HISTORY,

A STRING OF FIZZING CHAMPAGNE BUBBLES, FLUTTERING FLAPPER DRESSES, AND BOW-TIED GLITZY, JAZZ MUSIC.

BUT NOW THE ECONOMY WAS LURCHING, AND THOSE CLEAN SHIRTS AT THE COALFACE OF THE COUNTRY'S COMMERCIAL SECTOR WERE STARTING TO SWEAT.

TOO MANY COMPANIES WERE PRODUCING TOO MANY GOODS, TOO MANY FARMS WERE PRODUCING TOO MANY CROPS, AND TOO MANY BANKS WERE LENDING MONEY THEY DIDN'T HAVE.

PRICES FELL...

AND WITH THEM,

PEOPLE'S LIVELIHOODS.

As the economy rocked, swayed, and finally collapsed, Woody continued strumming his chords, lost in his own world of rhythm and rhyme.

It took a good year or two for the Depression to hit the south country,

and Woody, with no money to lose, remained unscathed.

He had started meeting some other boys down at the barbershop, to listen to and learn the ear music from an old spidery bluesman who played there for tips.

He played the old blues tunes from the low countries, whose saucy melodies dripped with a visceral violence and carnal passion that shocked the churchgoers...

It was in a hustling b-joint where the Mississippi run,

Stackolee killed Billy de Lyons with a smoking forty-one.

and roused a primal force in Woody that he'd not yet experienced in the flesh.

A WHILE BACK, A TALL, STOOPY FELLOW BY THE NAME OF MATT JENNINGS HAD COME TO UNCLE JEFF'S TO TUNE AN OLD FIDDLE HE'D BOUGHT IN A PAWNSHOP, AND THOUGH HE COULDN'T PLAY A NOTE, WOODY HAD SNAPPED HIM UP:

HE WANTED A BAND OF HIS OWN.

AFTER A WHILE, WOODY AND MATT WERE JOINED BY A GUITAR PLAYER CALLED CLUSTER BAKER, AND WHEN WOODY SWITCHED TO THE MANDOLIN TO COMPLEMENT THE SOUND, HE THOUGHT THEY REALLY HAD SOMETHING.

Woody, there's no way in hell we're ready to play fer folks— Matt here can barely scratch a squeal from his fiddle, and you just picked up that there mandy box.

Yessir!!! That may be true— but we got all the heart in the whole damned world!

Woody, we're rough. Rougher than a coondog's bark.

Rough and sweet. Like a big juicy corncob. That's us, then, the Corncob Trio.

Far away from that barbershop in Pampa,

the lines started to form in the cities: bread lines, soup lines, lines for the closing banks, lines for the Red Cross hospitals.

And as the bank managers boarded up their windows and slid silently out of town...

The Corncob Trio practiced their songs.

AS THE CITIES STARTED CRUMBLING,

AS THE ELECTRICITY WAS CUT FROM THE POOREST PARTS OF THE TOWN,

AS PEOPLE LOST THEIR JOBS, LOST THEIR HOMES, AND MADE FUTILE RUNS ON THE BANKS TO PLUNDER THE EMPTY VAULTS, WOODY'S TRIO KEPT AT IT.

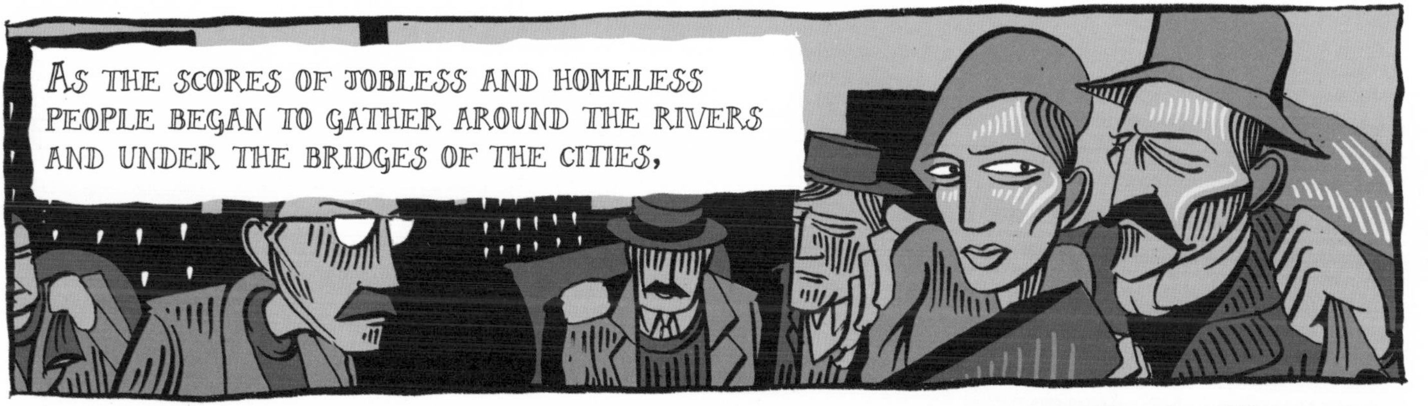
AS THE SCORES OF JOBLESS AND HOMELESS PEOPLE BEGAN TO GATHER AROUND THE RIVERS AND UNDER THE BRIDGES OF THE CITIES,

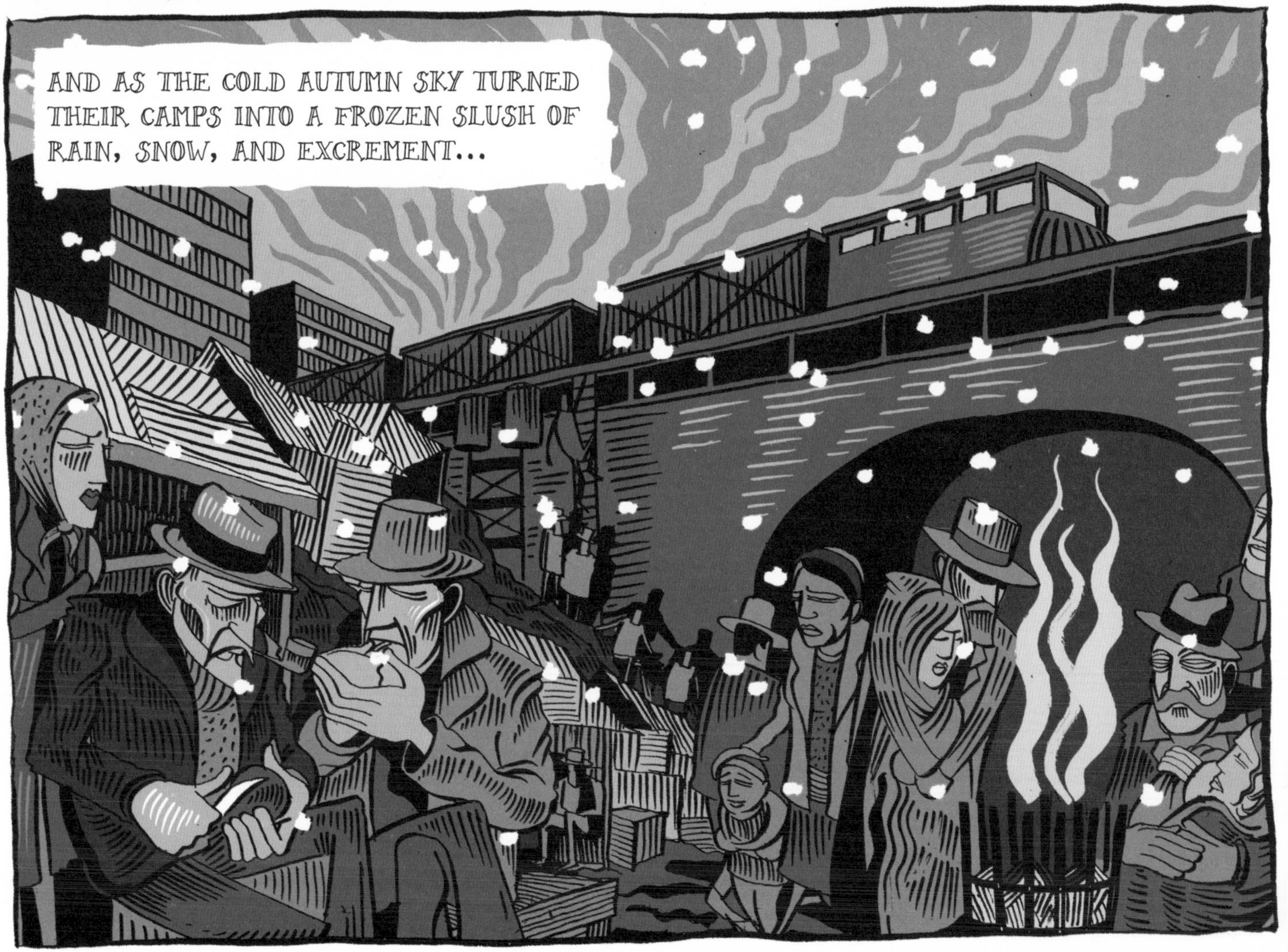
AND AS THE COLD AUTUMN SKY TURNED THEIR CAMPS INTO A FROZEN SLUSH OF RAIN, SNOW, AND EXCREMENT...

WOODY AND HIS CORNCOB TRIO STARTED PLAYING THEIR FIRST PUBLIC EVENTS:

THEY GOT AN EVENING SLOT ONCE A WEEK AT THE LOCAL ICE RINK.

An' this is my sister, Mary.

Hello, Woody.

You hanging 'round to see us tonight?

Ma, Pa, and m' sisters all came to see our Matt.

Well, I kinda hope you might be lookin' my way, too.

THEY WOULD OPEN FOR A STRING OF OTHER BANDS ON THOSE NIGHTS—COWBOY CROONERS, JUG BANDS, STRING BANDS, ANY KIND OF RHYTHM TO GET THE ICE-SKATERS MOVING.

LESS POLISHED THAN ANY OF THE OTHER ACTS, THE CORNCOB TRIO SANG OLD FIRESIDE SONGS, SIMPLE AS NURSERY RHYMES, AS WORN AND FAMILIAR AS AN OLD FAMILY QUILT.

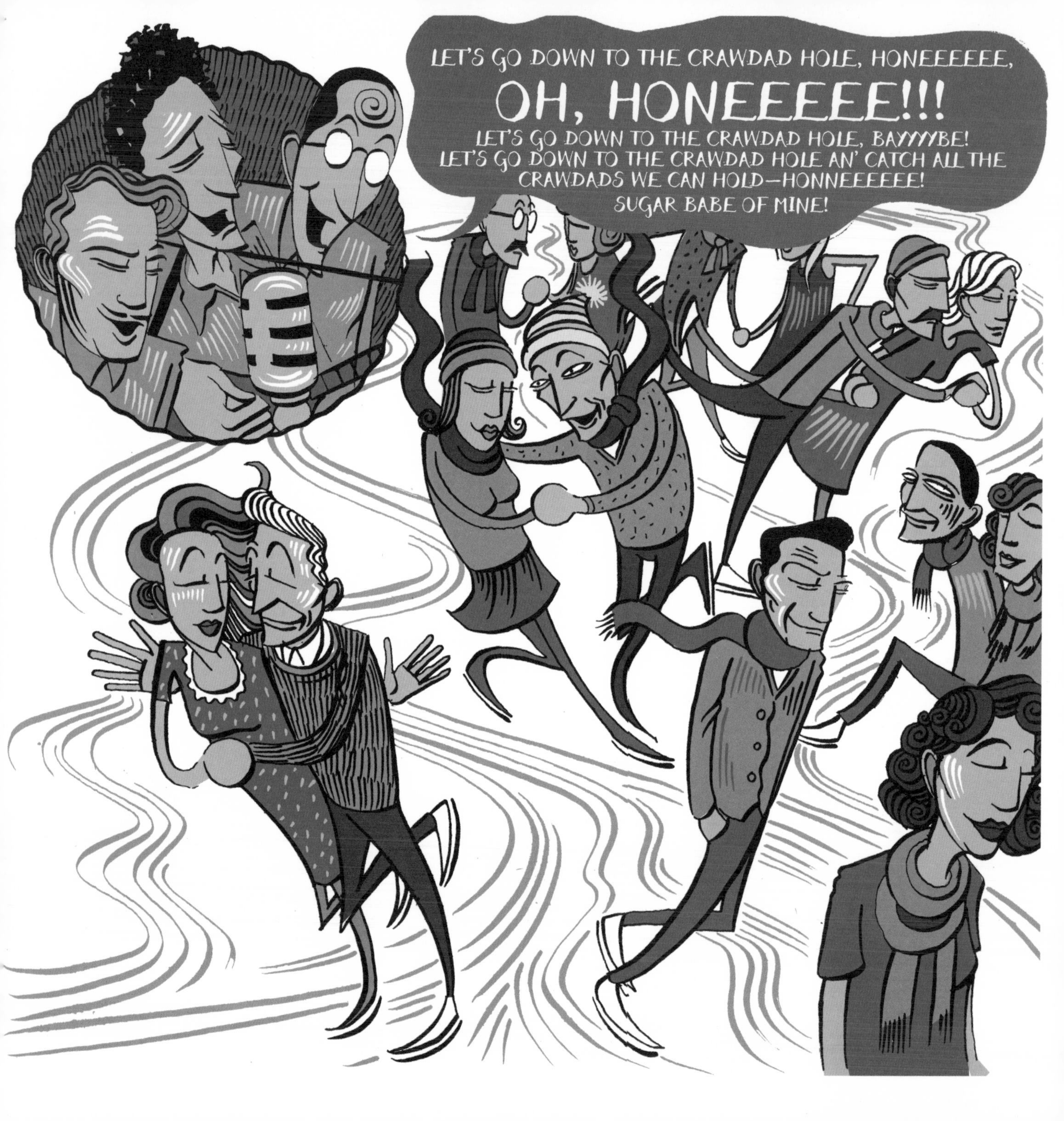
LET'S GO DOWN TO THE CRAWDAD HOLE, HONEEEEEE,
OH, HONEEEEEE!!!
LET'S GO DOWN TO THE CRAWDAD HOLE, BAYYYYBE!
LET'S GO DOWN TO THE CRAWDAD HOLE AN' CATCH ALL THE CRAWDADS WE CAN HOLD—HONNEEEEEE!
SUGAR BABE OF MINE!

NO ONE HAD WRITTEN THESE SONGS DOWN.

THERE WAS NO OFFICIAL VERSION, NO ONE SET OF LYRICS; THE SONGS WERE SIMPLY A STRUCTURE OF MELODY AND RHYTHM THAT ALLOWED ITS SINGER TO IMPROVISE TO THE SETTING.

THEN SUDDENLY, LIKE A STORM BREAKING,

THE DEPRESSION HIT THE SOUTH.

AND WITH THE DROP OF A LETTER ON THE FLOPHOUSE PORCH, WOODY'S MOTHER WAS DEAD. THERE WAS A DOLLAR FROM THE ASYLUM—HIS MOTHER'S LIFE SAVINGS—AND THEIR CONDOLENCES.

AND THAT WAS THAT.

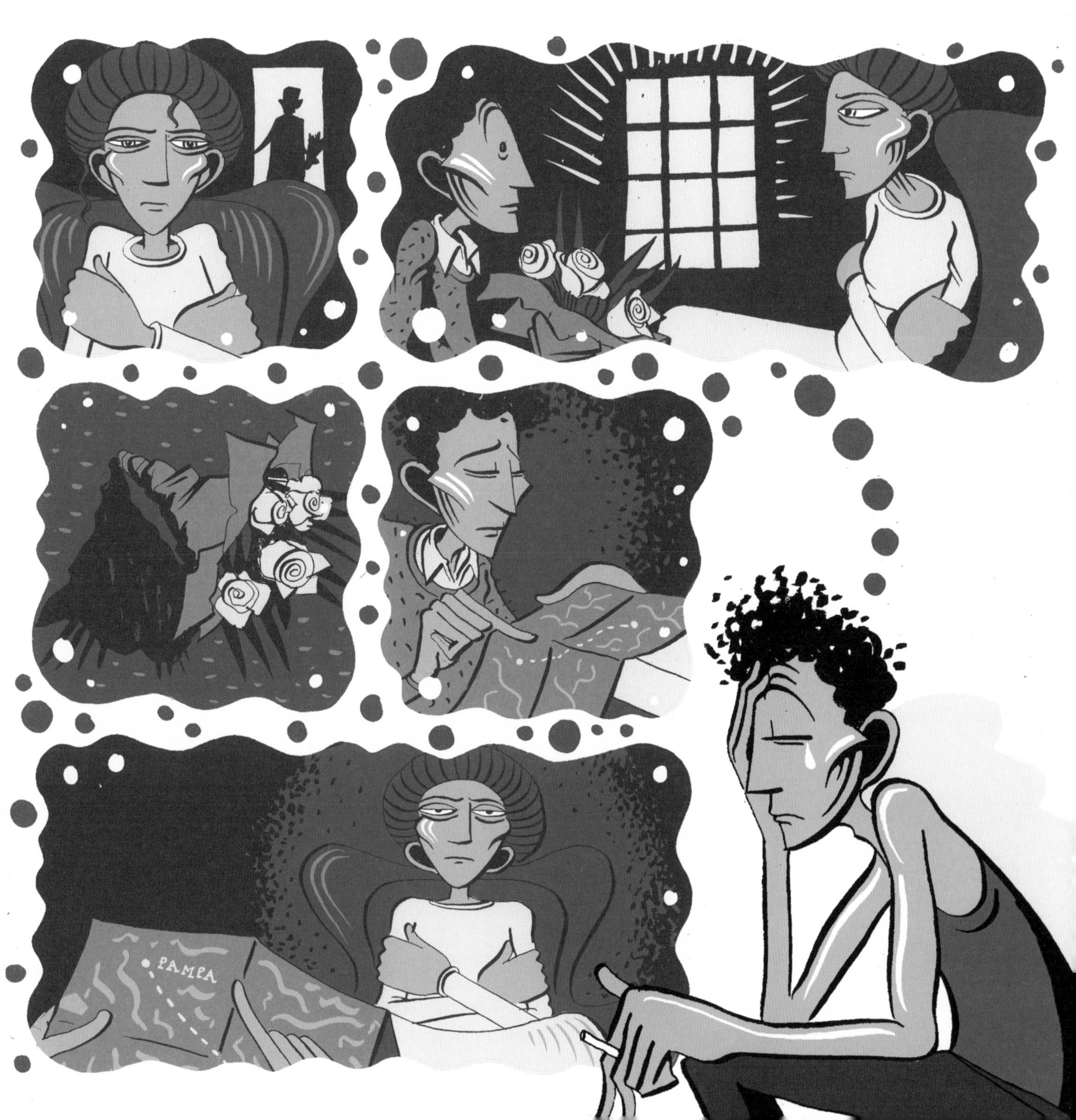
PAMPA

THE THRUM OF PAMPA WAS STILLED. THE STREETS NO LONGER FLOWED WITH COMMERCE BUT LAY STAGNANT, LINED WITH PEOPLE WITH NOWHERE TO BE.

PEOPLE MILLED AROUND THE BANKS, WAITING IN VAIN FOR THEM TO OPEN.

PEOPLE HUNG AROUND THEIR OLD OFFICES, WAITING TO SEE THEIR OLD BOSSES ABOUT SOME PART-TIME WORK.

AND AT THE END OF THE DAY, THEY ALL WENT HOME EMPTY-HANDED.

IT WAS AROUND THIS TIME THAT JEFF SUGGESTED THE TRIP.

FOR YEARS, A STORY KEPT RESURFACING IN THE GUTHRIE FAMILY FOLKLORE, A TALE OF CHARLEY AND JEFF'S FATHER, JEREMIAH PEARSALL GUTHRIE, THE COWHAND THAT HAD BROUGHT HIS FAMILY WEST TO TEXAS IN THE FIRST PLACE.

YEARS BEFORE HE WAS MARRIED, HE WAS HERDING CATTLE IN THE CHISOS MOUNTAINS, A DAY'S RIDE FROM THE MEXICAN BORDER. EACH BROTHER TOLD THE LEGEND A DIFFERENT WAY, BUT THE SUM OF IT WAS THAT HE SOMEHOW STUMBLED UPON A ROCK WITH A THICK VEIN OF SILVER STRUCK THROUGH IT, LIKE A BOLT OF LIGHTNING.

NO ONE OWNED THIS DESERTED WASTELAND, AND SO, IN THE SPIRIT AND LEGISLATURE OF THOSE TIMES, IT WAS UP FOR GRABS. JERRY P. HAD HASTILY SCRAWLED A MAP ON A SCRAP OF PAPER THAT UNCLE JEFF STILL KEPT IN HIS WALLET, AND HAD ETCHED HIS INITIALS IN A ROCK THAT HE PLACED UNDER A ROOT BY THE CREEK, WHERE, AS THE STORY WOULD ALWAYS END, IT LAY TO THIS DAY.

This again!...

I'm a-tellin' you! It's true, every bit of it. That rock is there, and it's got our name on it.

We find it, we dig that earth—hoo-boy!—we're back in the money.

It's a pipe dream. A needle in a haystack.

The old man died with that there mine on his mind—his last breath was on that mine... And Jerry P. weren't no liar... Charley, you'll be your own boss again, your own man. Like the old times...

AND SO IT WAS DECIDED.

THEY WOULD GO, ONCE AND FOR ALL, AND CHASE THIS STREAK OF SILVER, THIS FLASH OF HOPE IN A BARREN LANDSCAPE. JERRY P. HAD LEFT THAT MINE BEHIND TO CHASE THE LAND RUSH IN TEXAS, LAND THAT WAS NOW BOUGHT UP BY THE BANKS AND DRIED UP BY THE DROUGHT. HE HAD NEVER RETURNED TO TEST THIS DREAM, AND HAD PASSED HIS MAP ON TO HIS SONS AS THEIR BIRTHRIGHT, A PROMISE ON A PIECE OF PAPER.

SO CHARLEY, UNCLE JEFF, WOODY, AND HIS BROTHER ROY TAPPED A LOAD OF GASOLINE FROM A LOCAL PIPE,

FILLED FIVE OR SIX JARS WITH HOMEBREWED HOOCH,

AND HEADED SOUTH, DOWN PAST THE RIO GRANDE, ON A TWO-DAY JOURNEY TO THE CHISOS MOUNTAINS.

THEY PASSED THROUGH WHEAT COUNTRY, THROUGH COTTON COUNTRY, THROUGH CATTLE COUNTRY, AND THEN FINALLY ONTO THE SPARSE ROCKY DESERT, WHERE THE MOUNTAINS ROSE BEFORE THEM.

Woody's eyes were as wide as the sky. He had never been this far south before, never walked mountains so high, never seen so many crags, cliffs, canyons, cornices, and coves, such a chaos of color and animal cries that sent his pulse racing.

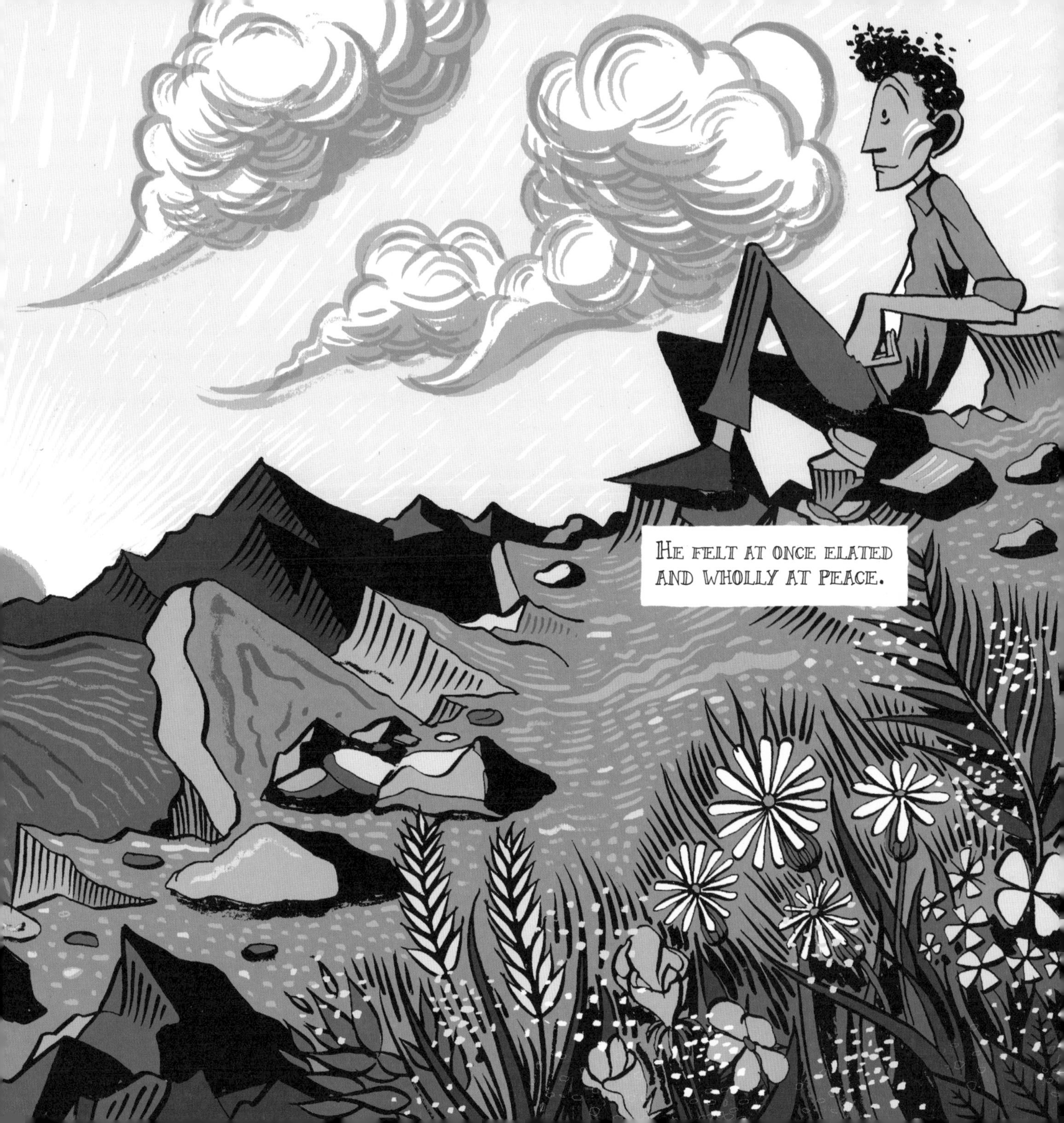
HE FELT AT ONCE ELATED AND WHOLLY AT PEACE.

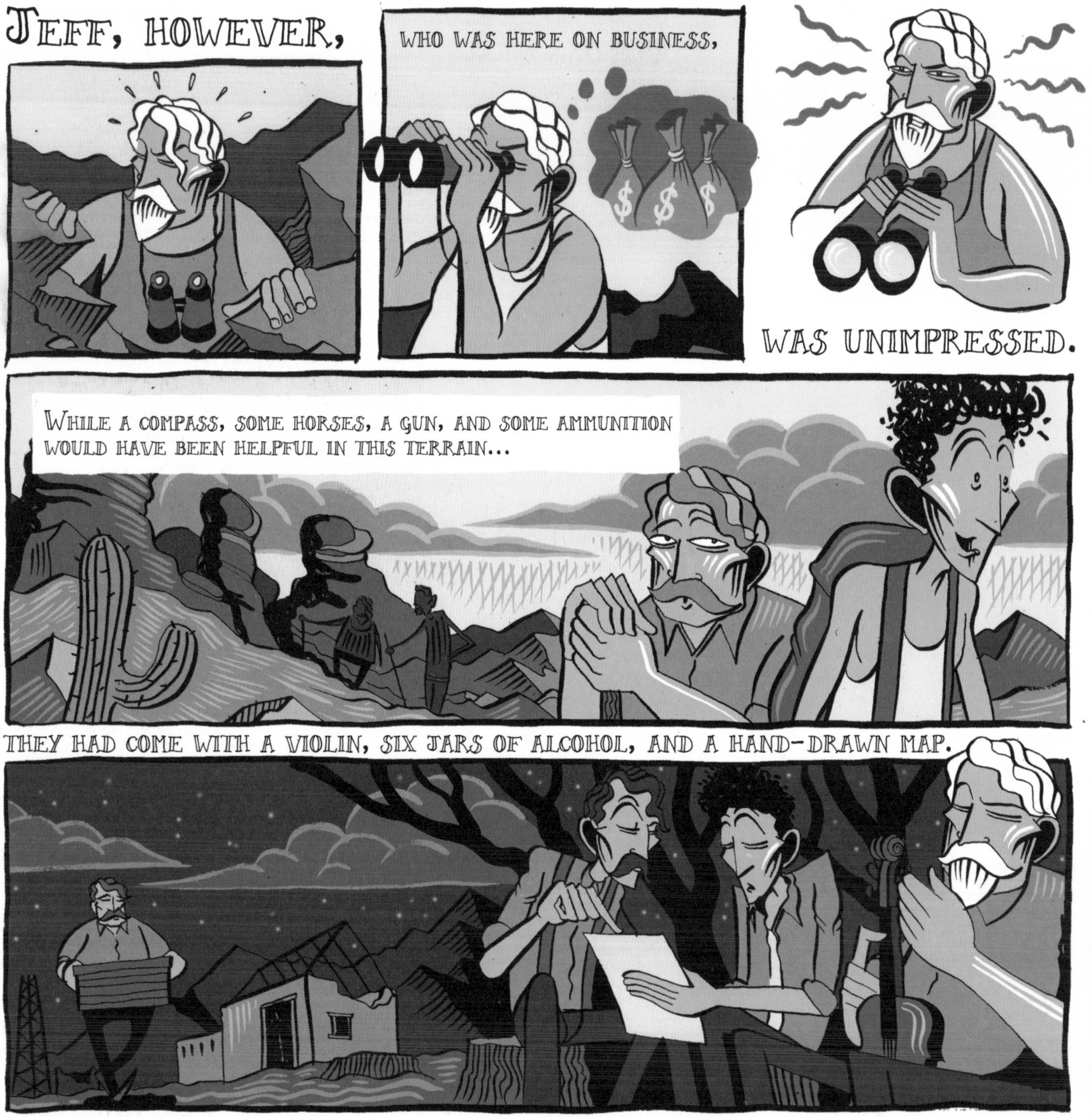
JEFF, HOWEVER,
WHO WAS HERE ON BUSINESS,
WAS UNIMPRESSED.
WHILE A COMPASS, SOME HORSES, A GUN, AND SOME AMMUNITION WOULD HAVE BEEN HELPFUL IN THIS TERRAIN...
THEY HAD COME WITH A VIOLIN, SIX JARS OF ALCOHOL, AND A HAND-DRAWN MAP.

BUT THE DAYS PASSED LIKE A DREAM, A WORLD APART FROM THE LIFE WOODY WAS USED TO...

AND THERE, IN THEIR ANCESTRAL HEARTH, FOR THAT BRIEF MOMENT,

THEY FELT LIKE A FAMILY ONCE MORE.

AND SO, A FEW DAYS LATER, THEY RETURNED AS THEIR WOMEN HAD SAID THEY WOULD, EMPTY-HANDED AND UNWASHED.

BUT FOR WOODY, THE TRIP WAS NOT WASTED; SOMETHING ABOUT THOSE CHISOS MOUNTAINS, SOMETHING ABOUT THEIR CRYSTAL AIR AND THE TIMELESS ARC OF THE STARS IN THE DARK HAD AFFECTED HIM.

AND ONLY LATER WOULD HE FIND THE WORDS FOR IT.

WHEN THEY RETURNED, THOUGH THEIR ABSENCE WAS BRIEF, IT WAS AS IF THE WHOLE OF PAMPA HAD CHANGED.

THEY WERE CONFRONTED WITH A THIN VEIL OF DUST THAT HUNG IN THE AIR AND POWDERED THE HOUSEHOLD FURNITURE.

MORE MEN LINED THE STREETS WITH THE FURIOUS PANG OF HUNGER RACKED ACROSS THEIR FACES.

THEIR EYES WERE BLANK AND RED-RIMMED WITH CANNED HEAT...

THEY WERE STUCK LIKE SCARECROWS TO THE GROUND, RAGGED AND BLANK.

BUT WOODY HAD TO SHAKE THIS DUST FROM HIS HEAD.

THE CORNCOB TRIO WAS PLAYING ITS BIGGEST GIG TO DATE, THE LOCAL PARISH HOEDOWN. MARY WOULD BE THERE TONIGHT, WITH THE WHOLE OF MATT'S FAMILY, PROUD AS PUNCH TO SEE THEIR SON ONSTAGE.

WOODY SAT IN THE EMPTY BARN AND WATCHED THE BUNTING GO UP. THE STAGE BEGAN TO FILL WITH ALL MANNER OF INSTRUMENTS — PARLOR GUITARS, MANDOLINS, FIDDLES, BANJOS, FAMILY HEIRLOOMS PASSED FROM WRINKLED HAND TO PUDGY FINGERS, SOME OF THEM ALMOST TWO HUNDRED YEARS OLD.

AND AMONG THESE INTRICATELY CRAFTED HEIRLOOMS WERE THE IMPROVISED INSTRUMENTS THAT THEY USED WHEN THERE WAS NOTHING ELSE TO PLAY: MAMA'S WASHBOARD, A PAIR OF SPOONS FROM THE KITCHEN DRAWER, SEVERAL OLD CERAMIC LIQUOR JUGS, AND TWO PAIRS OF BUFFALO RIB BONES, LEFT ON AN ANTHILL YEARS AGO TO CLEAN THEM OF THEIR MARROW; SANDWICHED BETWEEN THE FINGERS, THEY WERE CRICKED AND CRACKED AGAINST EACH OTHER, LIKE GRUESOME CASTANETS.

AND THOSE SAME SCARECROWS FROM THIS MORNING TRAIPSED IN, BANDAGED UP IN STARCHED SHIRTS BY THE WIVES WHO FOLLOWED THEM. AND AS THEIR KIDS TRIPPED AT THEIR ANKLES, AND AS NOISE ENTERED THE BARN,

WOODY AWOKE FROM HIS REVERIE, FALLING FROM THE CHISOS MOUNTAINS TO THE DUSTY BARN FLOOR.

AND WHILE THE OLD BOYS TUNED UP AND SCRATCHED A COUPLE OF WARM-UP TUNES ON THEIR FIDDLEBOXES, THE ATMOSPHERE REMAINED MUTED. EVERY TIME THAT BARN DOOR OPENED, THE CLIMATE OUT-SIDE—THE DROUGHT, THE HARD TIMES—SEEMED TO COUGH IN ANOTHER DRY CLOUD OF DUST AND CHOKE THE AIR INSIDE.

SO, IN THE END, IT WAS THE OLD FOLK THAT STARTED IT. AND SUDDENLY THE KIDS WERE POINTING AND LAUGHING. IT WAS RARE TO SEE GRANDMA HITCH HER SKIRTS, LET ALONE WATCH HER FEET TAP THE TWO-FOUR OF THE FIDDLE REEL.

AND WHEN SHE CLIMBED TO THE STAGE FOR THE NEXT SONG, AFTER NOT SO VERY MUCH COAXING, SHE HAD ON HER WOODEN CLOGS, THE ONES THAT USUALLY SAT ON THE SHELF IN THE SITTING ROOM, THE ONES THE CHILDREN HAD THOUGHT WERE ORNAMENTS.

AND WHEN THOSE CLOGS CLICKED AND CLACKED AGAINST THE HARD WOODEN SLATS OF THE STAGE, THERE WERE CHEERS FROM THE CROWDS. AND THE BAND TOOK THEIR CUE, AND LAUNCHED INTO AN OLD FAVORITE...

I GOT A GIRL AND SHE LOVES ME, SHE'S AS SWEET AS SHE CAN BE, SHE'S GOT EYES OF BABY BLUE, MAKES MY GUN SHOOT STRAIGHT AND TRUE!!!

FOR THE NIGHT HAD JUST BEGUN.

There has t' be close to two hun'ert 'n' fitty peoples out thar...

Biggest shindig I ever bin to, let alone be playin'.

Folks, hushanow! Hush now, please. Laydeees and kind gentlemen, for your esteemed pleasurrre,

THE CORNCOB TRIO.

And the barn held its breath. And the boys took the stage. And as one they raised the roof.

HARD AIN'T IT HARD AIN'T IT HARD T' LOVE SOMEONE THAT NEVER DID LOVE YOU...

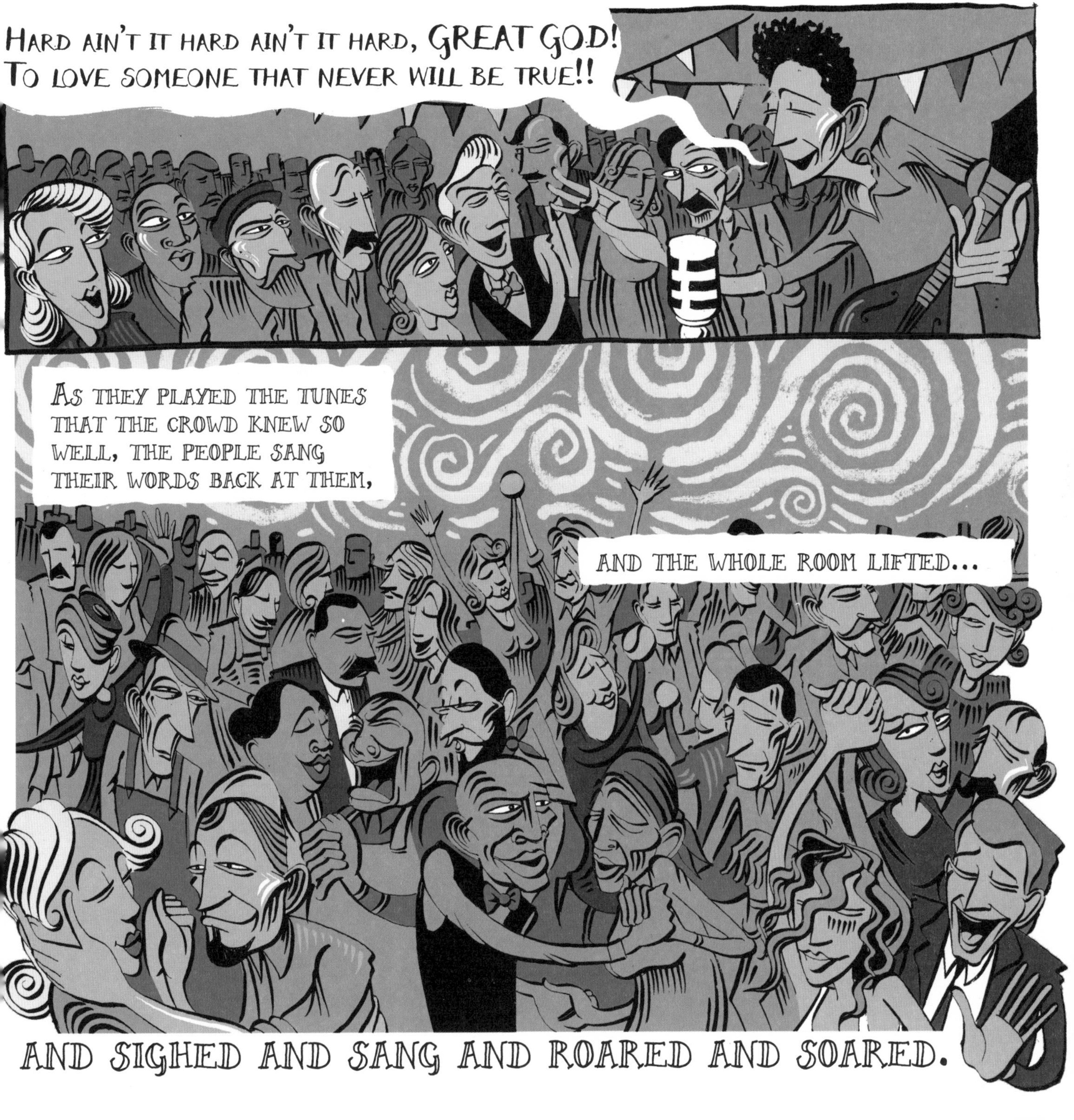
HARD AIN'T IT HARD AIN'T IT HARD, GREAT GOD! TO LOVE SOMEONE THAT NEVER WILL BE TRUE!!
AS THEY PLAYED THE TUNES THAT THE CROWD KNEW SO WELL, THE PEOPLE SANG THEIR WORDS BACK AT THEM,
AND THE WHOLE ROOM LIFTED...
AND SIGHED AND SANG AND ROARED AND SOARED.

THERE WAS AN ALCHEMY IN THIS NOISE AND EXULTATION:

SPELLBOUND IN THE
SORCERY OF THESE
SONGS, *I* BECAME
WE, *ME* BECAME *US*.
FOR THERE WAS AN
EMPOWERMENT IN
THIS EMPATHY, A
CATHARSIS IN THIS
ENERGY, AS IF EACH
MAN HAD GATHERED
THE BARE BONES
OF HIS PERSONAL
CIRCUMSTANCES
AND WAS BANGING
A RHYTHM OUT OF
THEM, A RHYTHM
THAT SANG WITH
THE FEROCIOUS
ENERGY OF SURVIVAL,
A HEARTBEAT THAT
SAID THEY WEREN'T
BEAT.

BECAUSE SINGING WAS BREATHING AND DANCING WAS MOVING, AND BREATHING AND MOVING WERE FOR THE QUICK AND NOT THE DEAD. AND SUDDENLY, THE AIR WAS FULL OF WET— DAMP WITH BREATH AND SWEAT. FACES WERE DRIPPING, ARMS WERE FLAILING, KIDS WERE KISSING, PAS WERE CUSSING, AND MAS WERE LAUGHING, AND ALL WERE SWAYING IN A WAY THAT HAD SOMETHING TO DO WITH THE HOMEBREW, SOMETHING TO DO WITH THE MUSIC, WITH THE WAY THINGS ARE, WITH THE WAY THEY SHOULD BE, AND WITH THE WAY THEY ALWAYS HAVE BEEN. AND QUIETLY BEHIND HIS SONG,

WOODY WATCHED IT ALL REFLECTED IN THE EYES OF MARY JENNINGS.

CHAPTER 4

As parched summer turned to dry winter,

WOODY MARRIED MARY JENNINGS.

THE WINDS WERE UP WHEN THEY RAN FROM THE SMALL CHURCH TO THE DIME STORE TO PRESERVE THEIR MOMENT IN CHEAP SEPIA SNAPS.

MARY'S FATHER, THOUGH NOT HAPPY WITH THIS NEW UNION, SLOWLY WARMED TO WOODY AND BOUGHT THEM ONE OF THE SHOTGUN SHACKS BEHIND HIS HOUSE.

THE SHACK WAS OLD AND RICKETY, GRIMED WITH THE DUST THAT WAS FLOWING THROUGH THE AIR. IT RATTLED IN THE WINTER WINDS, AND HAD FEWER FLOORBOARDS THAN WAS STRICTLY NECESSARY. BUT WITH AN OIL STOVE IN THE FRONT ROOM, AND WET TOWELS ALONG THE WINDOW FRAMES TO KEEP OUT THE DUST,

WOODY AND MARY NESTED THE WINTER THROUGH,

FLUSHED WITH THE WARMTH OF NEW LOVE.

BUT OUTSIDE, THE WIND SCREAMED AND THE DUST RAILED AGAINST THE WINDOWPANES, GRITTING THE GLASS LIKE HAIL.

THERE WAS A NEW PRESIDENT IN WASHINGTON, AND NEW PROMISES IN THE PAPERS, BUT THE PEOPLE OF THE HIGH PLAINS WERE DESPERATE.

IT STILL HADN'T RAINED.

THE WHEAT HARVESTS HAD FAILED, AND MUCH OF THE GROUND LAY FALLOW.

TOWNS WERE EMPLOYING CHARLATAN ENGINEERS TO POINT GUNS AT THE SKY AND FILL THEM WITH EXPLOSIONS THAT THEY CLAIMED WOULD BLOW THE HEAVENS OPEN. THEY LEFT TOWN BEFORE THEIR GUARANTEES RAN OUT.

THOSE WHO HAD HOGS SLAUGHTERED THEM...

THOSE WHO HAD GODS PRAYED TO THEM...

AND THOSE WITH SUPERSTITIONS NAILED SNAKES TO THEIR FENCE POSTS AND DAUBED THE LINTELS OF THEIR HOMES WITH BLOOD. ANYTHING TO SEE THEM THROUGH THE NEXT FEW MONTHS.

WOODY KEPT WITH HIS MUSIC, PICKING UP MORE INSTRUMENTS, TURNING HIS HAND TO STRING, HORN, AND IVORY.

HE JOINED UNCLE JEFF IN HIS NEW STINT AS A MAGICIAN, HELPING HIM EXECUTE HIS SLEIGHT-OF-HAND MIRAGES TO THE PALTRY CROWDS, AND DEVELOPED A GOOFER'S ACT WITH HIS WASHBOARD, CHOMPING CIGARS, FALLING OVER HIS FLOWING TROUSERS, AND TELLING CORNY JOKES THAT EVERYBODY HAD HEARD A HUNDRED TIMES BEFORE.

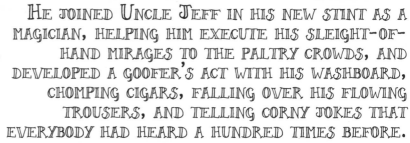

I stopped with a family that had twin boys. One was named Pete and the other... Re-pete!!!

At another place they had twin girls. One they called Kate...the other Dupli-kate!!!

HE CLUNG TO THE MEMORY OF HIS MOTHER'S FACE, FLICKERING IN THE JEWEL PICTURE HOUSE, WATCHING THE GLIMMERING SLAPSTICK OF CHARLIE CHAPLIN.

CRYING WITH LAUGHTER, HER SHOULDERS WOULD HEAVE WITH DELIGHT.

HE REMEMBERED HER FACE BY THE WIRELESS, WAITING FOR WILL ROGERS'S NEXT PUNCHLINE, EYES FULL OF TWINKLE, SUSPENDED IN A MOMENT OF TINGLING HOPE AND EXCITEMENT.

AND IN THE BLANK FACES IN ALL THE AUDIENCES HE PLAYED FOR,

WOODY SOUGHT THAT LOOK.

CHARLEY GUTHRIE ALSO HAD A NEW BRIDE, AND LIKE MOST OF HIS SELF-IMPROVEMENT SCHEMES,

SHE HAD COME BY MAIL.

HE HAD REPLIED TO AN AD IN THE LONELY-HEARTS COLUMN, AND FOLLOWING TWO RATHER FORMAL, PRAGMATIC EXCHANGES, BETTY JEAN MCPHERSON HAD ARRIVED AT THE STATION IN PAMPA AND HEADED WITH CHARLEY TO THE CHURCH. SHE WAS A FEROCIOUS-BOSOMED, TOBACCO-STAINED, HEAVING HULK OF A WOMAN WHO STIFLED THOSE AROUND HER WITH HER REGAL AURA AND EUCALYPTUS PERFUME.

BUT TO WOODY, SHE BECAME AN OPEN DOOR TO THE OTHER SIDE.

FOR BETTY JEAN WAS A SELF-PROCLAIMED SPIRITUALIST WHOSE POWDERED HEAD HELD THE MYSTERIES TO A HUNDRED OCCULT PRACTICES.

SHE PRACTICED TELEPATHY AND HYPNOTISM...

SHE COULD READ PEOPLE'S MINDS, THEIR PALMS, AND THEIR FUTURES FROM A CRYSTAL BALL, AND INTERPRET THE CARDS THEY PICKED ON HER BAIZE TABLE...

IN HER HANDS, SHE HELD THE SECRET OF MAGNETIC HEALING.

AS SHE TRACED THE CREASES OF THEIR PALMS AND READ A BRIGHTER FUTURE, HE SAW A HOPE IN THEIR EYES, A LIGHT THAT PIERCED THROUGH THEIR GLOOMING CATARACTS. BECAUSE THESE WERE NO ORDINARY PROMISES. THERE WAS A SURETY IN HER LINK TO THIS OTHER SIDE THAT WARRANTED HER CUSTOMERS SAFETY. FOR BETTY'S WORDS WERE BACKED BY THE STEADFASTNESS OF THE DEAD, THE VASTNESS OF THE HEAVENS, THE TIMELESS SPAN OF INFINITY.

THERE WAS SOMETHING OF THE CHURCH IN THIS, SOMETHING OF A MOTHER'S EMBRACE IN THIS, AND TO WOODY, THERE WAS SOMETHING THAT CHIMED WITH THOSE CHISOS MOUNTAINS AND THE STARS THAT LIT THEM.

WOODY BECAME FASCINATED BY THIS OTHER SIDE, THIS GREAT SCOPE OF EXISTENCE, THAT LINK OF LIFE THAT BROUGHT EACH AND EVERY BEING TOGETHER IN DEATH. HE BEGAN TEARING THROUGH THE PAGES OF BOOKS IN THE LIBRARY, LEAFING THROUGH HISTORY BOOKS, PHILOSOPHICAL TRACTS, SPIRITUALIST WRITINGS, SEARCHING FOR AN OLDER WISDOM THAT MIGHT CURE THE TOWN OF ITS DESPONDENCY.

DAY BY DAY HE WOULD VISIT THAT LIBRARY, RUN HIS FINGER DOWN THE CORRIDORS OF LEATHER SPINES, AND MARVEL AT THE SHEER NUMBER OF WORDS AND THOUGHTS HIDDEN AWAY IN THIS OLD BUILDING IN PAMPA.

EVERY ONCE IN A WHILE, HE PULLED OUT TITLES THAT TUGGED AT HIS IMAGINATION AND SAT FOR HOURS AS HIS EYES FED HIS HUNGRY MIND. AND IN THAT LIBRARY, AS HE SPREAD THE PAGES OF THESE BOOKS, HIS MIND OPENED ITS WINGS AND TOOK OFF OUT OF PAMPA.

It flew up high into that vast vault of blue and looked down upon Texas, Oklahoma, Kansas, upon all of the Great Plains, and saw a horizon that stretched across the entire history of America.

CARRIED ALOFT ON THESE PRINTED WORDS, HE SAW THE PLAINS AS THEY WERE BEFORE MANKIND: A VAST INLAND OCEAN THAT SPREAD OUT FROM BENEATH HIS FEET TO THE VERY NORTH OF AMERICA, FLANKED TO THE WEST BY THE ROCKIES, AND TO THE EAST BY THE APPALACHIANS.

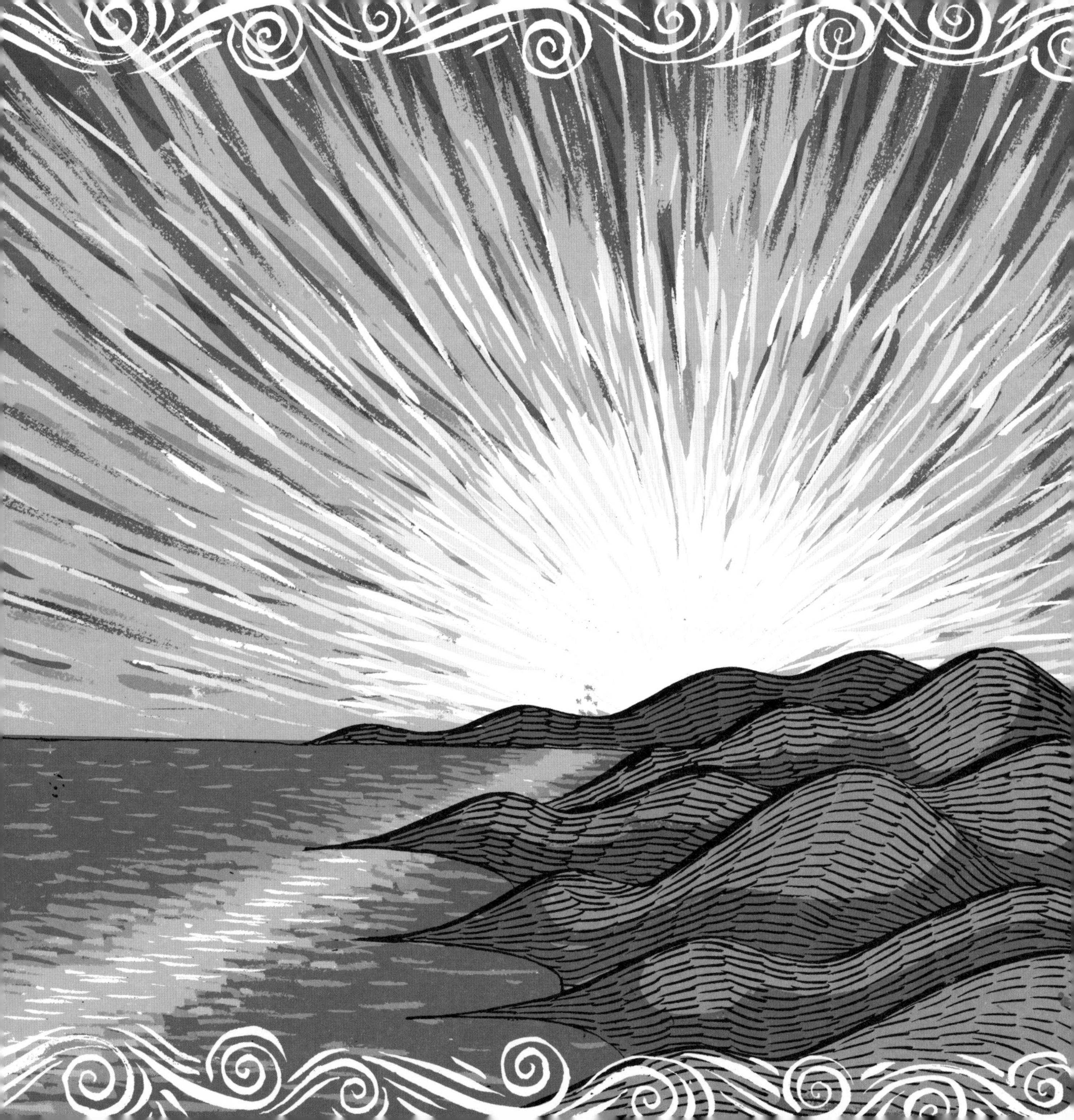

HE FELT THE AEONS ROLL IN HIS STOMACH AND WATCHED THE SEA RECEDE INTO A RICH ALLUVIAL PLAIN AS FLAT AS THE OCEAN THAT WANED.

HE FELT THE RUSH OF WIND IN HIS HAIR AND STARTED SINKING LOWER TO THE LAND,

AND THE HURRICANES AND TORNADOES SHRIEKED AMID HIS HEAD, WHIPPING THE GRASSES INTO RUSTLING WAVES.

DESCENDING STILL, HE SAW MASTODONS SWAYING UNDER THEIR MAMMOTH WEIGHT,

SABER-TOOTHED TIGERS SLINKING THROUGH THE BRISTLING GRASSES,

HERDS OF HORSES, GIANT SLOTHS,

AND A LONE AMERICAN LION.

HE FELT THE DIZZYING RUSH OF TIME IN HIS GUT ONCE AGAIN,

AND AS HIS FEET TOUCHED GROUND,

HE SAW THE ANIMALS TURN TO GHOSTS.

WALKING FORWARD, HE FOUND HIMSELF ENMESHED IN A VAST WORLD OF NETTED GRASS AND TANGLED ROOT. TO HIS WEST HE SAW PLAINS OF SHORT-TUFTED BLUE GRAMA GRASS, TUSSETS OF SPIKY FESCUE, FEATHERY DROPSEED, AND GALLETA.

BEFORE HIM, THE GRASS WAS BIGGER, A KNEE-HIGH MESH OF NEEDLEGRASS, PRAIRIE THREE-AWN, SOAPWEED, AND YUCCA. DELICATE BRIGHTLY PETALED FLOWERS OF POPPY MALLOW, BUTTERWEED, AND SUNDROP ROSE FROM THE THORNY BRISTLING STEMS OF THE SAGEBRUSH, SALTWORT, AND RUSSIAN THISTLE.

And to the northeast edge of the plains, he saw the big bluestem grass, the switch grass, and Indian grass that towered into the sky, eight feet high.

He bent to one knee, took a large snatch of the bluestem in one hand, placed his other on the land, and pulled with all his might. The grass tore reluctantly from its roots, bringing with it clods of crumbling black chernozem soil. Woody dug with his hands, tearing at the thick weave of stringy white roots until his hands bled and he found no space beneath him that wasn't tightly bonded with this mat of interwoven root. Beneath the vicious winds of the plains, these roots kept the grassland grounded. In the flash fires that scourged the plains, these roots gave life to the charred, blackened grassland. And in the harsh eras of drought, these roots plunged deep into the earth, to its ancient store of water and minerals, and kept the land alive.

THERE WAS A HAND ON HIS SHOULDER, AND HE TURNED.

A MAN THE COLOR OF RED CLAY, WITH STREAKS OF VEGETABLE DYE ON HIS FACE, BONES AROUND HIS NECK, AND FEATHERS ON HIS HEAD THAT STROKED THE SKY, PEERED INTO HIS EYES.

OTHERS EMERGED FROM THE GRASSES AND WALKED WITH HIM TO THEIR CAMP. TEPEES OF BUFFALO HIDE WERE STRETCHED OVER PORTABLE FRAMES, WOMEN WERE DIVIDING UP THE FOOD, AND CHILDREN WERE WATCHING THEIR FATHERS STRING BOWS.

IN THE DISTANCE, A HERD OF BISON SLID ACROSS THE HORIZON, AND WOODY WATCHED AS THESE TRIBESMEN PACKED UP THEIR CAMP AND FOLLOWED THE HERD NORTH.

Still, the winds blew. And Woody watched with the tribes— the Blackfoot, Crow, Sioux, Cheyenne, Arapaho, and Comanche— as new figures entered the landscape, figures on horseback, with gleaming armor.

He watched as they bartered with the Indians and produced large parchments of paper promises and payment assurances.

He watched as they came again, in greater number, flags flying, to stain their swords and drive the Indians away.

He watched the tribesmen resist, he watched as they ambushed the wagon trails of settlers, pacing the ground like the silent ghosts of the extinct American lions, and he watched as they sang their victories and buried their dead.

LIKE CLOUDS, THE CENTURIES ROLLED OVER WOODY'S HEAD, AND SUDDENLY THERE WERE MORE MEN, LIGHTER-SKINNED, WHO CAME AGAIN ON HORSEBACK, THOUGH THIS TIME WITH GUNS.

LIKE THOSE BEFORE THEM, THEY WANTED THE LAND: NOT A SHARE OF THE LAND, NOT RIGHTS TO THE LAND, BUT DOMINION OVER THE LAND, POSSESSION, OWNERSHIP.

AND FOR THAT, IT COULDN'T BE SHARED.

SO IN THE END, THE INDIANS WERE GONE.

UPROOTED AND BLOWN TO THE CORNERS OF THE PLAINS.

And all the while, the cities that had sprouted around these Great Plains were sending prospectors to survey the land, calculating its economic value. Shareholders in England, Holland, and Germany, waving the same paper parchments that had been signed on the plains, demanded a return on their investments, and the settlers were contracted to turn the land into profit.

So they hammered in steel railways that brought in cattle by the millions,

They rolled millions of miles of barbed fence lines across the land,

And Woody watched the XIT cowboys birth, herd, and slaughter their livestock. To make way for these great factory ranches, the bison of the plains, all twenty-five million of them, were chased down and killed, their skulls piled into mountains by the rail yards, to be taken away, powdered, and used as fertilizer.

AND THEN A HARD WINTER HIT THE PLAINS,

THE FIRST SINCE THE BISONS' DISAPPEARANCE,
AND THE COWS IN THE SOUTH, WHOSE THIN
HIDES WERE UNSUITED TO THIS PLUMMET
IN TEMPERATURE, DIED IN DROVES.
IT WAS SAID YOU COULD WALK FOUR
HUNDRED MILES ALONG THE
CANADIAN RIVER INTO NEW
MEXICO AND NEVER STEP OFF
THEIR CARCASSES.
BECAUSE COWS WERE NO LONGER A VIABLE COMMODITY,
THE CITIES SOUGHT FOR SOMETHING ELSE TO HARNESS THE WEALTH OF THIS LAND.

THEY CHOSE WHEAT. SOW THE EARTH WITH WHEAT
AND IT WILL GROW GREEN, AND TURN GOLD IN THE SUN.

WHEAT WAS THE VERY COLOR OF WEALTH.

SO THEY PLOWED THE LAND.

FIRST WITH HORSE PLOWS, THEN
WITH A ONE-DISK MACHINE THAT
SLICED THE ROOTS OF THE BUFFALO
GRASS FOR THE FIRST TIME IN FIFTY
MILLION YEARS.

THEY TURFED THE PLAINS UPSIDE DOWN, CLUMPED IN
SEVERED CLOTS, ROOTS FACING UP TO THE BLUE SKY.

AND WOODY WATCHED AS THE WHEAT GREW.

ITS SHALLOW ROOTS TOOK TO THE TOPSOIL AND DRAINED IT OF ITS NUTRIENTS.

WOODY WATCHED AS GREAT MACHINE COMBINES THRESHED THE WHEAT TILL IT POURED LIKE GOLDEN STEAM INTO THE WAGONS, TO BE SHIPPED OFF TO FEED A NEW WORLD WAR.

AND AS ITS MARKET VALUE INCREASED, BACKED BY THE GOVERNMENT, THE TOWNS SWELLED AND FILLED WITH PEOPLE WHO CUT FARTHER INTO THE PLAINS, BITING AWAY AT THE BUFFALO GRASS WITH A PETROL-DRIVEN EFFICIENCY.

AND NOW, FOR THE FIRST TIME SINCE THE BUFFALO GRASS DISAPPEARED, A DROUGHT HAD SETTLED IN.

THE LAND HAD STARTED TO CRACK, THE SOIL HAD STARTED TO FAIL, AND THE HOWLS OF THE BLUE NORTHERS ONCE AGAIN WHIPPED THROUGH THE HOLLOW TOWNS LIKE AVENGING ANGELS.

WITHOUT THE ROOTS OF THE GRASS TO GROUND IT, THE EARTH TOOK TO THE SKIES. A GHOST-LIKE SHROUD OF DUST PEPPERED THE AIR, THICKENING EVERY DRY BREATH, AND STINGING THE EYES; IT MADE THE CHILDREN COUGH, IT MADE THE ANIMALS WEAK, AND PAMPA, LIKE EVERY TOWN AROUND IT, WAS CATALEPTIC.

IN THE EVENING, THE WOMEN JOINED THE MEN ON THE PORCH TO REFLECT THE EMPTY SKY WITH THEIR FACES.

WOODY KEPT SEEING HIS MOTHER IN THESE VACANT STARES.

HE REMEMBERED THE CHANGE THAT WOULD COME OVER HER WHEN THEY WERE PLAYING IN THE YARD OR SETTING THE TABLE.

AT TIMES, SHE WAS A SATURDAY-MORNING FARMERS' MARKET IN PAMPA, BUSTLING WITH ENERGY, BRIMMING WITH CONVERSATION, BUT MORE GRADUALLY, AFTER THE FIRST FIRE, AND MORE OFTEN TOWARD THE LAST, HER FACE WOULD CONTORT, TWISTING A SMILE INTO A SNARL, AND HER EYES WOULD EMPTY AND SHE WOULD SIT FOR HOURS STARING INTO THE NEAR DISTANCE.

AS WOODY SAW HIS NEIGHBORS' FACES CONTORT INTO THE HARDENED GRIMACES OF HIS MOTHER'S LAST YEARS, HE RETREATED INTO HIS NEW HOME.

HE WOULD COME HOME FROM HIS SHOWS WITH UNCLE JEFF AND SIT WITH MARY UNDER THE PATCHWORK QUILT. THEY WOULD LISTEN TO THE OLD-TIME SONGS ON THE RADIO—THE WARM-HEARTED DITTIES OF CHARLIE POOLE, THE PIERCING HARMONIES OF THE CARTER FAMILY.

WRAPPED IN THE COMFORT OF MARY'S BLANKET, HER ARMS AROUND HIM, WITH THOSE BITTERSWEET MELODIES FILLING THE ROOM, THERE WAS SOMETHING OF HIS CHILDHOOD, A MEMORY THAT MESMERIZED HIM.

I stand on my stepstone at eventide now,
The wind whistles by with a moan...

His mother had called these the facts-of-life music. The melodies had that haunting beauty of a vulture circling the wind eddies, or the glimmer of the moon on a lake. The lyrics spoke of demon lovers, outlaws and border raids, seafaring heroes lost to the seas, broken hearts and dispossessed peoples.

THESE WERE SONGS OF LOSS.

And as they played through the radios, they spoke to every family on Pampa's skid row. The families of German and Dutch immigrants whose grandfathers had left their motherland for America, the Scots and Irish whose ancestors had come over with the pilgrims, the black families whose heritage was one of kidnap from the West African coasts.

Each household was reminded of what their ancestors had lost, making them cling ever tighter to their children, to their hope for the future.

As Woody's mother sang these old Scots ballads, Irish laments, and African spirituals, the room filled with the ghosts of human experience, called from the graves of lost lands, touching the living with the value and fragility of their lives.

Two years into the drought, many of Pampa's residents, these migrants and travelers from other lands, were once again on the get-go.

FOLLOWING THE CRASH

ON WALL STREET, MANY BANKS WERE CLAIMING UP THE LAND THEY OWNED FROM THE TENANT FARMERS, BULLDOZING THEIR MATCHBOX LIVELIHOODS FOR GREAT BIG FACTORY FARMS. THOSE WHO RENTED, OR HADN'T PAID THEIR FULL MORTGAGE, WERE OUSTED FROM THE LAND THEY WERE BORN ON, TO MAKE WAY FOR THESE NEW, VAST OCEANS OF WHEAT. LAND COMPANIES, BANKS, AND SHAREHOLDERS DIVIDED IT AMONG THEMSELVES, CUT IT UP LIKE A LIVING CARCASS, MECHANIZED IT, COMMODIFIED IT, AND BLED IT OF ITS ASSETS.

AND NOW WITH THE DUST,

THE LIFE OF THE LAND HAD BEEN BLOWN TO THE WIND,

LEAVING THE PEOPLE UPON ITS HARD SHELL AS ROOTLESS AS THE SHALLOW WHEAT THAT HAD BEEN PLANTED IN THEIR PLACE.

AS THESE DISPOSSESSED FARMERS TOOK TO THE ROADS, THEY WERE MIGRANTS ONCE MORE. THIS TIME, THEIR MOTHERLAND WAS NOT BEHIND THEM, BUT DEAD BENEATH THEIR FEET.

DAY AND NIGHT, WOODY WATCHED THEM PASS HIS DOOR AND HEARD THE CARTER FAMILY STRIKE UP THAT FAMOUS SONG AGAIN ON THE RADIO:

"Good-bye to my stepstone, good-bye to my home,
God bless the ones that I leave with a sigh;
Fields will be whitening
And I will be gone,
to ramble this wide world alone."

CHAPTER 5

THE DROUGHT HAD SEIZED THE HIGH PLAINS AND HELD A CHOKING GRIP.
THE SKY HAD TURNED FROM BLUE TO A DAZZLING WHITE, AND PRESSED LIKE MARBLE UPON THE GROUND, BURNING THE EYES OF ITS ONLOOKERS. CRACKING UNDER THIS HIGH PRESSURE, THE LAND WAS REACTING WITH A STRANGENESS THAT WAS NEW TO ITS RESIDENTS.

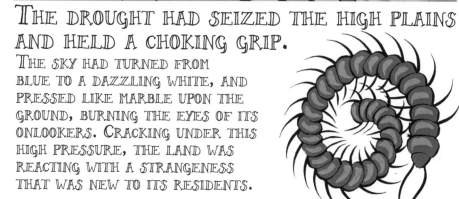

THE FLOORS AND WALLS OF THE HOUSES CRAWLED WITH A PROFUSION OF CENTIPEDES, GRASSHOPPERS, BLACK WIDOWS, AND TARANTULAS, WHICH WERE EXCAVATED BY THE BUCKET LOAD. THE HEAT BROKE ALL RECORDS.

STRANGE STORMS WERE BEING REPORTED ACROSS THE PLAINS: BLIZZARDS OF BLACK DUST WOULD APPEAR AT THE EDGES OF THE TOWNS, ROLLING LIKE MOUNTAINOUS SEAS OF DIRT.

THEY WOULD BLISTER THROUGH THE TOWNS, SNUFFING THE SUN, AND DEPOSIT TONS OF TORRID TOPSOIL IN DESERT DUNES ACROSS THE LANDS. WHEAT FIELDS WERE CRUSHED, AND THOSE THAT REMAINED WERE DEVOURED BY THE INSECTS, WINGING AND CRAWLING THEIR WAY ACROSS THE PLAINS.

BECAUSE TODAY WAS A SUNDAY AND MOST OF SHORTY'S CUSTOMERS WERE EITHER AT CHURCH...

OR CRACKING THE SKULLS OF RABBITS.

SINCE THE DROUGHT, RABBITS HAD BEEN TAKING ADVANTAGE OF THE MOUNTAINS OF TOASTING GRAIN LEFT TO SPOIL AROUND EVERY TOWN AND THEY WERE BREEDING LIKE A BIBLICAL PLAGUE. ALL ACROSS THE PLAINS, FOLK HAD STARTED TO ROUND UP THE RABBITS IN THE NEAREST FIELDS AND CLUB THEM TO EXTINCTION.

WHETHER THEY THOUGHT THIS WAS POSSIBLE, OR SIMPLY WANTED TO KICK BACK AT THE BOUNTY OF A LAND THAT HAD DESERTED THEM,

THESE DROVES HAD BECOME MORE AND MORE POPULAR, INSPIRING AN ALMOST CARNIVAL ATMOSPHERE.

TODAY, THE DRUNKS HAD ABANDONED SHORTY'S STORE FOR THE CORN LIQUOR THAT NOW ACCOMPANIED THESE RABBIT-BASHING FETES.

WOODY, HOWEVER, WAS PAINTING THE SIGN.

You not drovin' them jackrabbits?
No, sir, I have no interest in bashin' bunnies. Sweating in the sun fer no good purpose... that ain't my idea of fun...
People gotta do sumthin'. I keep looking t' the sky for that old sun dog; sum sign to tell me the rains is on their way. But they keeps not comin'.
I figure folks jest want t' be out on the land. Them pollitishuns say you cain't plant no more crops, there's too much wheat, they say— you gotta stop. People jest don't know whattado. They're paying people to sit on their haunches, and watch their land wither beneath 'em.
So many folks is leavin'...It ain't right. You cain't just turn yr back on a place like that.
They ain't got no choice left to make.

RTY'S

Them handbills they keeps waving: Work in California. Good clean orange pickin', lettuce pickin', prune pickin'. A man can clear make a fortune, following that sun to harvest.

That what them handbills say. Nuttin' but promises writ on a piece of paper.

PAMPA HERALD

AND JUST THEN, A BIRD FELL FROM THE SKY.

BOTH MEN LOOKED UP. FLOCKS OF SCISSOR-TAILS, PLOVERS, AND JACKDAWS WERE HEADING SOUTH, DRIVEN BY A COLD WIND THAT BEGAN TO TUG AT THE MEN'S SHIRTS.

THE BIRD WAS GRIMED, FEATHERS HEAVY WITH GRIT.
This in't right.
There ain't nuttin' about this town that's right no more...
No, I mean, this ain't right.
BIRDS WERE FILLING THE SKY IN NUMBER NOW, URGENTLY FLEEING THE WIND THAT BEGAN TO HOWL ABOVE THE MEN'S HEADS.

THE WIND WAS BLASTING THEIR FACES WITH A GRIT THAT CHOKED THEIR THROATS. THIS WAS NO ORDINARY TWISTER.

WOODY RAN OUT INTO THE STREET. HE LOOKED SOUTH AND COULD SEE NOTHING BUT SKY AND BIRDS.

HE LOOKED NORTH AND HIS JAW DROPPED.

THE SKY BEFORE HIM WAS BLACK, ROILING AND WRITHING, A SEA OF SNAKES TUMBLING TOWARD HIM. FORKS OF LIGHTNING CRACKED THE BLACK WITH GREAT STATIC SPEARS OF LIGHT, DANCING AND FLASHING THROUGH THE CLOUDS; TINY TYPHOONS RIPPED AND ZIPPED ACROSS THE DUSTY HIGH STREET, SCORING SMOKE-LIKE LINES BEHIND THEM, AND TETHERED HORSES BEGAN TO WRESTLE THEIR MANES, STRAINING AGAINST THEIR ROPES, EYEBALLS WHITE WITH TERROR, WHINNYING IN THE WIND.

WOODY'S HOME WAS UPWIND, MARY WAS THERE, AND HE HAD TO GET BACK.

LIKE IRON WOOL ON PEELED PEACHES, THE GUSHING GRIT SCRAPED HIS EYES, SCOURED HIS FACE, AND TURNED HIS MOUTH TO MUD.

THE PEOPLE OF PAMPA WERE RUNNING, TOO, SCATTERING TOWARD THEIR HOMES, TO ANY PLACE WHERE THEY COULD CATCH SOME BREATH.

AS HE RAN AGAINST THIS STAMPEDING WIND OF EARTH, WOODY HEARD THE SIGN OF THE PHARMACY STORE SLANGING AGAINST THE METAL LAMP, KNELLING A WARNING TO THE PEOPLE BELOW.

GOD FORGIVE US!!!! PEOPLE! THIS IS YOUR RETRIBUTION!
WITH THE WIND HAS COME OUR JUDGMENT!
DROWN PEOPLE! DROWN!
WE HAD THIS A-COMIN' FROM THE MOMENT WE SET FOOT ON THESE GREAT PLAINS.
LIKE THEM HEATHEN ISRAYELITES, PEOPLE, THIS DEAD SEA STORM IS A-COMIN' TO US, AND IT'S GUNNA CLEAN YOU OF YOUR SINS.
GOD SAYS: "THE LAND SHALL NOT BE SOLD FOREVER: FOR THE LAND IS MINE; FOR YE ARE STRANGERS AND SOJOURNERS WITH ME." LEVITICUS 25, PEOPLE.

As the darkness ingested Woody, he could see the barbed-wire fences glowing red in the dark, charged with the static that cracked through the air.

THE STORM WAS NOW UPON THE TOWN, CHOMPING THROUGH THE STREETS LIKE A HAIRY, BLACK-BACKED BEAST, ENVELOPING THE BUILDINGS, SWALLOWING THE RUNNING PEOPLE.

HE PUSHED THROUGH THE ROAR AND FOUND HIS FRONT DOOR.

MARY WAS RUNNING THE TAP OVER THE LAST OF THEIR TOWELS TO PRESS AGAINST THE BASE OF THE WINDOWS.

BABY!

AS SHE HELD HIM, THE GRAVELED MESH OF WIND SEEMED TO RUSH FASTER AGAINST THE WINDOW-PANES, THE ROOM GREW SUDDENLY DARKER, AND THE HOUSE WENT COLD.

Jeezus, Mary! I ain't never seen a thing more wilder in my waking days.

What should we do?

T'ain't nothing we can do.

There's a lady out there.

She's rantin' and ravin' and she's saying it's our judgment.

Woody... you don't believe in no Judgment Day...

I don't know Mary-gal—there's sumthin' out there that's wild—it's got a spirit to it—it may come from the Lord, or the sky, or the land, it don't matter, but it ain't got no love for us.

It's angry...

IN THAT COLD, DARK ROOM, SHAKING AND RATTLING IN THAT VICIOUS WIND, MARY HELD WOODY ON THEIR SOFA, AND THEY PRESSED CLOSE TO EACH OTHER'S WARMTH BENEATH HIS MOTHER'S QUILT.

THEY SAT MUTELY, LISTENING TO THE RADIO, AS REPORTS CAME IN ON THE STORM.

THIS OCEAN OF DUST NOW DROWNING PAMPA SPREAD FROM ALBUQUERQUE TO TULSA, A FRONT OF NEARLY SEVEN HUNDRED MILES.

IT WAS PICKING UP THOUSANDS OF TONS OF DRY, LOOSE TEXAN TOPSOIL AND BLASTING IT THROUGH OKLAHOMA, KANSAS, AND COLORADO.

AS THE STORM SNAPPED THE POLES OF THE ELECTRIC WIRES SOME MILES NORTH,

THE RADIO IN THE GUTHRIES' HOME SUDDENLY FIZZLED DEAD, AND THEY SAT IN SILENCE FOR THE REST OF THE AFTERNOON AS THE WIND BLEW ITSELF OUT.

At some point toward the evening, with Mary asleep, her arms still around him, an old melody slipped into Woody's mind.

And with that melody, **A MEMORY.**

Years ago, when his mother was alive, a cyclone had struck their home.

They had run from the house to the pine shelter his pa had dug into the ground,

And waited as the whirlwind whipped the boards off the barn roofs.

His mother had sung an old song about such moments, a song she called "The Sherman Cyclone," and slowly, the words began to filter through his mind.

We saw the storm approaching, The clouds looked deathly black,
And through our little city, It made its dreadful track.
We saw the lightning streaming, We heard the thunder roll,
It was but the shortest moment, And the story soon was told.

The song had been written forty years or so before, after the wind had claimed over a hundred lives. Written to commemorate the dead, it had calmed Woody on his mother's lap, and it calmed him now.

There was a security in those old words, a warmth of a mother's wisdom. The song suggested a survival, a voice that had lasted through the storm, and singing it now was a spell of assurance. The storm would pass. They would sit it out.

BUT AS WOODY SANG THAT SONG, LIKE A LULLABY, AS THE STORM WANED AROUND HIS SHOTGUN SHACK, NEW WORDS ENTERED HIS MIND, AND THEY FITTED EASILY, UNCONSCIOUSLY, INTO THAT OLD MELODY.

GENTLY, HE LEFT MARY AND THE QUILT ON THE SOFA, AND WENT TO THE WINDOW, WHERE HIS GUITAR WAS PERCHED. ITS WOODEN BELLY SLOTTED INTO HIS LAP, AND HIS FINGERS FOUND THE CHORDS.

AS HE PLAYED THE MELODY OUT ON THE GUITAR, THE CHORDS RINGING THROUGH THE HOLLOW CAVERN INTO THE CHAMBER OF HIS CHEST, THE WORDS SLID INTO HIS HEAD AND ONTO THE PAPER BEFORE HIM, A STREAM OF CONSCIOUSNESS.

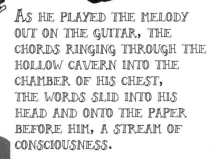

On the 14th day of April of 1935,
There struck the worst of dust storms
That ever filled the sky.
You could see that dust storm comin',
The cloud looked deathlike black,
And through our mighty nation,
It left a dreadful track.

From Oklahoma City to the Arizona line,
Dakota and Nebraska to the lazy Rio Grande,
It fell across our city like a curtain of black rolled down,
We thought it was our judgment,
We thought it was our doom.

THE NEXT DAY, THEY WOKE TO A HAZE OF DUST.

IT HUNG IN THE AIR OF THEIR SHACK;

IT HUNG IN THE AIR OUTSIDE.

TOGETHER THEY CLEARED THE MUDDY TOWELS FROM THE WINDOWS, COUGHING AS THEY WENT, PACING SLOWLY THROUGH THE SUNLIT LINT OF OKLAHOMAN DIRT.

THEY STEPPED OUT TO WASH THE TOWELS.
AS IF SNOW HAD FALLEN, THE LANDSCAPE WAS SWADDLED IN A NEW SHAPE, A STATIC OCEAN OF RISING AND FALLING WAVES, RIPPLED INTO RIDGES BY THE WIND.

THE RUTS IN THE LAND WERE FILLED INTO HILLS, FENCE POSTS STOOD SUBMERGED IN DUNES, WHICH IN SOME PLACES REACHED THE EAVES OF THE BARNS. FARTHER INTO THE DISTANCE, THE WHEAT STALKS STUCK OUT OF THE GRIT DRIFTS LIKE BURNED MATCHES, SCORCHED BY THE ELECTRICITY IN THE AIR.

As Woody and Mary walked, they heard news about the storm from around their town. The telephone poles were down. Cars were left stranded on the highways, half-buried in dirt.

A train had been derailed just outside of Pampa.

People who had been stranded in their cars for the night were returning home in soiled suits, faces charred.

They went to check in on neighbors, and take in this new world. They saw the cows in one corner of a field.

They were piled on top of one other, where they had huddled to the end. A farmer stood by them, a knife in his bloodied, muddied hands:

There's no words...
They're stuffed full of it.
Stomachs like sandbags.

FARTHER OUT INTO THE PLAINS, IN THE EMPTY SPACES THAT HAD ONCE BEEN WHEAT FIELDS, THE GROUND HAD OPENED UP ITS MAW, AND RELICS AND RUINS HAD BEEN UNEARTHED.

INDIAN BURIAL SITES HAD BEEN BLOWN OPEN, REVEALING SKELETONS STILL ADORNED WITH FEATHER BRACELETS.

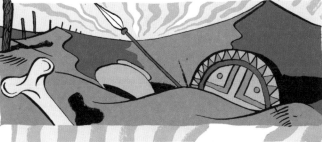

AND FARTHER STILL, THE BONES OF PREHISTORIC SEA CREATURES LAY JUTTING OUT OF THE DIRT...

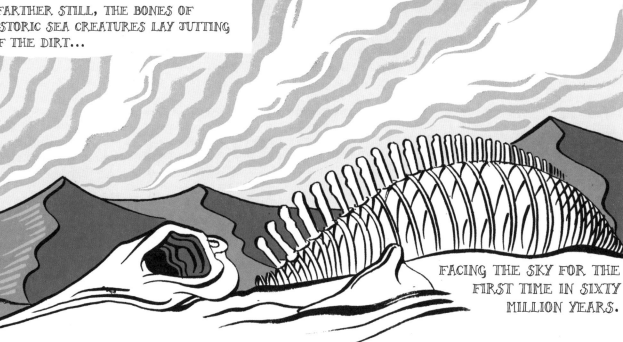

FACING THE SKY FOR THE FIRST TIME IN SIXTY MILLION YEARS.

WHEN WOODY RETURNED HOME WITH MARY, THEY WERE BOTH SILENT.

WOODY WENT STRAIGHT FOR HIS NOTEBOOK AND PEN.

OVER THE LAST COUPLE OF YEARS, HE'D BEEN REWRITING THE WORDS OF VARIOUS OLD TUNES, TO PLAY WITH MATT AND CLUSTER, OR JEFF AND HIS WIFE.

THEY WERE NONSENSE RHYMES, OFTEN DERIVED FROM FUNNY LITTLE NOTIONS HE'D HAD AT SHORTY'S, ANECDOTES HE'D HEARD, OR THE ODD THINGS HIS MIND PRESENTED HIM WITH WHEN HE FORGOT THE LYRICS ONSTAGE.

HE HAD BOUND THEM TOGETHER INTO A BOOK, AND GIVEN IT A GRANDIOSE TITLE, BEFITTING HIS CLOWNISH ONSTAGE PERSONA:

ALONZO.M. ZILCH'S
Collection of
Original Songs

BUT THE SONG HE HAD WRITTEN LAST NIGHT WAS DIFFERENT. IT BIT LIKE THE GRIT OF THE STORM THAT INSPIRED IT AND FIT SO SNUGLY INTO THAT OLD MELODY THAT IT SEEMED LIKE A RESPONSE, SOME KIND CONTINUED CONVERSATION WITH THE WISDOM OF OLD.

HE WANTED TO FINISH IT, AND SAT DOWN AGAIN TO HIS BOOK BY THE WINDOW.

HE DREDGED UP THE LYRICS TO HIS MOTHER'S SONG, AND TRIED THE LAST VERSE IN HIS HEAD.

Soon the storm was over, The people gathered round;
And there the dead and dying, Lay prostrate on the ground.
The good people of our city, You may safely be assured,
We will nurse the sad afflicted, Till health may be restored.

BUT THE LAST COUPLET GRATED. IT DIDN'T SEEM RIGHT ANYMORE.

THE VIEW FROM HIS WINDOW OFFERED NO ASSURANCE...

AND THOSE DROVES OF DRIFTING SANDS WOULD NEVER BE RESTORED. TOO MUCH HAD GONE; IT SEEMED IRREDEEMABLE.

He looked out the window, and the words came...

The storm took place at sundown, It lasted through the night,
When we looked out next morning, We saw a terrible sight.
We saw outside our window, Where wheat fields they had grown,
Was now a rippling ocean, Of dust the wind had blown.

It covered up our fences,

It covered up our barns,

It covered up our tractors in this wild and dusty storm.

We loaded our jalopies, And piled our families in,

We rattled down that highway, To never come back again.

U.S. 66

CHAPTER 6

AND THE DUST STORMED ON.

YOU COULD TELL THE DIRECTION OF THE WIND BY THE DUST THAT GATHERED AT YOUR WINDOWSILL. BLACK DUST FROM KANSAS, RED DUST FROM OKLAHOMA, AND THE TAN-COLORED DUST THAT HAD BLOWN IN FROM COLORADO.

A MONTH AFTER PAMPA'S STORM, ANOTHER GREAT WIND HIT THE PLAINS AND DUMPED ITS LOAD TWO THOUSAND MILES AWAY IN NEW YORK. THE STATUE OF LIBERTY DISAPPEARED THAT DAY, LOST IN THE BILLOWING GRIT OF ITS LAND.

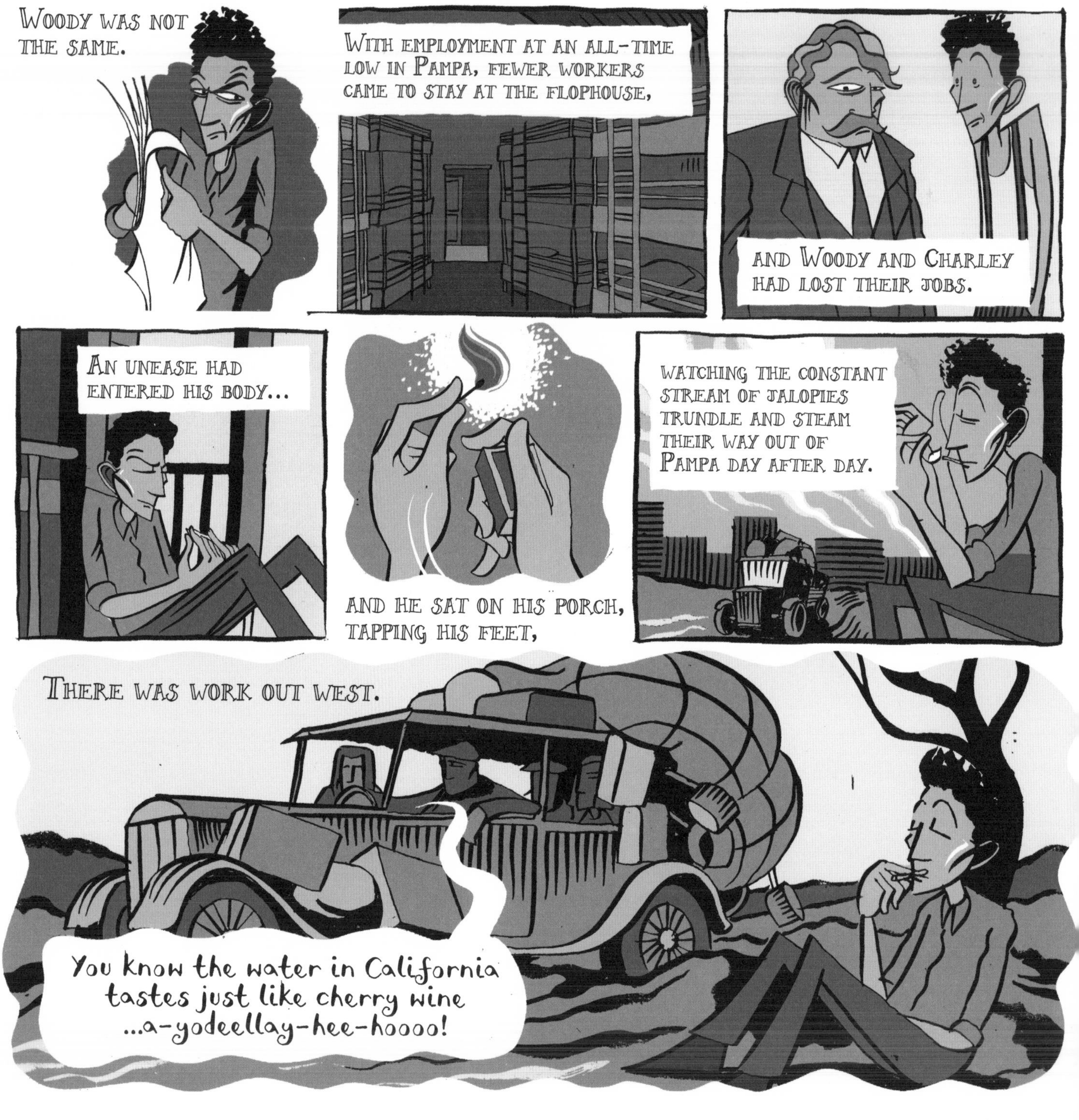
WOODY WAS NOT THE SAME.
WITH EMPLOYMENT AT AN ALL-TIME LOW IN PAMPA, FEWER WORKERS CAME TO STAY AT THE FLOPHOUSE,
AND WOODY AND CHARLEY HAD LOST THEIR JOBS.
AN UNEASE HAD ENTERED HIS BODY...
AND HE SAT ON HIS PORCH, TAPPING HIS FEET,
WATCHING THE CONSTANT STREAM OF JALOPIES TRUNDLE AND STEAM THEIR WAY OUT OF PAMPA DAY AFTER DAY.
THERE WAS WORK OUT WEST.
You know the water in California tastes just like cherry wine ...a-yodeellay-hee-hoooo!

LIKE THE EARTH IN THE AIR, THE PEOPLE WERE ON THE MOVE.

It seemed like the towns were emptying just as fast as they had filled when the booms had struck.

And Woody shared their restlessness.

He let his hair grow long, smoked furiously, and shambled around the back alleys of town, kicking cans, lost in the mist of his mind.

He was apathetic with his music, and even the birth of his first daughter in November...

Did little to shake him from his haze.

JUST AFTER CHRISTMAS, WOODY GOT A LETTER FROM CHARLEY.

IT ANNOUNCED THAT BETTY JEAN HAD LEFT HIM.

THEIR DOMESTIC LIFE HAD NEVER BEEN COMFORTABLE:

TWO BULL-HEADED BEASTS WITH BURDENOUS PASTS TRAPPED IN A RICKETY SHACK,

IT WAS INEVITABLE THAT WHEN THEY FOUGHT, THE WALLS WOULD COME DOWN.

BETTY JEAN WAS OUT SOMEWHERE IN THE GREAT PLAINS, HOPPING FREIGHT TRAINS WITH THE HOBOS, PEDDLING HER MIRACLE CURES,

AND CHARLEY HAD MOVED BACK TO OKLAHOMA, INTO A SHOTGUN SHACK ON ITS CRUMBLING SKID ROW.

HE WAS KNOCKING ON DOORS, SELLING KNIVES TO PEOPLE THAT COULD AFFORD THE FOOD TO CHOP...

AND SPENT MOST OF HIS SAVINGS ON HIS RENTED OFFICE.

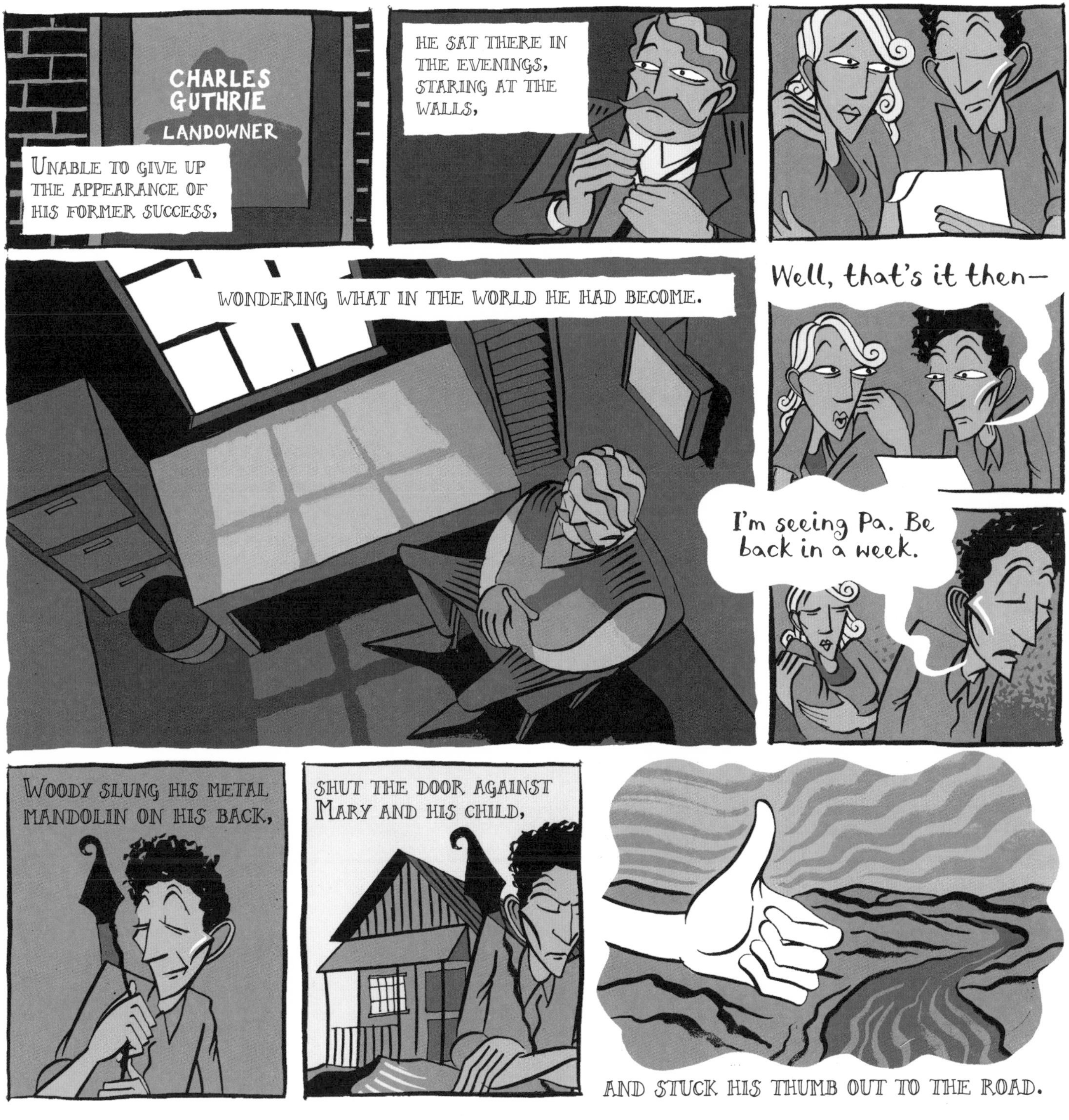
CHARLES GUTHRIE
LANDOWNER
UNABLE TO GIVE UP THE APPEARANCE OF HIS FORMER SUCCESS,
HE SAT THERE IN THE EVENINGS, STARING AT THE WALLS,
WONDERING WHAT IN THE WORLD HE HAD BECOME.
Well, that's it then—
I'm seeing Pa. Be back in a week.
WOODY SLUNG HIS METAL MANDOLIN ON HIS BACK,
SHUT THE DOOR AGAINST MARY AND HIS CHILD,
AND STUCK HIS THUMB OUT TO THE ROAD.

A FARMER'S TRUCK TOOK HIM OUT OF PAMPA,

AND AT ROUTE 44, WHEN THE TRUCK TURNED WEST TO CALIFORNIA, HE CROSSED THE ROAD TO HITCH A RIDE EAST, TO OKLAHOMA.

IN THE OPPOSITE DIRECTION, LINES OF CARS STREAMED ALONG THE HIGHWAY,

POSSESSIONS STRUNG TO THE ROOFS,

CHILDREN BALANCING WITH GRANDMOTHERS ON THE BACK,

FAMILIES FROM KANSAS CITY, OMAHA, AND TULSA ALL LEAVING THE SAME EMPTY BARNS AND BARREN FIELDS, ALL HEADING TOWARD THE LINCOLN HIGHWAY, EVERY SINGLE ONE OF THEM DRIVEN BY THE PROMISE OF GREENER GRASS IN CALIFORNIA.

THE GOING WAS TOUGH.

THE HIGHWAY WAS A DESICCATED OCEAN,

AND THE JALOPIES, SLIDING AND SKIDDING ON THE SURFACE, LEFT A WAKE OF CLOUDING DIRT.

THE FIELDS ON EITHER SIDE OF THE HIGHWAY WERE SWATHED IN DUNES OF DUST, AND A CONSTANT FLUME OF POWDER POURED UP FROM THEIR CRESTS, LIKE SNOW SMOKING OFF A MOUNTAIN PEAK.

ALL ALONG THE ROAD TO OKLAHOMA, WOODY SAW HOMESTEADS, FARMS, AND BARNS BURIED ALIVE,

AS IF THE GROUND HAD RISEN UP TO SWALLOW THEM.

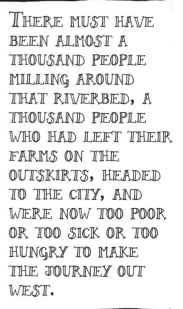

THE TRUCK DROPPED WOODY JUST INSIDE THE CITY LIMITS, BY THE CLOYING REMAINS OF THE OKLAHOMA RIVER.

IT HAD STARTED TO RAIN, THE USUAL FAINT-HEARTED PATTER OF THE DROUGHTS, AND AS HE STEPPED INTO THE MUD, HE WISHED HE'D BROUGHT A JACKET.

THERE MUST HAVE BEEN ALMOST A THOUSAND PEOPLE MILLING AROUND THAT RIVERBED, A THOUSAND PEOPLE WHO HAD LEFT THEIR FARMS ON THE OUTSKIRTS, HEADED TO THE CITY, AND WERE NOW TOO POOR OR TOO SICK OR TOO HUNGRY TO MAKE THE JOURNEY OUT WEST.

THEY CROUCHED UNDER RASPS OF CORRUGATED STEEL,

PEERED OUT FROM BROKEN ORANGE CRATES,

AND TOOK SCANT SHELTER FROM THE MAKESHIFT SHACKS THEY HAD BUILT FROM THE NEIGHBORING GARBAGE DUMP.

Many of them wore Red Cross masks, which had been handed out in the city center,

Trying in vain to ward off that rattling cough they named dust pneumonia— the dry hacking of dirt from their lungs.

As Woody passed through this shanty town,

seeing children dressed in the burlap sacks potatoes were sold in, he walked into the districts of cheap housing and two-bit bars. He saw grocery stores with their fronts smashed in, plates of shattered glass on the floor, and empty, ransacked shelves.

He thought of the piles of wheat outside the city limits, withered and husked by the sun, rotting in the muddy rain, and the guns of the company men that protected them.

Five years ago,

America had produced the largest wheat harvest the world had ever known, the greatest harvest in all of nature, and today its children's bellies were distended in hunger.

He met his father in a cheap bar along Skid Row.

There was distemper in the air, a discontent that erupted every now and then in the sounds of smashed glass and cracked jaws.

Many years ago, standing at his sister Clara's deathbed, he had promised her never to cry, never to break down,

BOY!!!

So when he saw his father in the corner of the bar, he quickly folded his reaction into himself.

CHARLEY WAS DRESSED IN HIS BUSINESS CLOTHES, THE SUIT HE HAD BOUGHT WHEN HE HAD RUN FOR OFFICE TWENTY YEARS BACK. THE COLLAR OF HIS SHIRT WAS SOILED WITH PAST TIME, HIS OLD BOXING HANDS WERE CLAWED INTO HIS WRISTS, AND HIS HEAD WAS SUNK LOW ON HIS SHOULDERS.

Boy!!! si'down!

I got a bottle right here for the pair of us, an' we're gunna sup it up till we cough it up.

That's fine by me, Pa.

This first one is to congratulate you, boy...

You went 'n' made a baby girl, and that's a fine thing to do in life.

Yessir—I will rinky-drink to that.

She's a purty li'l gal, sir,

the light of life in her eyes.

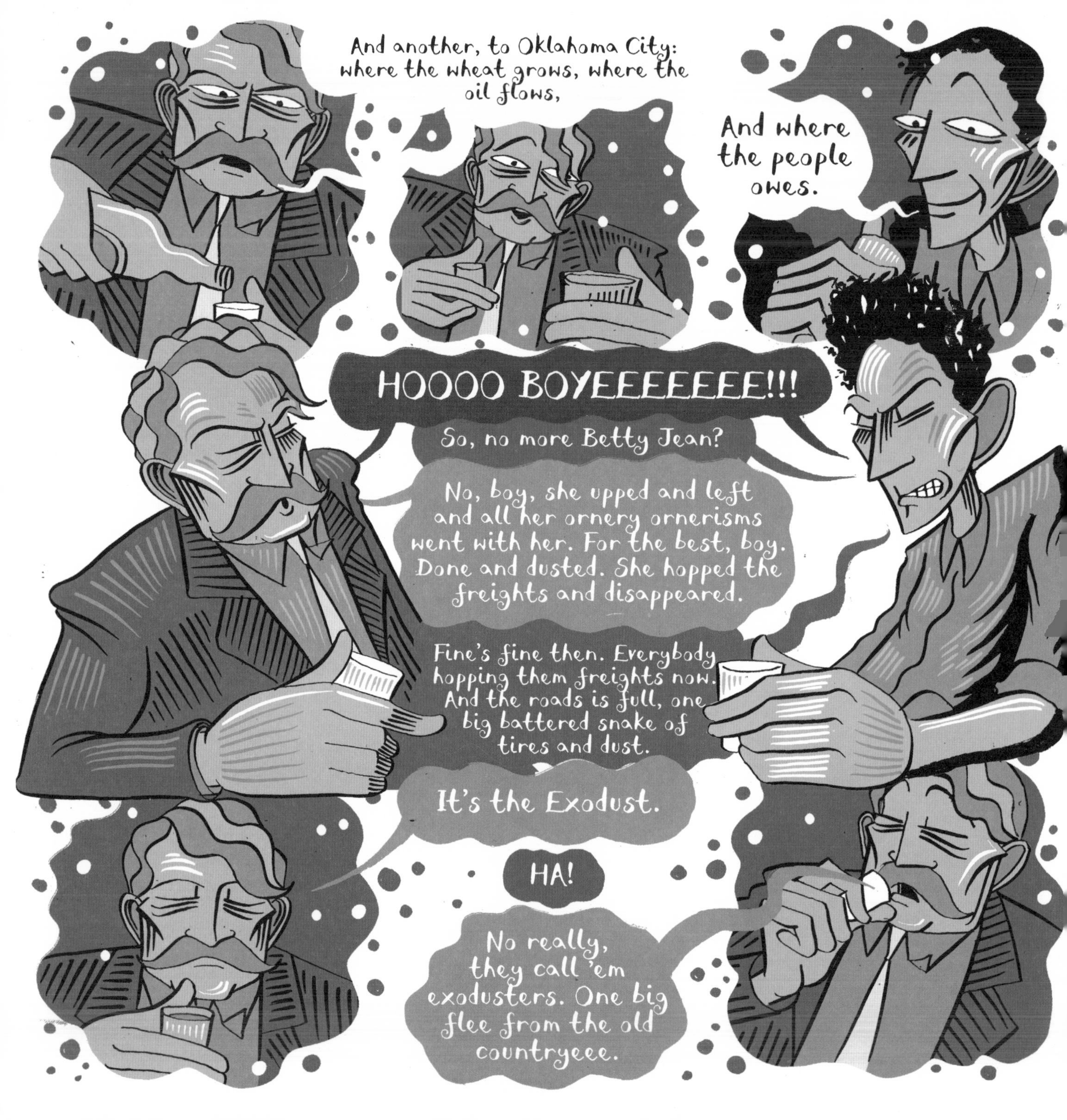
And another, to Oklahoma City: where the wheat grows, where the oil flows,
And where the people owes.
HOOOO BOYEEEEEEEE!!!
So, no more Betty Jean?
No, boy, she upped and left and all her ornery ornerisms went with her. For the best, boy. Done and dusted. She hopped the freights and disappeared.
Fine's fine then. Everybody hopping them freights now. And the roads is full, one big battered snake of tires and dust.
It's the Exodust.
HA!
No really, they call 'em exodusters. One big flee from the old countryeee.

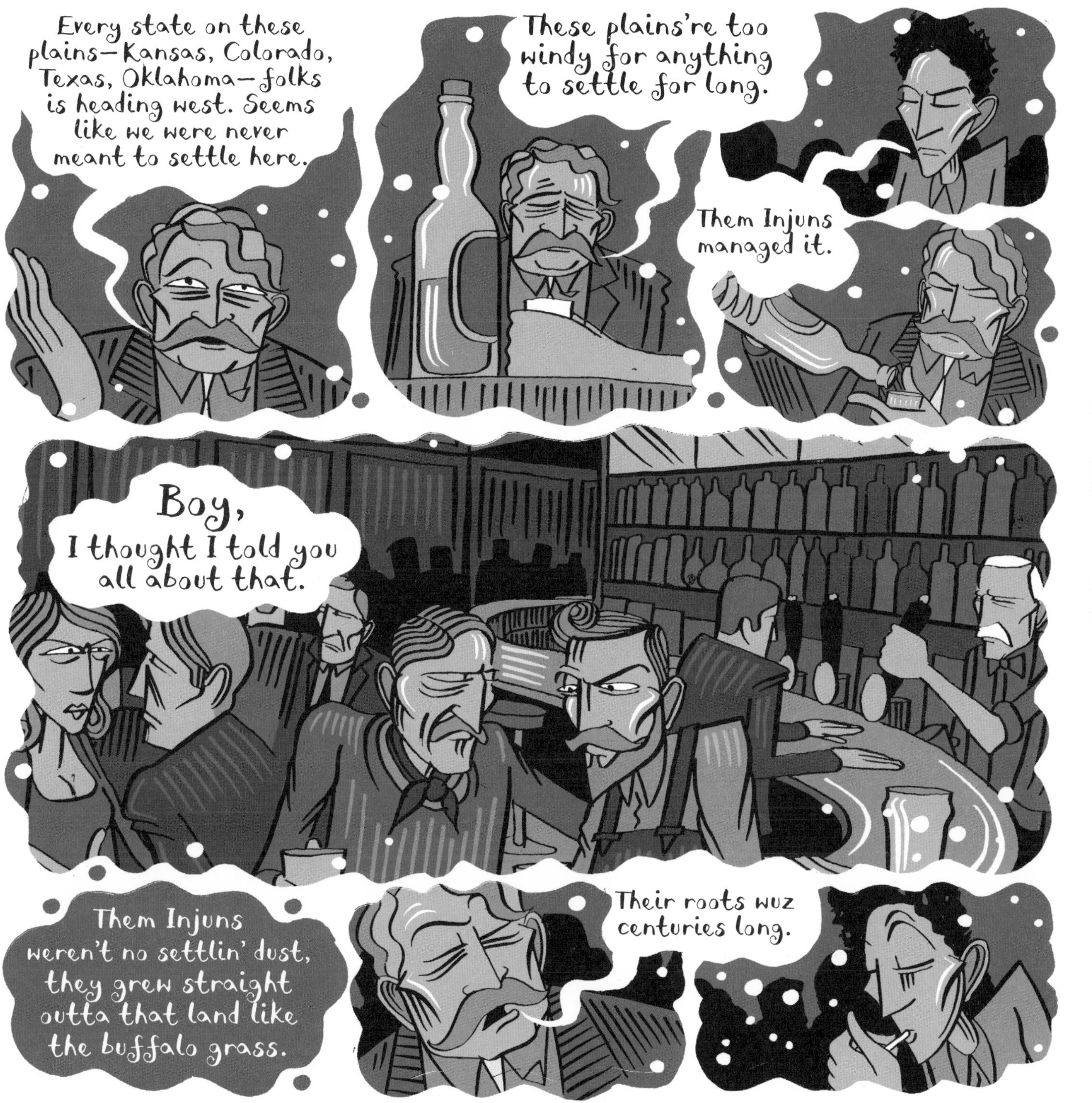
Every state on these plains—Kansas, Colorado, Texas, Oklahoma—folks is heading west. Seems like we were never meant to settle here.
These plains're too windy for anything to settle for long.
Them Injuns managed it.
Boy, I thought I told you all about that.
Them Injuns weren't no settlin' dust, they grew straight outta that land like the buffalo grass.
Their roots wuz centuries long.

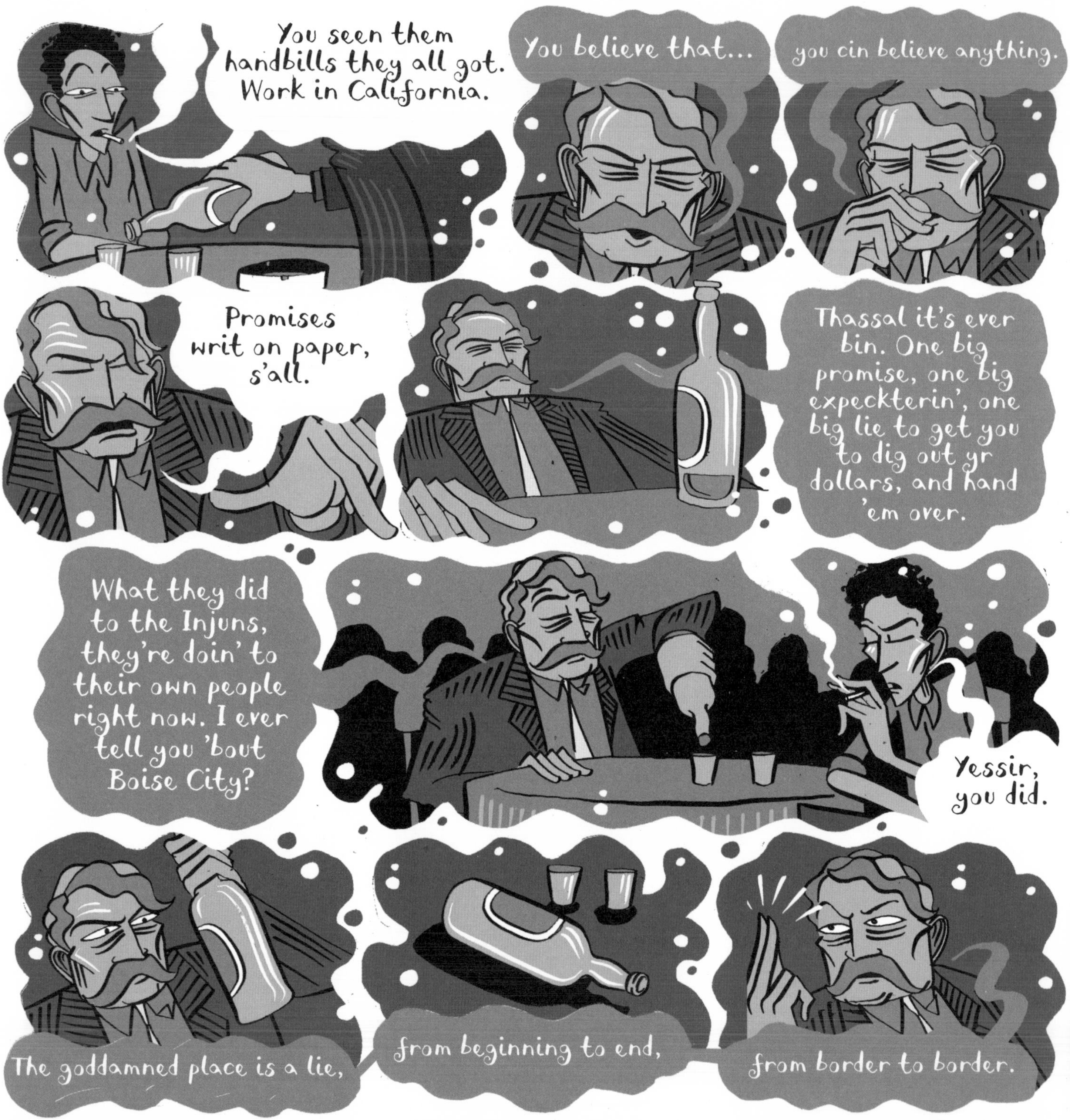
You seen them handbills they all got. Work in California.
You believe that...
you cin believe anything.
Promises writ on paper, s'all.
Thassal it's ever bin. One big promise, one big expeckterin', one big lie to get you to dig out yr dollars, and hand 'em over.
What they did to the Injuns, they're doin' to their own people right now. I ever tell you 'bout Boise City?
Yessir, you did.
The goddamned place is a lie,
from beginning to end,
from border to border.

That there town lay in what they called no-man's-land. One bit of dry Injun land that no state much wanted. That flat bit of land was way outta the way of any place, a day's ride from any water. There's stories of mule carriages trading through there, cutting a short from the Santa Fe Trail through no-man's-land and then running so short of water they cuts the ears off their mules, and wus drinking the blood from their heads. And where there's nothing, there's no sheriff, and where there's no sheriff, there in't no law, and that's where there's outlaws. The Coe gang lived up there, Frank 'n' Jesse James, them an' their whores and nothing else but sky and grass. Then Oklahoma decides she wants this scrap of land. Wants to own it. Ain't no good to nobody just lying around. So, Oklahoma, in her great wisdom, she takes it. And she fences it. And it's hers. But it still ain't no damned good to her if it ain't bringin' in the green.

Them damned Anglo shareholders put a call in from London and they tell the landman they need him to make some money from the land. So, he prints up a load of paper bills. And he sends them all over. Up north, through the cities, out west. He calls 'em "broshurrres." He says there's land sellin' in Boise City, give-away prices, and that you gotta go now t' make yer fortune.

He has a little drawing on that paper, there's trees, there's brick houses, there's paved streets, and there's a big well right in the center. Says the land's full of water, full of potential. Says the panhandle is the greatest wheat country in the world, says you got corn bigger than saw logs and watermelons bigger than humpback whales.

And there STILL ain't nuthin' there.

Boise City. You know what Boise City means? "Boise" is French for trees. 'Cept there were no trees in Boise City and there weren't no city. Jus' a promise on a piece of paper. Them people bought up that land all right. Bought the land and came to live in the city, dressed up in frilly skirts and bowler hats. Then they saw Boise City, all right. No houses, no railroads. No paving slabs and no well. Stakes in the ground and flags flappin' in the wind.

They arrested the developers, o' course. They routed 'em and they hanged 'em. But there wus still a whole town load of people with no town to live in. Fed promises by profiteers.

A TUNE STARTED PLAYING ON THE JUKEBOX...

A TUNE THAT WOODY RECOGNIZED, A JIMMY COX RECORD FROM FIFTEEN YEARS BACK, SUNG BY SOMEONE NEW.

HER VOICE WAS STRONG AND SAD, LIKE SHE'D JUST DRIED HER EYES.

SHE HAD A HORN SECTION BEHIND HER, TROMBONES BLONTING LIKE A DRUNKEN TRUDGE, MUTED TRUMPETS WAWWING AND COOING LIKE A QUIVERING BOTTOM LIP, AND THE SONG'S SADNESS SEEMED ALMOST TO MOCK CHARLEY'S WORDS.

Once I lived the life of a millionaire,
Spending all my money, I didn't care,
I carried my friends out for a mighty good time,
Buying bootleg liquor, champagne, and wine...

All these people here, they're from outta town, come here cuz their place is all dried up. Government brought 'em down here, told 'em to bring their families. Even gave 'em free train rides. Sure! Come one, come all. Every man his own boss they said. Every man a landlord. So they sold 'em the piece of paper with the land rights on it. And down they all came.

And they busted the sod, carved up the grass, and planted their wheat. When times wus gud, the businessmen told 'em to borrow money off old Nick the bankerman and buy their goods from the sell-ermen. New machines, more land, pretty things for the home.

But then I began to fall so low I didn't have no friend and no place to go.

And now the land don't give up no more. It's taken to the air like it wants out. Cuz they had no interest in the land. They wanted the dollar from the land. And what's a dollar? It's a promise printed on a piece of paper.
If I ever gets my hand on a dollar again, I'm gunna squeeze that dollar till that ol' eagle grins.
And when you've turned that land into gold, and turned that gold into dol-lar bills, and when you ain't got no more dollars, you don't got nuthin'. And then, America don't want to know you...
Till that eeee-eagle grins...

WOODY STAYED WITH CHARLEY FOR A COUPLE OF DAYS,

AND THEN TURNED HIS BACK ON OKLAHOMA.

HIS FATHER SEEMED LOST TO HIM, LOST AMONG A SEA OF RED-EYED, DIRTY-COLLARED, BITTER-HEARTED MEN, BENT DOUBLE OVER CHEAP LIQUOR.

BOOMERS ONCE, BOOMING FOR OIL, BOOMING FOR LAND, BOOMING FOR WHEAT;

BUT THE BOOM HAD BUSTED, AND DUSTED THEM DOWN.

WOODY WALKED THROUGH THE HOOVERVILLES AND JUNGLE CAMPS TO ROUTE 44, WHERE HE WOULD STICK OUT HIS THUMB AND JOIN THE FLOW WEST.

Named after the multimillionaire whose presidency had caused them to sprout up across the plains, the Hoovervilles were the mud churned up by the speeding truck of the twenties, a smear on the starched shirt of the economy.

Relief offices had begun to open up across the plains, alongside the emergency clinics, and every family that received a check had their name printed in the weekly paper.

If the tax-paying folk of America had to pay to keep these people alive, they had a right to know who was receiving their goodwill.

And every surname in those newspaper columns was branded with the scarlet letter of their misfortune, their hard luck, their failure to succeed.

And Woody saw his father in every one.

 As he hitched a lift home across three hundred miles of muddy desert, back to Mary and the baby, a fire rose in his chest, and words flared in his head.

That dust might get the wheat... but... it won't get me...

And as he neared home, the gobs of rain that splotched the windshield with mud became thicker, grittier, and turned to ice. Then the heavens opened, and great chunks of hail speared through the night air, drumming on the hood of the truck, battering the vehicle and slowing its progress to a crawl.

 When eventually he reached home, sleepless and harried, he had a list of verses, lines of angry defiance against the entire journey.

...it won't get me.

HE KISSED MARY
AND THE BABY, WHO
HAD JUST GOTTEN
UP FOR THE DAY,
FOLDED THE SONG
UP WITH THE OTHERS,
AND WENT TO BED.

HE SLEPT FOR DAYS.

CHAPTER 7

So long, it's been good to know yuh.

WOODY LASTED ABOUT A MONTH WITH MARY AND THE BABY.

HE KEPT COMING HOME FROM HIS GIGS WITH THE CORNCOB BOYS DRUNKER THAN THE NIGHT BEFORE.

HE HAD A NEW SONG, WRITTEN TO THE TUNE OF "BALLAD OF BILLY THE KID" AND HE SANG IT OVER AND OVER AGAIN, THROUGH THE STREETS AT MIDNIGHT, ON THE PORCH AT NOON, WHEN PEOPLE WERE AROUND, WHEN HE WAS ON HIS OWN.

THERE WAS SOMETHING IN ITS SIMPLE REFRAIN, ITS NAIVE NURSERY-RHYME MELODY, THAT FELT RIGHT. IN WOODY'S MOUTH, IT HELD A LASHING SARCASM THAT SEEMED TO TAUNT PAMPA AND ITS RESIDENTS.

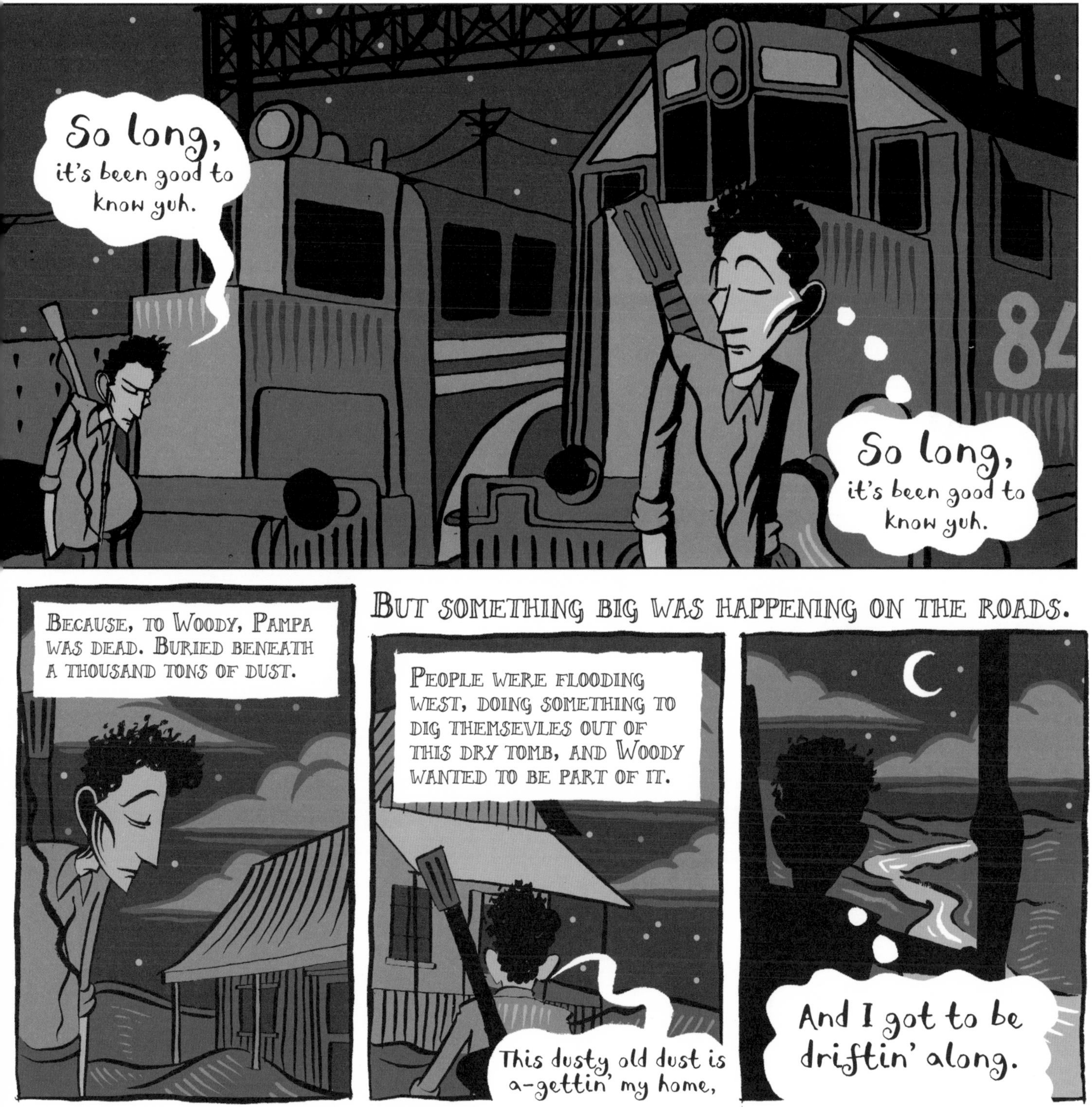
So long, it's been good to know yuh.
So long, it's been good to know yuh.
BECAUSE, TO WOODY, PAMPA WAS DEAD. BURIED BENEATH A THOUSAND TONS OF DUST.
BUT SOMETHING BIG WAS HAPPENING ON THE ROADS.
PEOPLE WERE FLOODING WEST, DOING SOMETHING TO DIG THEMSEVLES OUT OF THIS DRY TOMB, AND WOODY WANTED TO BE PART OF IT.
This dusty old dust is a-gettin' my home,
And I got to be driftin' along.

SO ONE DAY, HE LEFT. HE TOLD HIMSELF HE WAS HEADING TO FIND WORK, DOING RIGHT BY MARY AND THE CHILD, BUT THE TRUTH WAS, HE FELT TETHERED, AND WANTED OUT.

HE SLUNG HIS GUITAR ON HIS SHOULDER,

LEFT A NOTE FOR MARY, AND HIT THE ROAD.

BUT THE GOING WAS NOT AS EASY AS WOODY HAD HOPED.

IF ANYTHING, THE RUSTY LINE OF RATTLETRAP CARS, JALOPIES AND FARMERS' FLIVVERS HAD INCREASED IN DENSITY, BUT GOING WEST, THEY WERE STUFFED TO SPILLING WITH FAMILIES AND THEIR HOUSEHOLDS.

THERE WAS NO ROOM

AND IN THE COLD FEBRUARY WIND, HE DIDN'T LAST LONG ON THE HIGHWAY.

HE'D HEAD SOUTH, WHERE IT WAS WARMER, AND HE'D HOP A TRAIN TO GET THERE.

FOR WOODY,

THE FIRST TRAIN TOOK HIM TO AMARILLO.

THE SECOND THROUGH ROSWELL, ON TO CLOVIS, AND THEN ON TO ALAMOGORDO.

HERE ON THE BORDER OF MEXICO, HE WAS THE CLOSEST HE HAD BEEN IN YEARS TO THAT CHISOS TRAIL.

IN THE MEXICAN HEAT, WOODY WAS WARMING TO HIS TRAVEL, REMEMBERING THAT OLD SENSE OF FREEDOM IN THE MOUNTAINS. THE SKY NO LONGER SEEMED TO BEAR DOWN UPON HIM BUT SOARED WIDE AND VAST INTO INFINITY. AND THE EARTH NO LONGER BLEW SEAS UP INTO THE AIR.

THERE WAS A BALANCE HERE, THE CALM OF ETERNITY.

HE SLIPPED OFF THE SLOW-MOVING TRAIN TWO HUNDRED YARDS OR SO FROM THE STATION,

DUCKED UNDER THE FENCE,

AND MELDED INTO THE MORNING CROWD.

HE COULD THINK OF NOTHING BUT FOOD. THAT LAST BOWL OF CHILI WAS TWO DAYS DOWN THE TRACK AND HIS HEART THUMPED WITH URGENCY THAT MADE HIS HEAD SWOON.

Got anywhar to be, son?

Yessir, on my way to my aunt's.

And whar is she?

Oh, well, she lives just down the road a little.

Listen, son, you must be the fiftieth fleabag I run into this morning. We got bags o' soot like you crawling all over this neck o' the woods. I'll tellituyya plain. Tucson is a fine place, for fine people. If you ain't got a job, you ain't got a reason to be here.

'T'ain't no crime to be out of work.

Telling, the law is my job 'round these parts, not yours. You jest ain't welcome. And if that in't plain innuf fer ya, I got a skull-cracker here that talks purrty clear.

SO WOODY FLIPPED HIS HEELS AND WALKED BACK THE WAY HE CAME. HE CROSSED THE ROAD BY THE STATION, AND HEADED ON UP THE HILL, PAST BOX HEDGES AND WHITE-PAINTED HOUSES, PAST HOUSEWIVES WATERING THEIR HANGING BASKETS.

Got a job fer me? I cin clean yr porch, cut yr hedge, trim yr lawn for yiz. Happy to help for a sandwich.

THEIR EYES ALL FLICKED AWAY FROM HIM, LEAVING HIS QUESTION HANGING IN THE AIR. TURNING A CORNER, HE SAW TUCSON'S CHURCH, A LOCAL LANDMARK HE HAD HEARD OF EVEN IN PAMPA WHEN IT WAS BUILT JUST A FEW YEARS BEFORE.

IT WAS AS GRAND AS A CASTLE. IT GLEAMED IN THE SUN.

Howdy, ma'am! S'a beautiful day.

Yes. Thank the Lord.

Indeedy. I am wondering if there's any snub o' work I could rattle out for you t'day in exchange me'bee for a bowl of stew and a rusk o' bread.

There's no work here. We, the nuns, perform all of God's tasks for the day.

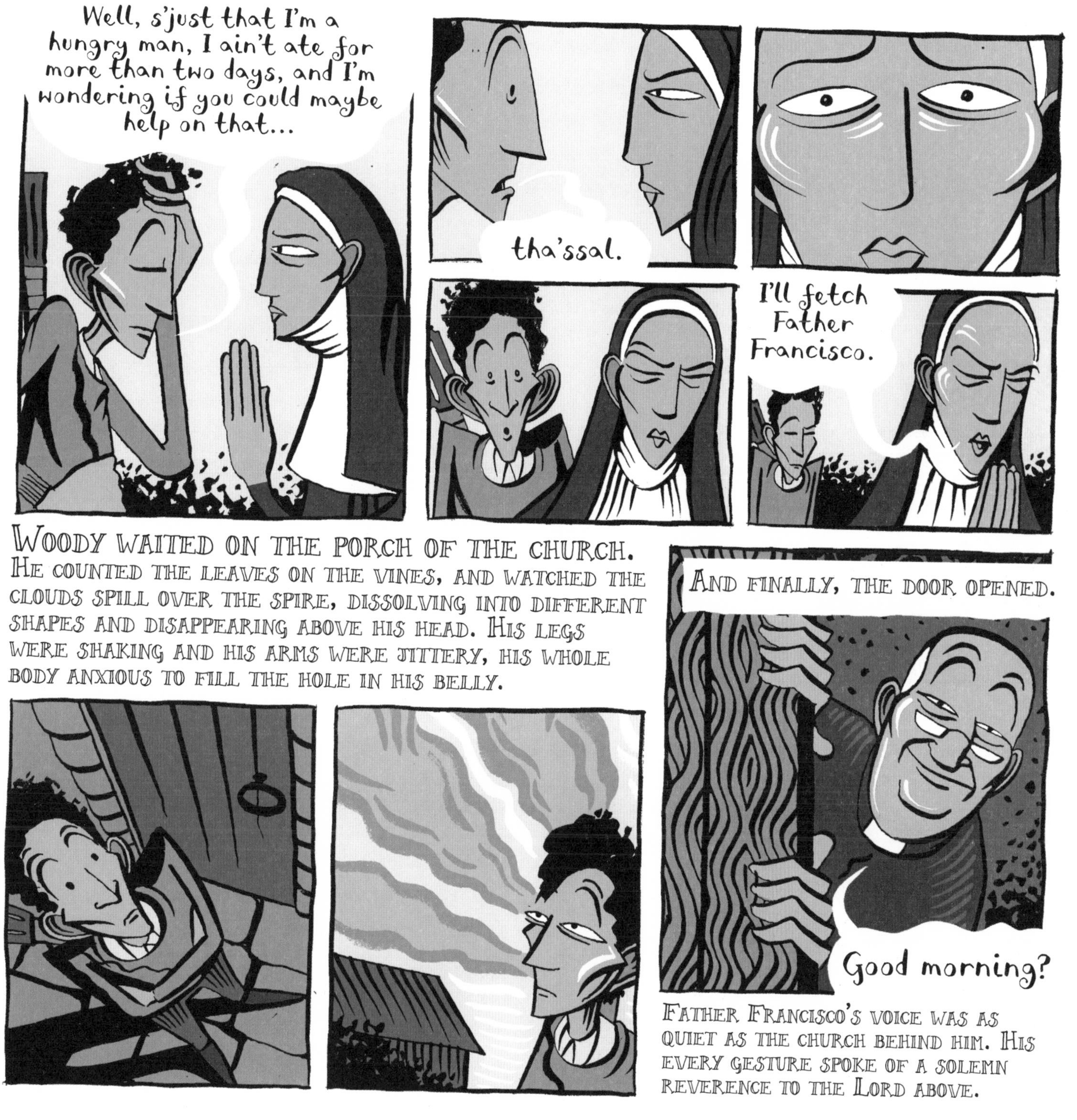
Well, s'just that I'm a hungry man, I ain't ate for more than two days, and I'm wondering if you could maybe help on that...
tha'ssal.
I'll fetch Father Francisco.
Woody waited on the porch of the church. He counted the leaves on the vines, and watched the clouds spill over the spire, dissolving into different shapes and disappearing above his head. His legs were shaking and his arms were jittery, his whole body anxious to fill the hole in his belly.
And finally, the door opened.
Good morning?
Father Francisco's voice was as quiet as the church behind him. His every gesture spoke of a solemn reverence to the Lord above.

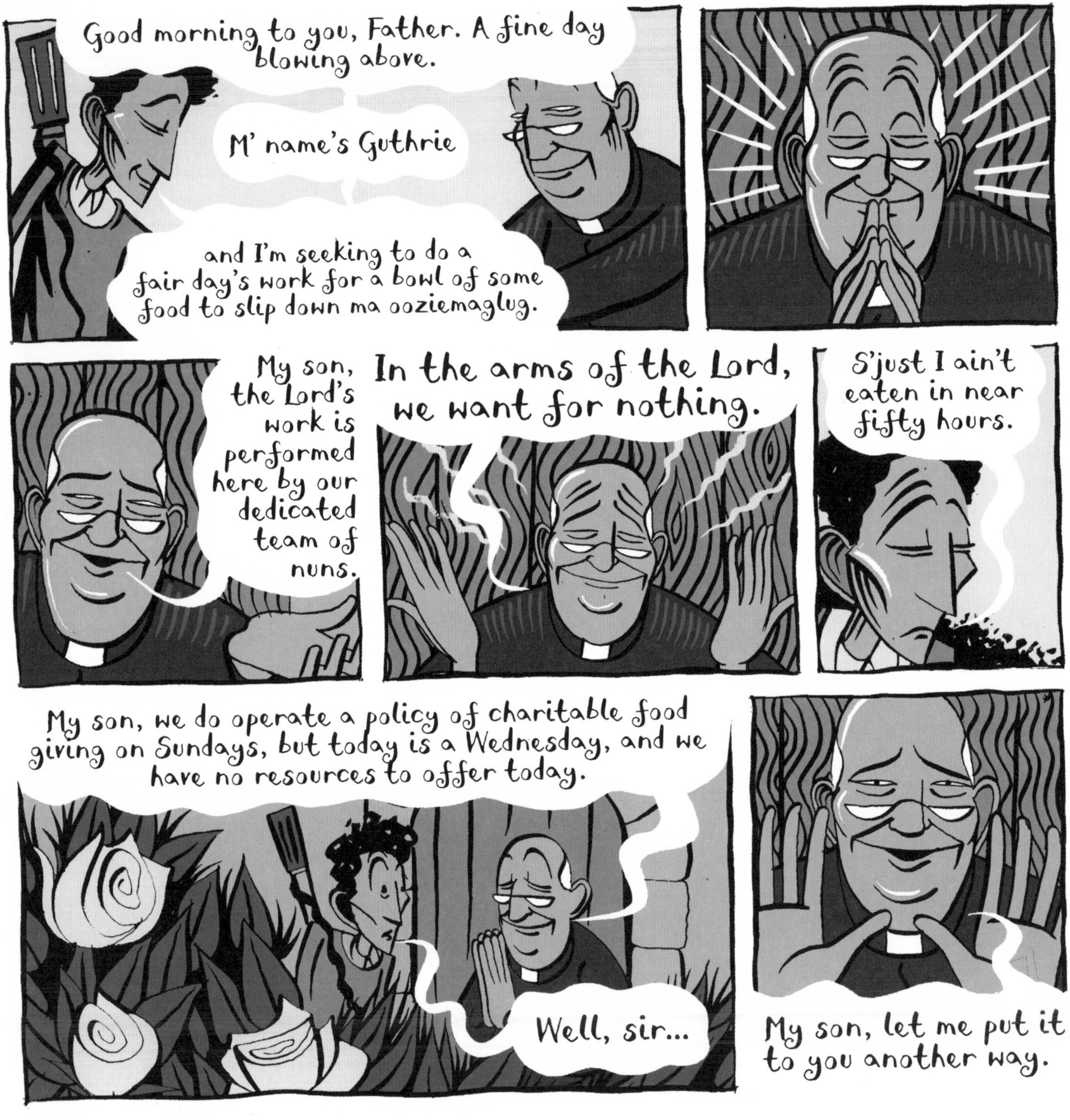
Good morning to you, Father. A fine day blowing above.
M' name's Guthrie
and I'm seeking to do a fair day's work for a bowl of some food to slip down ma ooziemaglug.
My son, the Lord's work is performed here by our dedicated team of nuns.
In the arms of the Lord, we want for nothing.
S'just I ain't eaten in near fifty hours.
My son, we do operate a policy of charitable food giving on Sundays, but today is a Wednesday, and we have no resources to offer today.
Well, sir...
My son, let me put it to you another way.

I applaud your approach. You come here offering work, as I can see you still have some pride. You know that it demeans you to ask for charity, as I can see you are better than that. I can fix you up a bowl of soup and that would feed you for now, but tomorrow, where would you be? Accepting my charity will only make you weaker, more reliant on me. And we cannot go feeding you forever.

FATHER FRANCISCO ANOINTED WOODY WITH A SERENE SMILE, AND BEGAN TO SHUT THE DOOR.

You know, they refused Jesus, too...

Well...you ain't him.

AND THE DOOR SHUT, WITHOUT A SOUND.

I'm goin' down this old dusty road,

I'm goin' down this old dusty road,

I'm goin' down this old dusty road,

An' I ain't a-gonna be treated this a-way.

WOODY WATCHED THE LITTER BLOWING DOWN THAT DUSTY ROAD AND THOUGHT AGAIN OF THAT OLD-TIME LYRIC SUNG SO MANY TIMES IN THE SALOONS BACK HOME. AS HE WALKED ON INTO TUSCON'S SKID ROW, NEW WORDS BEGAN TO SLIP INTO THAT OLD MELODY.

HE PASSED THE SUN-BLISTERED HOUSES WITH THEIR PEELING PAINT AND SUDDENLY TUCSON'S GLEAMING WHITE HAD FADED TO A DUSTY BROWN.

THE BUSTLE HAD GONE, AND EVERYWHERE, THE MEN STOOD ON THE RUBBLED SIDEWALKS, SILENT, LIKE MOURNERS BY A DUG GRAVE.

AFTER AN HOUR'S WANDER, WOODY FOUND HIS MEAL TICKET.

AN OLD COUPLE WERE CLEARING THEIR DINER AFTER LUNCH, AND HE STOPPED BY TO MOP THE FLOOR AND TAKE OUT THE TRASH.

THEY SAT WEARILY ON THEIR CUSTOMERS' CHAIRS AS HE WHIZZED AROUND THEM.

AFTER A BOWL OF CHILI, THE OLD WOMAN TOOK HIM TO ONE SIDE, PUSHED A PAPER BAG INTO HIS HANDS, AND WHISPERED IN HIS EAR.

Take these sandwiches,

but don't you dare tell the old man!

HE SMILED QUIETLY AND THANKED HER WITH HIS EYES.

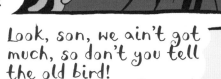

AS HE LEFT THE DINER, THE OLD MAN TOOK HIM BY THE ARM, AND LED HIM OUTSIDE.

Look, son, we ain't got much, so don't you tell the old bird!

But here's a little sumthin' to help ya down the road.

AND HE PRESSED A QUARTER INTO WOODY'S HAND.

THE ROAD TOOK HIM BY A RAILWAY SIDING, AND AS HE PASSED, HE SAW A HUDDLE OF TEN OR TWELVE MEN CROUCHING IN THE LONG GRASS.

You got one comin'?

Next fifteen minutes or so. But for chrissakes, hide that geetar 'n' keep yr head down, 'less you want us taken by the bulls.

HE CROUCHED WITH THEM AND HELD HIS BREATH.

AND SOON ENOUGH, HE FELT THE RUMBLE IN HIS GUT.

THE ENGINE APPROACHED AND CHUFFED PAST THEM, WITH THE RAILROAD BULLS HANGING FROM THE SIDES, HEAVY STICKS IN THEIR HANDS, SURVEYING THE LAND FOR HOBOS.

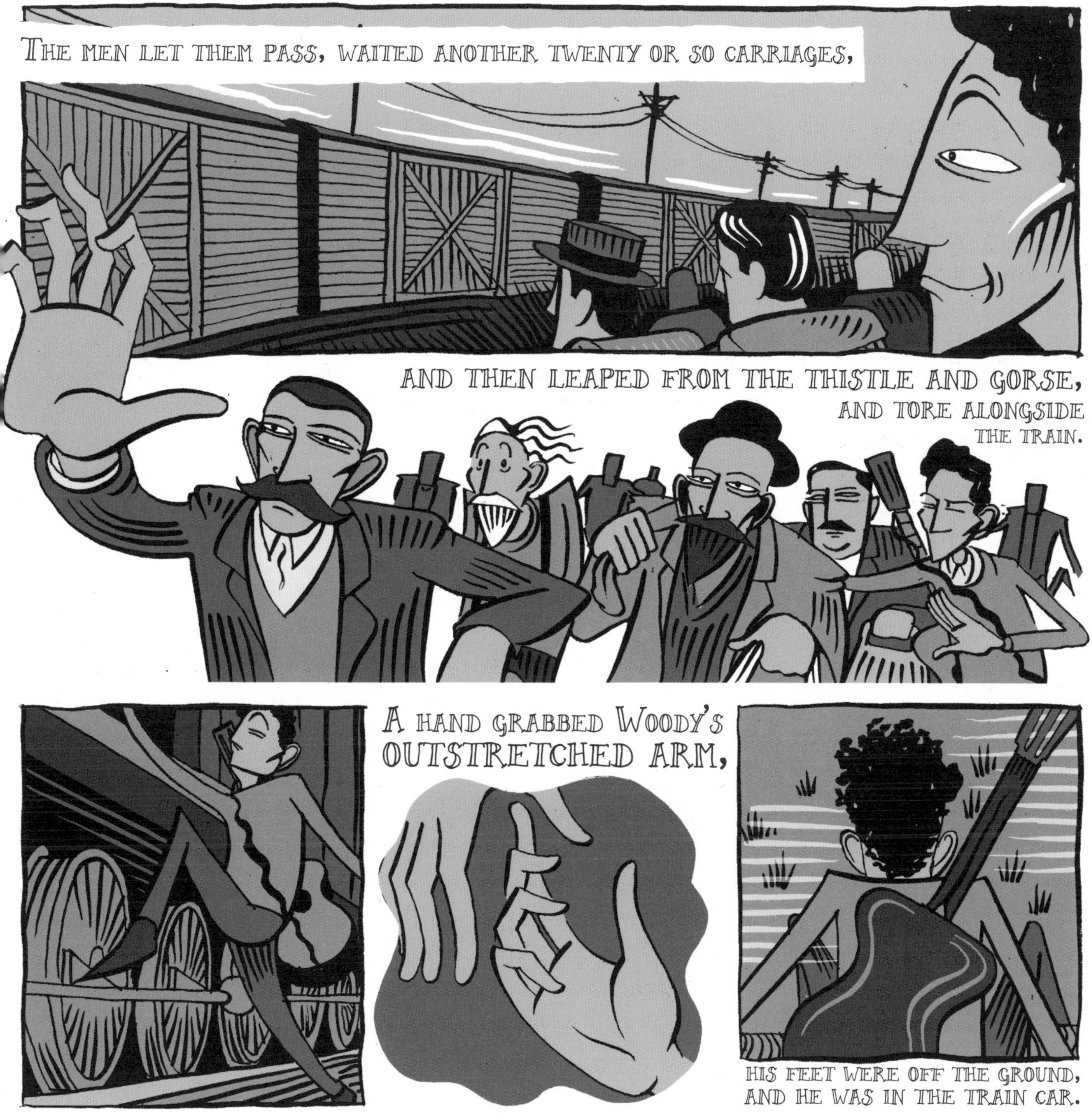
THE MEN LET THEM PASS, WAITED ANOTHER TWENTY OR SO CARRIAGES,
AND THEN LEAPED FROM THE THISTLE AND GORSE,
AND TORE ALONGSIDE THE TRAIN.
A HAND GRABBED WOODY'S OUTSTRETCHED ARM,
HIS FEET WERE OFF THE GROUND, AND HE WAS IN THE TRAIN CAR.

HIS PUPILS GREW TO THE GLOOM.

THERE WERE PERHAPS ANOTHER TWENTY OR SO MEN IN THE CAR, DIFFERENT AGES, DIFFERENT RACES, DIFFERENT SIZES, BUT ALL WEARING THAT SAME HARDENED LOOK OF THE ROAD.

ALL AROUND THE COUNTRY, FREIGHT-TRAIN CARS WERE FILLED WITH THESE MEN,

SOME NEW AND UNSURE OF THEMSELVES, OTHERS TIME-WORN BINDLE STIFFS FOR WHOM THE FREIGHT CAR WAS HOME.

Howdy y'all...

SOME OF THE MEN MUTTERED A RESPONSE, OTHERS STARED OUT THE SIDECAR DOOR, WATCHING THE LAND BLUR. THE MAN NEXT TO HIM WAS ROLLING A THIN CIGARETTE FROM HIS BULL DURHAM POUCH, AND WOODY LEANED TOWARD HIM TO BEG A SMOKE.

'T'ain't no bother...

but there's nuttin' but mousies' whiskers in there.

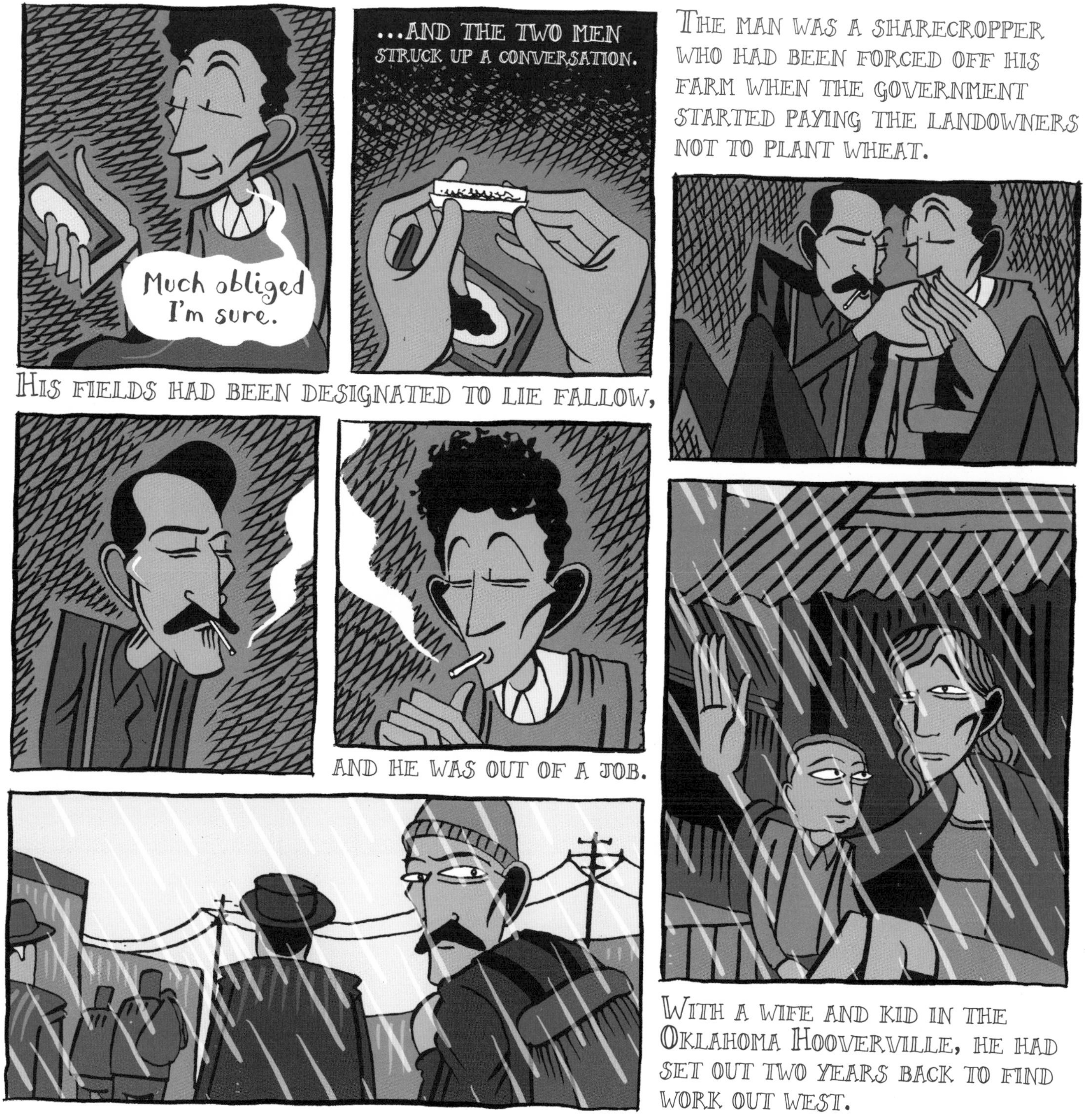
Much obliged I'm sure.
...AND THE TWO MEN STRUCK UP A CONVERSATION.
THE MAN WAS A SHARECROPPER WHO HAD BEEN FORCED OFF HIS FARM WHEN THE GOVERNMENT STARTED PAYING THE LANDOWNERS NOT TO PLANT WHEAT.
HIS FIELDS HAD BEEN DESIGNATED TO LIE FALLOW,
AND HE WAS OUT OF A JOB.
WITH A WIFE AND KID IN THE OKLAHOMA HOOVERVILLE, HE HAD SET OUT TWO YEARS BACK TO FIND WORK OUT WEST.

Aimed to pass on to Los Angeles.

Out of the dust bowl, into the sugar bowl.

But them po-lees held a blockade there right when I was heading through.

Motorcycles and trucks blocking the road, wouldn't let nobody through 'less they had that dough in their back pocket. And if you ain't got that do-re-mi...you ain't getting through.

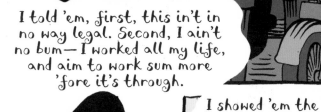

I told 'em, first, this in't in no way legal. Second, I ain't no bum—I worked all my life, and aim to work sum more 'fore it's through.

I read that...

I showed 'em the handbill I had in my pocket.

And they laughed,

PICKING WORK

said the farm's all full.

Look, fella—this caboose 's jus' too small, and this rail track is jus' too long for that kinda conversin'.

Whaddya say I have a little play on that gittar there, and cook us up something hot and juicy for the journey?

Sounds fine t' me...

THE MAN PICKED UP WOODY'S GUITAR, PINCHING THE STRINGS TOGETHER TO TEST THEIR TUNING.

WOODY PULLED OUT HIS MOUTH HARP.

Whatever it is, play it in D.

THE MAN BROKE INTO A FAST TRAIN-TRACK RHYTHM, A BLUES RIFF ON AN OLD GOSPEL SONG THEY'D ALL SUNG AS CHILDREN.

THIS TRAIN IS BOUND FOR GLORY!

AND BY THE LAST REFRAIN, THE CARRIAGE HAD WOKEN UP. TENOR AND BARITONE VOICES TOOK THE HARMONY, AND THOSE WHO COULDN'T SING SANG ANYWAY, THE WORDS BEING SO SIMPLE, THE MELODY SO ELEMENTAL, THAT IT SEEMED HARDER NOT TO.

AND WHEN THE SONG WAS SUNG, THE GUITAR WAS PASSED AROUND.

IF ONE KNEW THE WORDS, THE OTHER COULD FIND THE TUNE, THE CHORDS FOLLOWING SIMILAR CYCLES FOR EVERY SONG THEY KNEW. THEY SANG "JACK O'DIAMONDS," "OLD SMOKEY," AND "PRETTY POLLY," SONGS THEY HAD LEARNED ON THEIR FATHER'S KNEE. THESE SIMPLE SONGS, THEIR SIMPLE WORDS AND SIMPLE TUNES, HAD TAKEN ROOT IN THEIR YOUNG MINDS AND GROWN DOWN SO DEEP INTO THEM THAT THEY NO LONGER HAD TO THINK; THEY WERE A REFLEX.

THE GUITAR CAME BACK TO WOODY, AND WITH THE ATMOSPHERE IN THE CAR HOTTING UP, HE DECIDED TO PLAY SOMETHING WITH A BIT OF RAUNCH. HE THOUGHT OF "GYPSY DAVY."

It was late last night when the boss come home Asking 'bout his lady, The only answer that he got, "She's gone with the Gypsy Davy...

"She's gone with the Gypsy Dave."

THE MEN WHOOPED, WHISTLED, AND
JEERED, JOINING IN ON THE REFRAIN.

THE SONG TOLD AN ANCIENT STORY OF A RICH WOMAN WHO
WAS SEDUCED INTO THE WILDERNESS BY A GYPSY, WHO HAD
COME SINGING AND DANCING OVER THE PLAINS.

HER HUSBAND RETURNS HOME FROM THE HUNT TO FIND
HER GONE, AND GALLOPS OUT TO CLAIM HER. HE FINDS
HER IN THE FORESTS, SITTING AROUND THE GYPSY'S FIRE:

An' there by the light
of the campin' fire,
He saw her fair face beamin',
Her heart in tune to the big guitar
And the sound of the gypsy singin'
That song of the

Gypsy Dave.

WOODY HAD ALWAYS LOVED THAT LINE,
"HER HEART IN TUNE TO THE BIG GUITAR,"

Play it agin—
let's have it once more!

AND THAT VERSE ESPECIALLY ALWAYS BROUGHT HIM
BACK TO THOSE CHISOS MOUNTAINS, WHERE HE HAD SAT
WITH JEFF AND HIS FATHER, SINGING THE OLD SONGS.

Tellyawhat—that's a fine version of the song—but it in't nearly so ruff 'n' reddy as the one I got...

THERE WAS A LINGER OF THE SCOTTISH HIGHLANDS IN THIS VOICE, THE OWNER OF WHOM SNATCHED UP WOODY'S GUITAR. HE STRUMMED SOME CHORDS AS HE SPOKE.

Tha's an old Border ballad that one...s'far 's I know it, a clear three hundred years old. You Yanks took it and missed out half the details. He weren't no Davy—that gypsy boy's name was John Faa, hanged in the 1600s sumtime. He was known to the Kennedy clan as an outlaw, and he truly did it, he stole that Laird's wifey, Lady Jane.

THE MAN LAUNCHED INTO THE SONG, PICKING A MELODY SIMILAR TO WOODY'S, BUT WITH AN OLDER STYLE, A COLD ANCIENT AYRE THAT GUSTED THROUGH GRANITE-PAVED SCOTTISH MANOR HOUSES, AND OUT INTO CRAGGY OAK WOODS BRISTLED WITH LICHEN. THE STORY WAS THE SAME, BUT ACCENTED WITH DIFFERENT IDIOMS, THE DIALECT OF ITS SOURCE:

O saddle to me my milk-white steed, Go and fetch me my pony, O! That I may ride and seek my bride, Who is gone with the wraggle, taggle gypsies, O!

AND THE SONG LEFT A HAUNTING COLD IN THE AIR, A SILENCE THAT HUNG LIKE A SPELL.

THE MEN TRADED THESE SONGS THROUGHOUT THE NIGHT: "BLACK JACK DAVEY," "MATTY GROVES," "LIZZIE LINDSAY," "SEVEN YELLOW GYPSIES," "THE HOUSE CARPENTER'S DAUGHTER."

EACH SONG WAS A DIFFERENT EXPRESSION OF THE SAME ROOT, AN EVOLUTION OF A SPECIES OF SENTIMENT. EACH SONG HAD RISEN TO THE PRESENT MOMENT FROM THE DARK WATERS OF THE PAST. SUNG OVER CENTURIES, COUNTLESS MORE HAD SUNK WITHOUT TRACE; BUT THESE SURVIVED.

SOMETHING ABOUT THESE SONGS CONTAINED A TRUTH, A WAY OF SEEING THE WORLD, THAT CHIMED THROUGH THE PRESENT AS IT HAD THROUGH THE PAST.

AND IN THESE SONGS, THE LORD'S LADY ALWAYS CHOSE THE OPEN FIELD OVER THE GOOSE-DOWN BED.

AND THE GYPSY WAS NOT JOHN FAA, OR DAVY, BUT ALL THE MEN IN THE CABOOSE, AND EVERY MAN IN AMERICA WHO HAD BEEN FORCED TO THE FRINGES OF HIS NATION BY THE FACTORY FARMS AND BANK BUYOUTS.

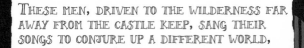

THESE MEN, DRIVEN TO THE WILDERNESS FAR AWAY FROM THE CASTLE KEEP, SANG THEIR SONGS TO CONJURE UP A DIFFERENT WORLD,

THESE SONGS WERE SECULAR PRAYERS THAT STEELED THEM THROUGH THE HARD TIMES, SHAMANIC SPELLS THAT STRENGTHENED THEIR NUMBER WITH EMPATHY.

AND IN THIS PREFERENCE, SHE **BLESSED** THE MEN THAT SANG THE SONG.

FOR SUNG INTO MYTH, SHE WAS NO LONGER THE WIFE OF A LONG-DEAD LORD, BUT GRACE ITSELF, THE SLENDER-ARMED EMBRACE OF HEAVEN.

A DREAMTIME WHERE THEY WERE ON TOP.

THESE SONGS WEREN'T WRITTEN TO SELL OR BE SOLD, THEY DIDN'T ADVERTISE MIRACLE CURES OR GET YOU A CAREER IN THE MUSICALS; THEY WERE EULOGIES TO THE MEN'S EXISTENCE, TESTIMONIES OF THEIR PAST AND THEIR PRESENT.

FOR SALE
BANK CLOSURE

AND UNLIKE THE LAND BENEATH THEIR FEET, THEY COULDN'T BE TAKEN AWAY.

As the moon rose above the Tucson Mountains, some men turned the collars of their coats up, nestled on the dirty train car floor, and tried to sleep.

And Woody watched the gloaming land blur by

...QUIETLY STRUMMING THE CHORDS.

HIS HEART IN TUNE TO THE BIG GUITAR, SINGING THE SONG OF GYPSY DAVY.

CHAPTER 8

WHEN WOODY FINALLY REACHED HIS AUNT IN TURLOCK, SHE BURNED HIS CLOTHES.

SHE SCRUBBED HIS SKIN,

DELICED HIS MATTED HAIR,

AND PUSHED HIM INTO A BILLOWING WHITE BED.

HE STAYED THERE, EMERGING INTERMITTENTLY TO PILLAGE THE FRIDGE, FOR ABOUT A WEEK.

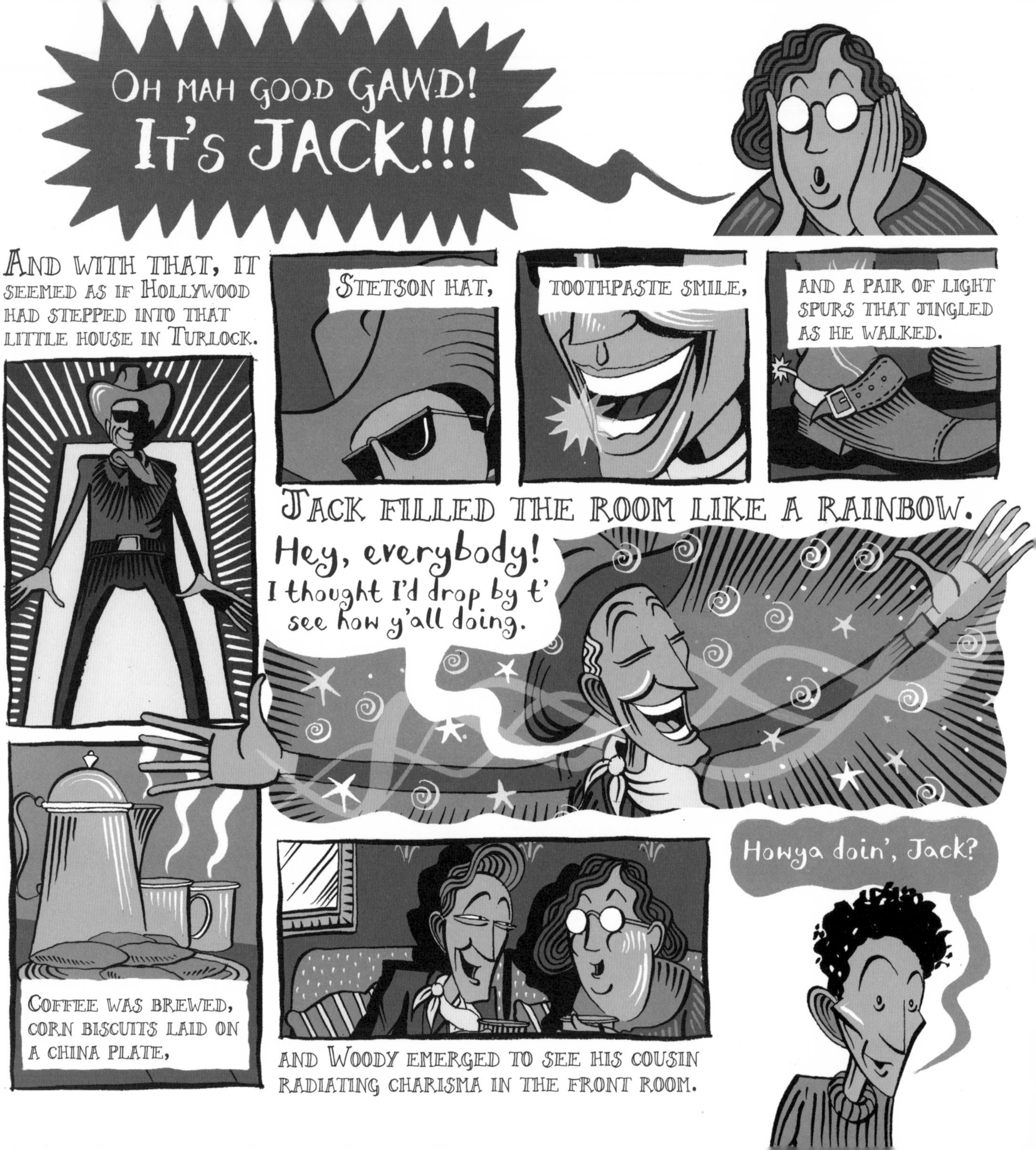

OH MAH GOOD GAWD! IT'S JACK!!!
AND WITH THAT, IT SEEMED AS IF HOLLYWOOD HAD STEPPED INTO THAT LITTLE HOUSE IN TURLOCK.
STETSON HAT,
TOOTHPASTE SMILE,
AND A PAIR OF LIGHT SPURS THAT JINGLED AS HE WALKED.
JACK FILLED THE ROOM LIKE A RAINBOW.
Hey, everybody! I thought I'd drop by t' see how y'all doing.
COFFEE WAS BREWED, CORN BISCUITS LAID ON A CHINA PLATE,
AND WOODY EMERGED TO SEE HIS COUSIN RADIATING CHARISMA IN THE FRONT ROOM.
Howya doin', Jack?

IN SPITE OF HIMSELF, WOODY COULD NOT HELP BUT BE WARMED BY JACK'S GLOW.

Well, strike-a-light if that ain't young Woodblock from way over east!

OVER THE PAST FEW YEARS, THE HOLLYWOOD PRODUCTION LINE HAD MANUFACTURED A NEW CINEMATIC PHENOMENON, A GENRE THEY CALLED

THE WESTERN MUSICAL.

TAPPING INTO A HEAVY-LIDDED NOSTALGIA FOR THE WILD WEST, IT PEDDLED ROMANTIC STORIES OF COWBOYS AND OUTLAWS, RIGHTING WRONGS ON HORSEBACK, STOPPING TO SING LONESOME LAMENTS AS THE SUN WENT DOWN, AND KISSING THAT GOOD OLD HOMEY GAL JUST BEFORE THE CREDITS ROLLED.

JACK HAD MOULDED HIMSELF IN THIS IMAGE,

AND WAS DOING WELL IN BARS, SINGING OILY LAMENTS AND SUGARY LOVE SONGS,

YODELING WITH THE SWEET-NESS OF A DISNEY BLUEBIRD.

OVER THE WEEK THAT JACK SPENT IN TURLOCK, HE AND WOODY PLAYED THEIR GUITARS AND SANG TOGETHER, FORMING AN UNLIKELY PARTNERSHIP OF SILK AND SACKCLOTH.

WHEN JACK LEFT FOR L.A.,

WOODY WENT WITH HIM,

AND BY THE TIME THEY REACHED MAGNOLIA, LOS ANGELES,

THEY HAD AN ACT.

WOODY RENTED A FLEAPIT ROOM IN GLENDALE, JUST DOWN THE ROAD FROM JACK, AND GOT A JOB SCRUBBING POTS IN A RESTAURANT.

JACK, WITH A WIFE AND A KID TO SUPPORT, WORKED HIS CONSTRUCTION JOB IN THE DAY,

AND THE TWO MET UP TO PLAY AT BARS IN THE EVENING.

WOODY RESUMED HIS WASHBOARD CLOWN ACT, AND CHOMPED HIS CIGAR AND TOLD DIRTY JOKES FOR THE MEN,

WHILE JACK LOOKED DEEP INTO THEIR GIRLS' EYES, AND LAUNCHED INTO ANOTHER MELODIC MELODRAMA.

Once I had a sweetheart, who meant the world to me, Then she went down to Deep Ellem, Now she's not the girl for me...

ON WEEKENDS, THEY WOULD GET IN JACK'S TRUCK AND HEAD TO THE CRISSMANS' HOUSE,

WHERE JACK HAD AN EYE FOR THE YOUNGER SISTER.

THE CRISSMANS WERE A MUSICAL FAMILY, AND WHILE THE CHILI WAS BUBBLING ON THE STOVE, THEY ALL SAT AROUND THE FRONT ROOM WITH MANDOLINS, DULCIMERS, AUTOHARPS, AND GUITARS AND STRUCK UP THE OLD TUNES.

AND WHEN MAXINE, THE CRISSMANS' ELDEST DAUGHTER, JOINED WOODY IN A RENDITION OF AN OLD GOSPEL SONG, THERE WAS A SENSATION IN THE AIR, SOMETHING LIKE STATIC, THAT PRICKLED THE BACKS OF THEIR NECKS.

There's a better, Home a-waitin' In the sky, Lord, In the sky...

THE WHOLE FAMILY PUT DOWN THEIR INSTRUMENTS AND DRANK TO THAT ONE.

So as Woody and Jack played the sugary songs to larger crowds at picture houses and square dances, Maxine and Woody would meet up more and more to play the old songs.

After a couple of months, Woody had practically moved in with the Crissmans.

He used to lie on the floor as the family moved around him, humming tunes to himself,

and clattering away at the typewriter late at night.

He had left his old songbook at home with Mary, but was rapidly filling the new one with new songs, his own compositions, the scenes of the past few months hoboing pouring out onto paper.

HE KEPT REWORKING ONE OF HIS FAVORITES, USING AN OLD NEGRO BLUES TECHNIQUE—A TRIPPING LITTLE CHORD PROGRESSION, BOUNCING UP THE STRINGS, WITH A LACONIC TALE DRAWLED OUT OVER THE TOP.

IT WAS A NONSENSE TALE, MORE ABOUT THE SOUND OF THE WORDS THAN WHAT THEY HAD TO SAY.

Down in the henhouse
on my knees,
I thought I heard
a chicken sneeze,
But it was only the rooster
sayin' his prayers,
Thankin' the Lord
for the hens upstairs.

AN ADULT NURSERY RHYME THAT FILLED THEIR WEARY HEADS WITH CARTOONS.

EVEN THE GRIMY SODBUSTERS IN THE FREIGHT CARS HAD LIKED THIS ONE.

And just as before, the words that came to Woody slipped easily into this walking, talking blues pattern, and over the weeks he spent at the Crissmans', he conjured up his own cartoon that told the story of every migrant farmer out west.

Back in Nineteen Twenty-Seven,
I had a little farm and I called that heaven.
Well, the prices up and the rain come down,
And I hauled my crops all into town...
I got the money, bought clothes and groceries,
Fed the kids, and raised a family.

Rain quit and the wind got high,
And the black ol' dust storm filled the sky.
And I swapped my farm for a Ford machine,
And I poured it full of this gas-i-line...
And I started, rockin' an' a-rollin',
Over the mountains,
out towards the old Peach Bowl.

Way up yonder on a mountain road,
I had a hot motor and a heavy load,
I's a-goin' pretty fast,
there wasn't even stoppin',
A-bouncin' up and down,
like popcorn poppin'...
Had a breakdown,
sort of a nervous bustdown of some kind,
There was a feller there, a mechanic feller,
Said it was en-gine trouble.
Way up yonder on a mountain curve,
It's way up yonder in the piney wood,
An' I give that rollin' Ford a shove,
An' I's a-gonna coast as far as I could...
Commence coastin', pickin' up speed,
Was a hairpin turn,
I didn't make it.

Man alive, I'm a-tellin' you,
The fiddles and the guitars really flew.
That Ford took off like a flying squirrel
An' it flew halfway around the world...
Scattered wives and childrens
All over the side of that mountain.
We got out to the West Coast broke,
So dad-gum hungry I thought I'd croak,
An' I bummed up a spud or two,
An' my wife fixed up a tater stew...
We poured the kids full of it,
Mighty thin stew, though,
You could read a magazine right through it.

Always have figured
That if it'd been just
a little bit thinner,
Some of these here politicians
Coulda seen through it.

HE SURPRISED HIMSELF WITH THAT LAST LITTLE KICK.

AND WHEN HE PLAYED IT TO THE CRISSMANS, HE WATCHED THEM BEHIND HIS HOLLOW BOX, CHUCKLING AT THE IMAGERY AS IF THE SONG WAS ONE LONG JOKE.

AND WHEN HE SPAT OUT THOSE FINAL WORDS, HE SAT IN SILENCE AS A CONVERSATION AROSE ABOUT THE FARMERS, THEIR BLIGHTED CROPS, THEIR LOST HOMELANDS, AND THEIR TREATMENT IN CALIFORNIA.

WOODY WAS INTRIGUED.

THERE WAS SOMETHING IN THIS SONG, SOME OLD BOY HUMOR, SOME HUMANITY, THAT REALLY CHIMED WITH PEOPLE. AND THAT FINAL LINE REALLY DID SOMETHING, MADE THEM SIT UP AND TALK.

AFTER SOME MONTHS OF THIS, JACK KNOCKED ON THE CRISSMANS' DOOR.

HE'D JUST LANDED AN AUDITION FOR KFVD RADIO,

A STATION OWNED BY J. FRANK BURKE,

WHO WAS FAMOUS AROUND THOSE PARTS FOR HIS ON-AIR SOCIALIST RANTS.

THEY GOT THE SHOW. AND BY SEPTEMBER, THEY WERE PLAYING TWICE A DAY, ONE SHOW BEFORE JACK'S CONSTRUCTION WORK, THE OTHER BEFORE THEY HIT THE BARS TO PLAY THEIR DOLLAR SETS.

WOODY WAS, FOR THE FIRST TIME IN HIS LIFE, STARTING TO EARN SOME REAL MONEY,

AND HE ENDED EVERY WEEK BY SEALING A WAD OF DOL-LARS INTO AN ENVELOPE, AND SENDING IT BACK TO MARY AND LITTLE GWENDOLINE.

KFVD

AFTER MONTHS ON THE ROAD, HE WAS FINALLY BEGINNING TO MISS THEM.

After a while, however, Jack's construction job took its toll.

He left the show and Woody went straight to Mr. Burke to ask for Maxine as a replacement.

Immediately, the show was transformed. Gone were Jack's smooth croons and in their place were the ancient songs of the hearth and home.

Bury me beneath the willow, 'Neath that weeping willow tree...

Laydees and gentlermen!!!

I am proud to be inno-dioosin t' y'all tonight for her first appearance before this here microber-phone:

Lefty Lou from South Mizoo...

She's long-winded and left-handed and she can jump a six-rail fence with a bucket of milk in each hand and never cause a ripple on the surface!

Woody hammed up his Okie accent, and strung the songs together with a monologue of what he called his cornpone philosophy.

Say, you know it but I'll say it agin, my name's Woody, and I'm from the buyootiful state of Texas, where the oil flows, the wheat grows, and where the people owes.
Bin around the country a few years, a hoboin' hillbilly, eating twice a week whether I was hungry or not.
I am a believer in everything and everybody, extry modern and extry old-fashioned.
And I got a song fer ya now, one that I wrote.
Lots of folks back east, they say, is leavin' home every day, Beatin' the hot old dusty way to the California line. 'Cross the desert sands they roll, gettin' out of that old dust bowl, They think they're goin' to a sugar bowl, but here's what they find Now, the police at the port of entry say, "You're number fourteen thousand for today."
Oh, if you ain't got the do re mi, folks,

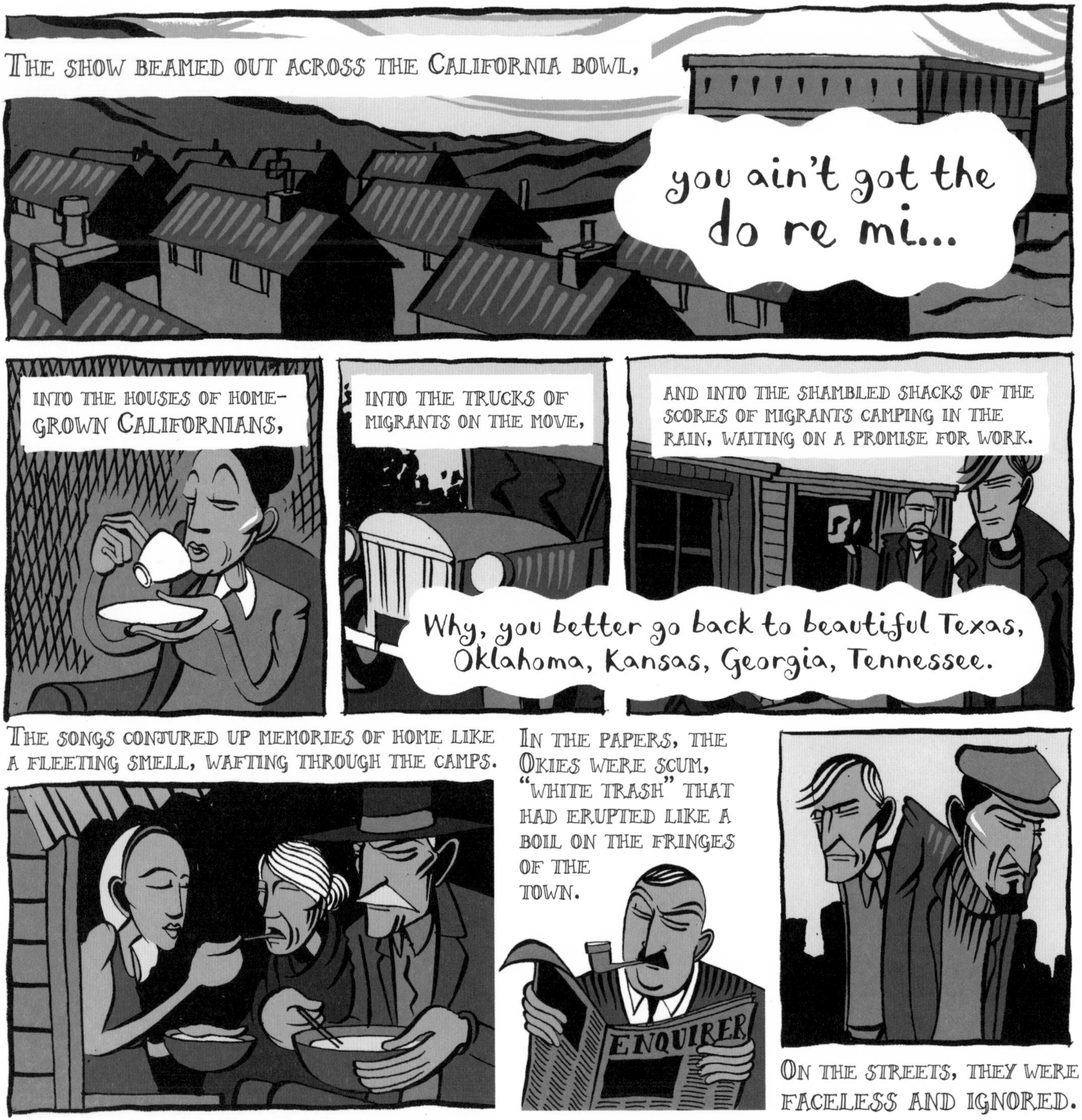

THE SHOW BEAMED OUT ACROSS THE CALIFORNIA BOWL,
you ain't got the do re mi...
INTO THE HOUSES OF HOME-GROWN CALIFORNIANS,
INTO THE TRUCKS OF MIGRANTS ON THE MOVE,
AND INTO THE SHAMBLED SHACKS OF THE SCORES OF MIGRANTS CAMPING IN THE RAIN, WAITING ON A PROMISE FOR WORK.
Why, you better go back to beautiful Texas, Oklahoma, Kansas, Georgia, Tennessee.
THE SONGS CONJURED UP MEMORIES OF HOME LIKE A FLEETING SMELL, WAFTING THROUGH THE CAMPS.
IN THE PAPERS, THE OKIES WERE SCUM, "WHITE TRASH" THAT HAD ERUPTED LIKE A BOIL ON THE FRINGES OF THE TOWN.
ENQUIRER
ON THE STREETS, THEY WERE FACELESS AND IGNORED.

BUT HERE, ON THE WOODY AND LEFTY LOU SHOW, THEY WERE THEMSELVES ONCE MORE.

BECAUSE THIS WAS ROOTS MUSIC...

California is a Garden of Eden, a paradise to live in or see;

THE WORDS AND MELODIES THAT HAD BEEN PASSED FROM GENERATION TO GENERATION.

THEY WERE THE SOUND OF HOG ROASTS ON THEIR FRONT PORCHES,

LULLABIES ON THEIR MOTHERS' LAPS,

THEY WERE THE RHYTHM OF A BLOODLINE THAT BEAT THROUGH THEM, FROM THEIR PARENTS AND ON TO THEIR CHILDREN.

But believe it or not, you won't find it so hot, If you ain't got that do re mi.

AND THOUGH THEIR FAMILIES HAD BEEN SCATTERED IN THE WIND, THESE TAPROOTS STILL RAN DEEP WITHIN THEM, SECURING THEIR SOULS TO THE SOILS OF THEIR PASTS.

THE SHOW WAS A HIT AND THE RADIO'S MAIL ROOM WAS FLOODED WITH SUPERLATIVES.

BURKE HAD MANAGED TO RAISE ADVERTISING REVENUE. HE SHARED IT WITH WOODY BY MEANS OF AN OFFICIAL CONTRACT,

AND WOODY STARTED SPEAKING TO MARY ABOUT COMING TO CALIFORNIA, TO SET UP A NEW HOME.

THINGS WERE REALLY STARTING TO HAPPEN FOR WOODY.

BUT TETHERED TO THIS SUCCESS, HE FELT A CERTAIN KIND OF GUILT.

HE HAD COME TO CALIFORNIA WITH THE DROVES OF DISPOSSESSED FARMERS AND JOB HUNTERS AND WAS NOW MAKING GOOD MONEY SINGING THEIR MISFORTUNE.

HE FELT THE PULL OF THE HOOVERVILLES AND JUNGLE CAMPS THAT LINGERED ON THE OUTSKIRTS AND KNEW THAT, FOR MANY, TIMES WERE HARDER THAN EVER.

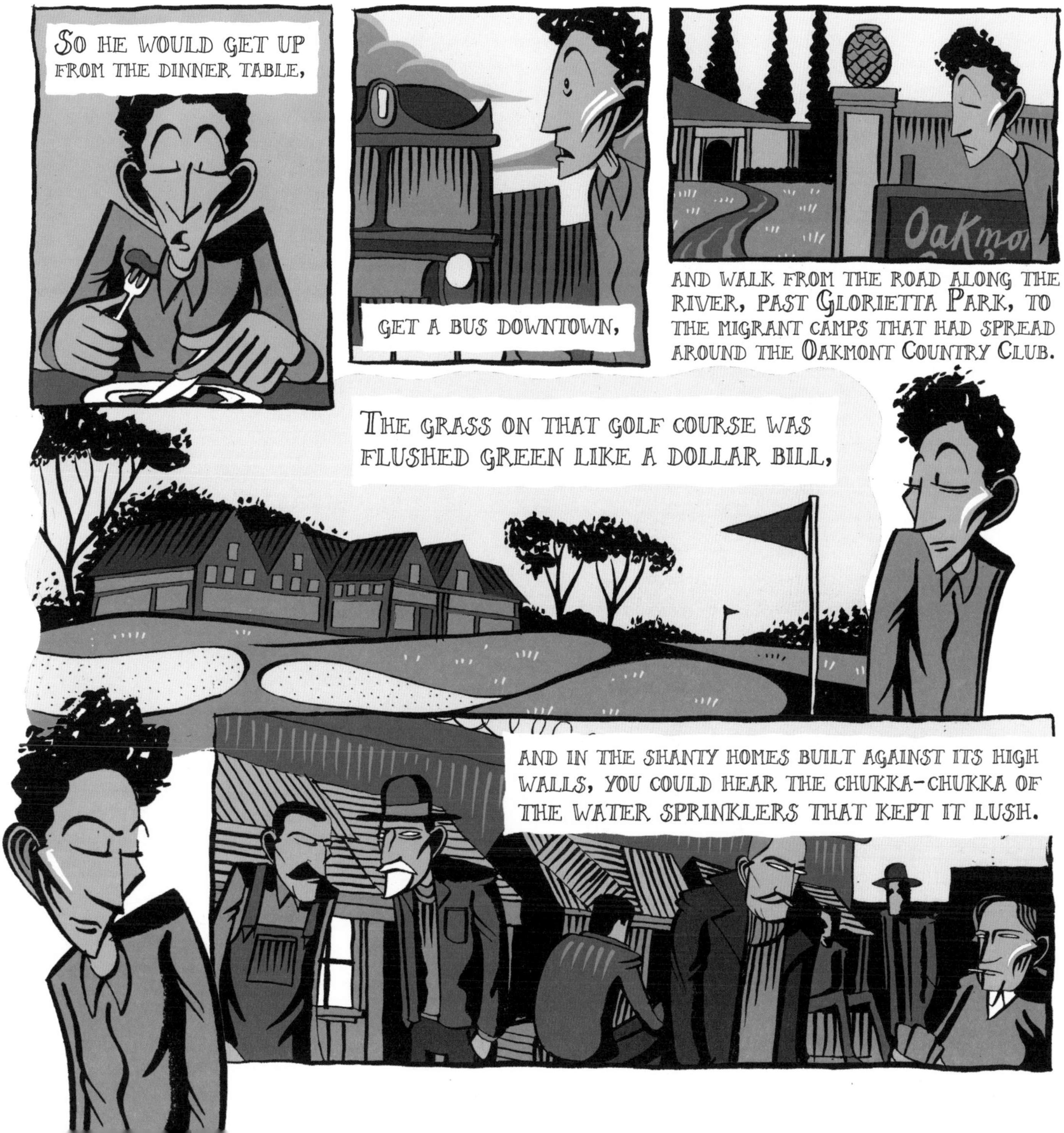
SO HE WOULD GET UP FROM THE DINNER TABLE,
GET A BUS DOWNTOWN,
Oakmon
AND WALK FROM THE ROAD ALONG THE RIVER, PAST GLORIETTA PARK, TO THE MIGRANT CAMPS THAT HAD SPREAD AROUND THE OAKMONT COUNTRY CLUB.
THE GRASS ON THAT GOLF COURSE WAS FLUSHED GREEN LIKE A DOLLAR BILL,
AND IN THE SHANTY HOMES BUILT AGAINST ITS HIGH WALLS, YOU COULD HEAR THE CHUKKA-CHUKKA OF THE WATER SPRINKLERS THAT KEPT IT LUSH.

AND AGAIN, IN THE GRIMY FACES OF THESE MIGRANTS,

WOODY SAW HIS MOTHER.

AND HE THOUGHT BACK TO THE FIRE THAT HAD BURNED DOWN THEIR FIRST HOUSE, WHEN WOODY WAS A CHILD. THAT HAD BEEN THE START OF IT ALL WITH NORA.

FROM THAT MOMENT ON, THE CONVULSIONS CAME UPON HER IN THE TIME IT TOOK TO POUR A CUP OF COFFEE; THEY TWISTED HER MOUTH INTO A SNARL, THEY CAUSED HER TO ERUPT IN FILTHY LANGUAGE AND SPITEFUL TIRADES.

THEY INSTILLED A FRENZY IN HER MIND, ON ONE OCCASION DRIVING HER TO EMPTY THE HOUSE OF FURNITURE, ON ANOTHER TO CHASE ROY AROUND THE HOUSE WITH A KNIFE. ONE DAY, WOODY'S SISTER CLARA HAD RETURNED HOME FROM SCHOOL TO FIND HER BABY BROTHER WRAPPED IN NEWSPAPER, CRYING IN THE OVEN.

As time wore on, these discolorations were upon her more often than not, and the neighbors started to notice.

They whispered and gossiped, they noted her behavior and they described it to their husbands and children over dinner tables.

And as several more fires flashed through the Guthries' lives, they reasoned that they must be connected with that woman's madness.

And in time, like the victims of plague, the Guthries were shunned.

Eyes lowered from Charley's gaze as he entered the barroom, children taunted Woody and his siblings at school, and customers left the store whenever Nora herself entered.

IN THE END, IT TURNED OUT THAT NORA WASN'T MAD.

THE DOCTORS EVENTUALLY AGREED ON THE DIAGNOSIS OF HUNTINGTON'S CHOREA, A RARE DEGENERATIVE DISORDER THAT CHEWED AWAY AT THE CORE OF THE BRAIN.

IT CAUSED INVOLUNTARY JERKS OF THE BODY, A TWISTING OF THE MUSCLES, AND SEVERE BOUTS OF DEPRESSION.

THIS HAD BEEN NORA'S STORY FROM HER THIRTIES ONWARD.

AS THE DOCTORS HAD GENTLY EXPLAINED TO CHARLEY AND HIS CHILDREN, HUNTINGTON'S WAS A GENETIC DISEASE, MEANING THEY HAD A ONE-IN-TWO CHANCE OF HAVING IT THEMSELVES.

IT WAS A TICKING TIME BOMB IN THE VERY CORE OF THEIR BRAINS,

POISED ON THE FLICK OF A COIN.

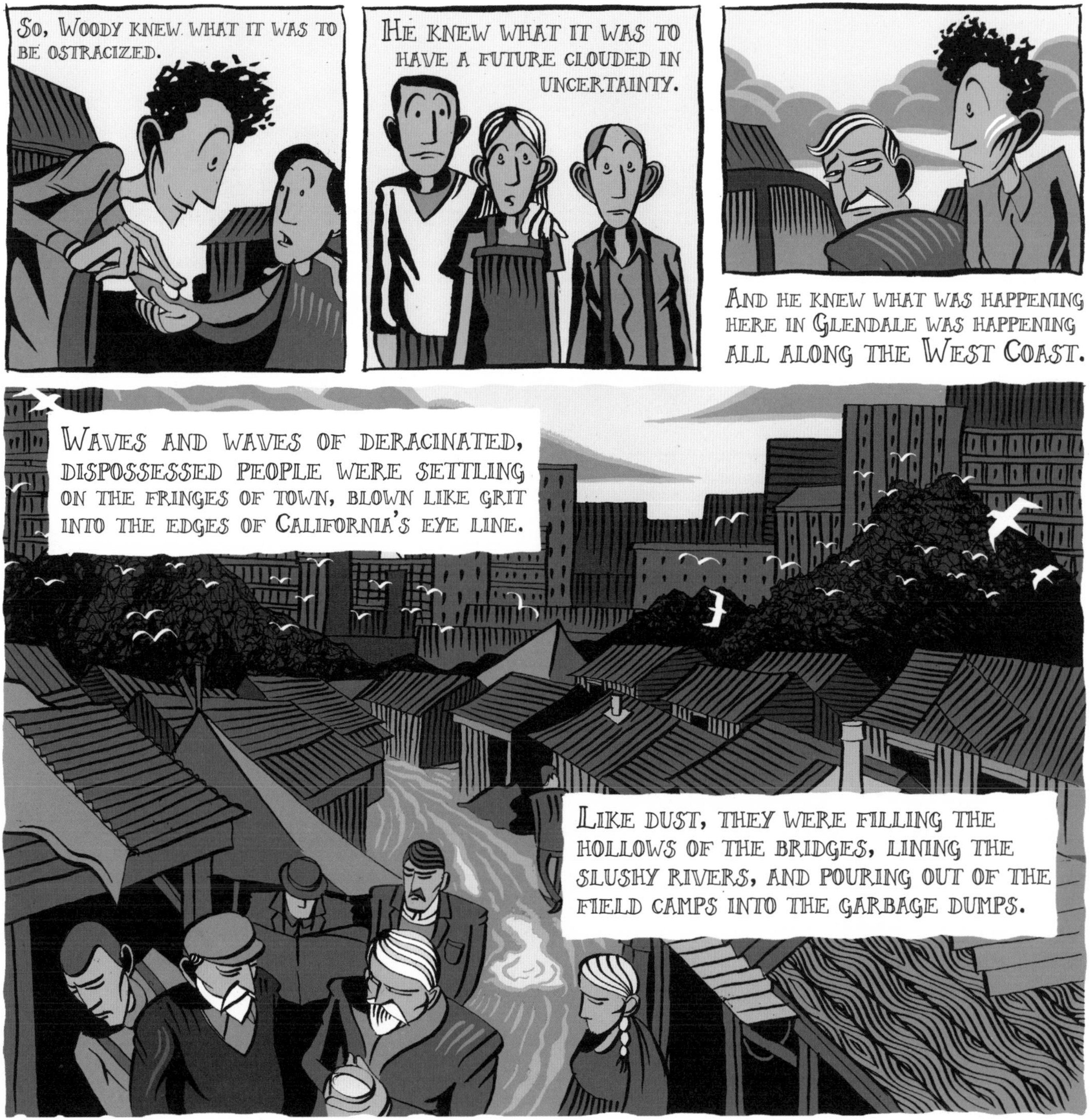
So, Woody knew what it was to be ostracized.
He knew what it was to have a future clouded in uncertainty.
And he knew what was happening here in Glendale was happening all along the West Coast.
Waves and waves of deracinated, dispossessed people were settling on the fringes of town, blown like grit into the edges of California's eye line.
Like dust, they were filling the hollows of the bridges, lining the slushy rivers, and pouring out of the field camps into the garbage dumps.

SITTING ON THE OUT-
SKIRTS OF GLENDALE
ONE DAY, OVERLOOKING
THE SAN GABRIEL
VALLEY, WOODY
THOUGHT OF THE OUT-
LAWS WHO HAD ROAMED
THESE HILLS BEFORE THE
TURN OF THE CENTURY.

THEY HAD HUNTED IN THESE HILLS,

THEY HAD SLEPT
IN THESE HILLS,

THE MURDERERS
WERE DEAD AND
GONE, BUT THEIR
LEGENDS LIVED
ON IN THE FOLK
SONGS.

THE MYTHS
HAD BLEACHED
THE BLOOD OFF
THEIR HANDS
AND LEFT ONLY
WHAT THE
PEOPLE NEEDED
FROM THEM:

AND LIKE THE BEASTS OF ANCIENT FOLKLORE, THEY HAD ONLY LEFT TO MURDER AND STEAL FROM THE SETTLEMENTS.

DEFIANCE AGAINST A SYSTEM THAT HAD NO ROOM FOR THEM.

AND LOOKING OVER THE LITTLE BOXES ON THE GLENDALE HILLSIDE, WOODY'S GUT CHURNED AT THE NEAT HYPOCRISY OF IT ALL, THE RIGID PROPERNESS THAT HAD WALLED OUT THE MIGRANTS.

GLENDALE WAS A GRID OF SQUARES, OF RIGHT ANGLES AND STRAIGHT LINES IMPOSED UPON THE LAND BY THE PEOPLE WHO HAD SETTLED THERE.

AGAIN, WOODY'S MIND TOOK TO THE SKY, AND HE SAW ALL THE TOWNS IN ALL OF AMERICA, ROULETTE TABLES IN A VAST CASINO OWNED BY THE BANKS.

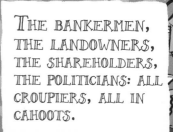

THE BANKERMEN, THE LANDOWNERS, THE SHAREHOLDERS, THE POLITICIANS: ALL CROUPIERS, ALL IN CAHOOTS.

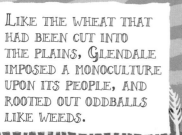

LIKE THE WHEAT THAT HAD BEEN CUT INTO THE PLAINS, GLENDALE IMPOSED A MONOCULTURE UPON ITS PEOPLE, AND ROOTED OUT ODDBALLS LIKE WEEDS.

FROM HIGH IN THE HILLTOPS, IT LOOKED LIKE A ROULETTE TABLE OF LINES AND NUMBERS, MANIPULATING ITS PEOPLE LIKE PLASTIC CHIPS, UNITS OF AN ECONOMY CONTROLLED BY THE SPIN OF THE BIG WHEEL IN THE CENTER.

THESE DAYS, THE CRIMINALS WERE NOT THE OUTLAWS IN THE HILLS, BUT THE SUITS IN THEIR OFFICES. YOU COULD ROB SOMEONE OF THEIR WAGES BY TAKING IT FROM HIS POCKETS, BUT IT WAS MORE EFFICIENT TO NOT PAY HIM IN THE FIRST PLACE.

Yes, as through this world I've wandered
I've seen lots of funny men;
Some will rob you with a six-gun,
And some with a fountain pen.

SITTING QUIETLY ON THAT HILL, HE WATCHED AS A MOTHER SERVED SOME THIN GRAVY INTO METAL PANS, CHIPPING AWAY AT A HARD HUSK OF CORNBREAD.

WOODY PULLED OUT HIS NOTEBOOK.

CUM GET IT!

WOODY WATCHED AS TWO CHILDREN EMERGED FROM THE TENT AND SAT AROUND THE FIRE.

AND AS AN OLD LADY WAS HELPED OUT BY A MAN, TO SIT ON THE UPTURNED PEACH BOX.

THE MAN TOOK ONE OF THE PLATES AND BEGAN TO SPOON THE GRAVY INTO HER MOUTH,

AS THE CHILDREN CLEANED THEIR PLATES IN SECONDS.

WHEN THE MAN HAD FINISHED FEEDING HER,

THE WOMAN PASSED HIM HIS PLATE,

AND THEY BOTH SAT BY THE FIRE.

WOODY THOUGHT OF THE HEARTH THEY HAD ONCE SAT BY, AND THE KITCHEN TABLE THEY HAD DESERTED.

THEIR BEDS, THEIR ORNAMENTS, THE VIEW FROM THEIR WINDOWS...

LOST TO THE ROLL OF THAT ROULETTE WHEEL.

And as through your life you travel,
Yes, as through your life you roam,
You won't never see an outlaw
Drive a family from their home.

CHAPTER 9

A MONTH OR TWO LATER, MARY AND THE BABY ARRIVED FROM TEXAS.

HER TRIP HAD BEEN PLANNED AND PAID FOR WEEKS EARLIER, BUT IN SPITE OF THIS, WOODY HADN'T ORGANIZED A PLACE FOR THEM TO STAY,

HE'D FORGOTTEN TO MEET THEM AT THE STATION,

AND HE'D ACCEPTED A JOB THAT WOULD TAKE HIM OUT OF L.A. FOR MONTHS.

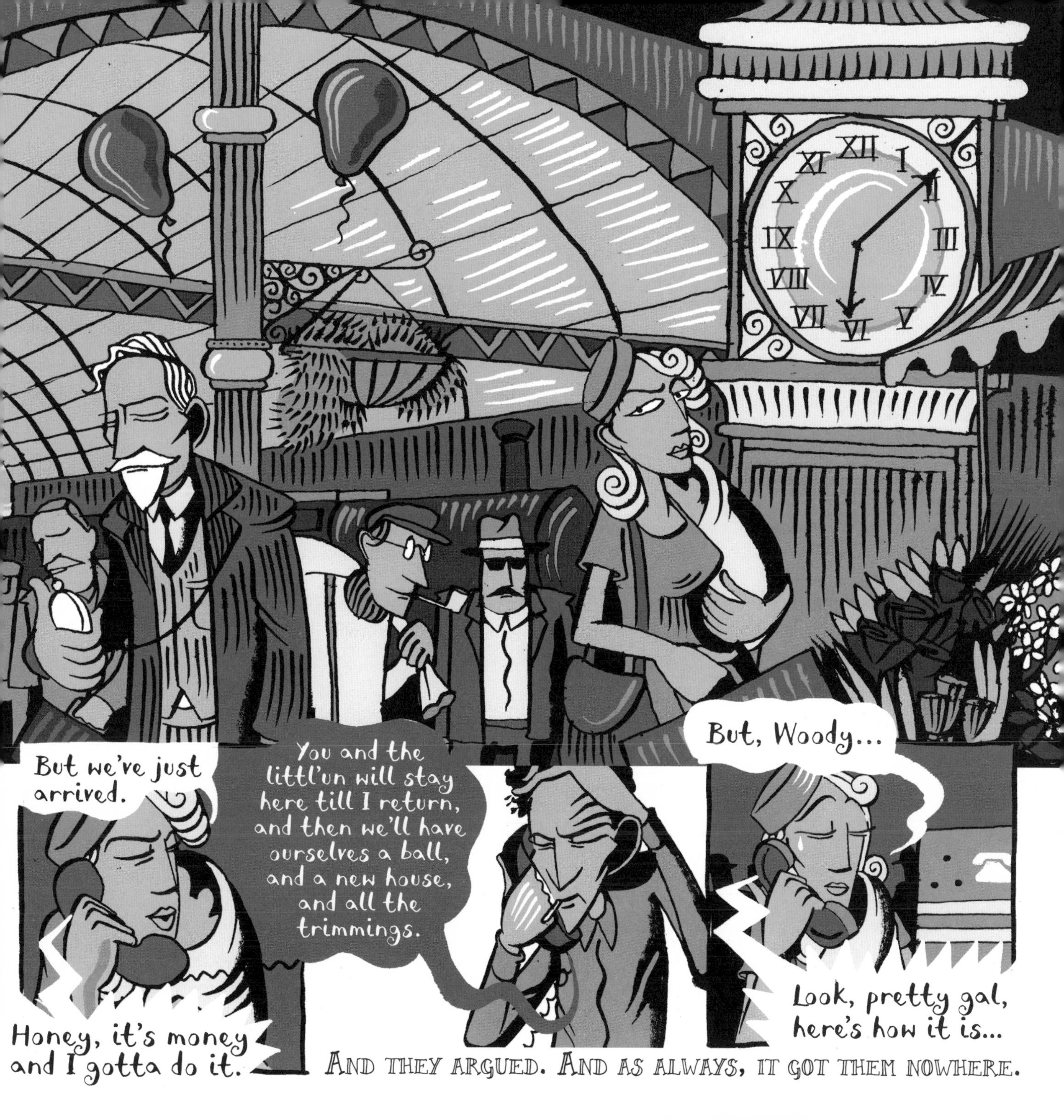
But we've just arrived.
Honey, it's money and I gotta do it.
You and the littl'un will stay here till I return, and then we'll have ourselves a ball, and a new house, and all the trimmings.
But, Woody...
Look, pretty gal, here's how it is...
AND THEY ARGUED. AND AS ALWAYS, IT GOT THEM NOWHERE.

OVER AT THE STATION, J. FRANK BURKE HAD BEEN INTRIGUED BY WOODY'S CORNPONE PHILOSOPHIZING, AND WANTED TO MAKE SOMETHING MORE OF IT.

I want you to git back inter them camps, and tell it how it really is.

I want you to go sing yr songs, make some interviews, get a feel for the workers in the camps, and write it all up for me.

We'll print a column a week in "The Light," and we'll see where it goes from there.

Sounds right enuff for me

Oh, and another thing...

"The Light" is a socialist paper—you know that, don't you?

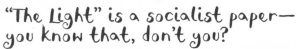

Left wing, right wing, west wing, chicken wing...

s'all the same to me!

SO, AFTER A YEAR OF CUSHIONED SOFAS AND CARPETED FLOORS,

WOODY WAS BACK HOBOING.

AND AS HE RETURNED TO THE MIGRANT CAMPS AND HOOVERVILLES OF THE WEST, AMONG THE SWARMS OF RAGGED, DISPOSSESSED PEOPLE, SITTING IN THEIR GARBAGE HOMES WITH THE ORANGE-CRATE WALLS AND MOLDY MATTRESSES,

WOODY WAS AGAIN REMINDED OF MRS. ATKINS'S SHACK ON THE OUTSKIRTS OF OKEMAH AND INSTANTLY FELT A SENSE OF HOME-COMING.

WOODY WAS WELCOMED INTO THE HOOVERVILLES AND JUNGLE CAMPS LESS LIKE A CELEBRITY AND MORE LIKE AN OLD FRIEND.

HE PASSED THOUSANDS OF MIGRANTS CAMPING ALONG THE ROADSIDE, BROKEN JALOPIES HALTING THEIR FLOW.

HE VISITED THE SWELLING FARM CAMPS SET UP FOR THE ALMONDS AND ARTICHOKES, AND A HUNDRED MORE CAMPS AROUND THEM, WITH THOUSANDS OF MIGRANTS WAITING ON A PROMISE FOR MORE WORK.

WARNING

WOODY'S GUT CHURNED AT THE SIGHT.

THEIR CARS WERE SOLD FOR FOOD, THEIR POSSESSIONS EXCHANGED FOR CREDIT AT THE LOCAL STORES, AND THEY WERE TRAPPED, LIKE FISH IN A PUDDLE, UNABLE TO HEAD HOME, AND PROHIBITED TO STAY WHERE THEY WERE.

STANDING BEHIND HIS GUITAR, HE SAW THE SAME FACES IN THESE CAMPS AS HE HAD SEEN A YEAR BEFORE, ONLY THERE WERE MORE OF THEM. THEIR FACES HAD HARDENED IN GRIM ANGER, AND THE QUIET WHISPERS AROUND EVERY CAMPFIRE SPOKE OF UNIONS AND UPRISING. BUT WHEREVER STRIKES WERE ATTEMPTED, THEY WERE EITHER CRUSHED BY THE LOCAL HIRED HANDS, HAPPY TO KICK OUT AT THE OKIE SCUM THAT HAD SETTLED AROUND THEIR PLEASANT PASTURES, OR BROKEN UP BY OKIES FROM OTHER CAMPS, WHO CARED MORE FOR TODAY'S EMPTY STOMACH THAN TOMORROW'S FAIR WAGES.

WOODY WAS AT ONE SUCH CAMP WHEN THE FIRE BROKE OUT. HE HAD HITCHED A LIFT TO REDDING WITH A FAMILY HE HAD MET ON THE ROAD. THEIR CAR HAD BROKEN DOWN ON THE WAY AND THEY AND A HUNDRED OTHER STRAGGLERS ALONG THE ROAD HAD BEEN DRIVEN TO THE NEAREST CAMP BY A COALITION OF POLICEMEN AND COMPANY THUGS. THEIR CARS WERE LEFT ON THE HIGHWAY.

THE TENSION IN THE SETTLEMENTS WAS PALPABLE, A STATIC OF AGGRESSION THAT PRICKLED THE AIR: THE WORD WAS THAT A STRIKE WAS DUE.

STORE

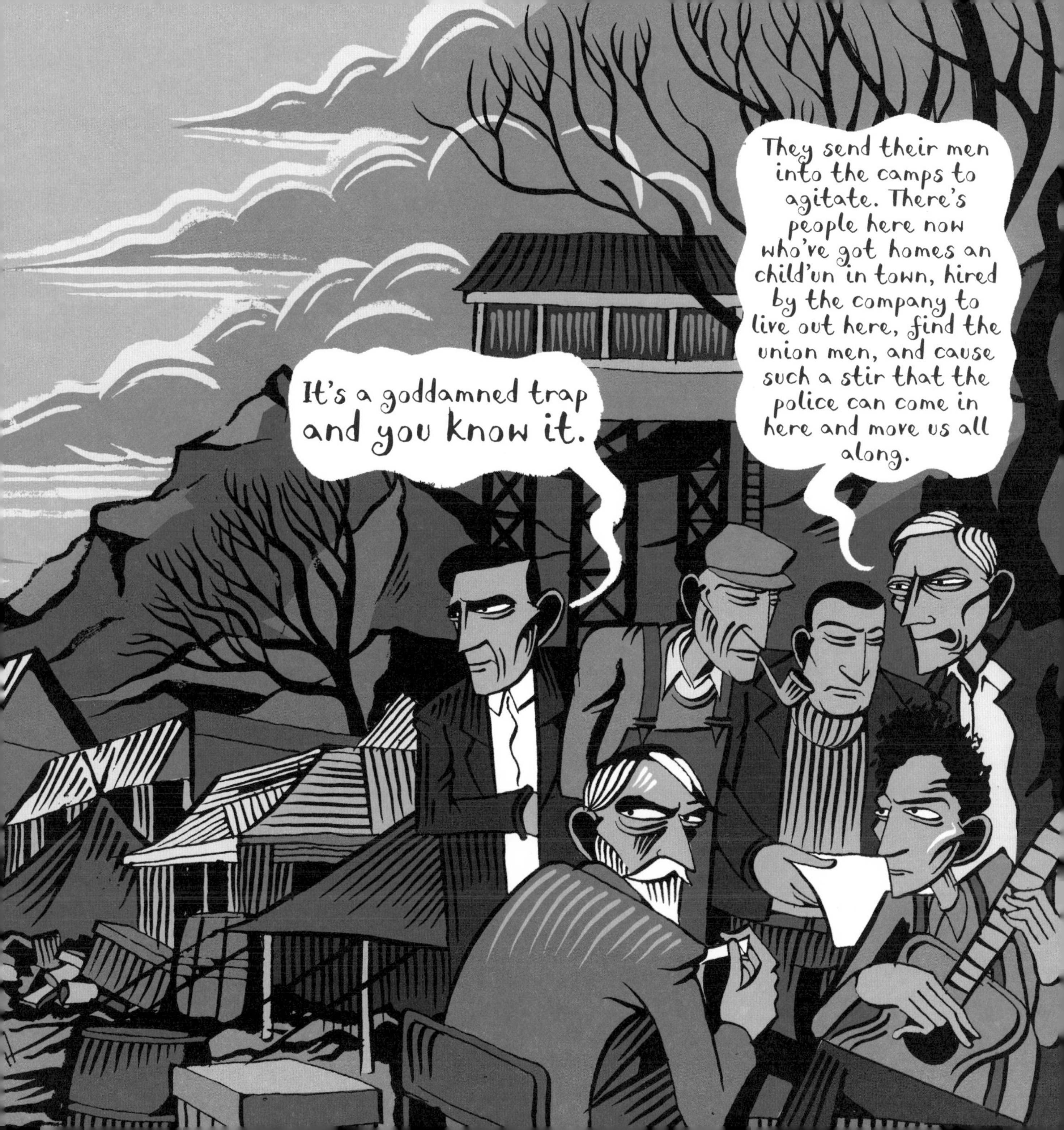
It's a goddamned trap and you know it.
They send their men into the camps to agitate. There's people here now who've got homes an child'un in town, hired by the company to live out here, find the union men, and cause such a stir that the police can come in here and move us all along.

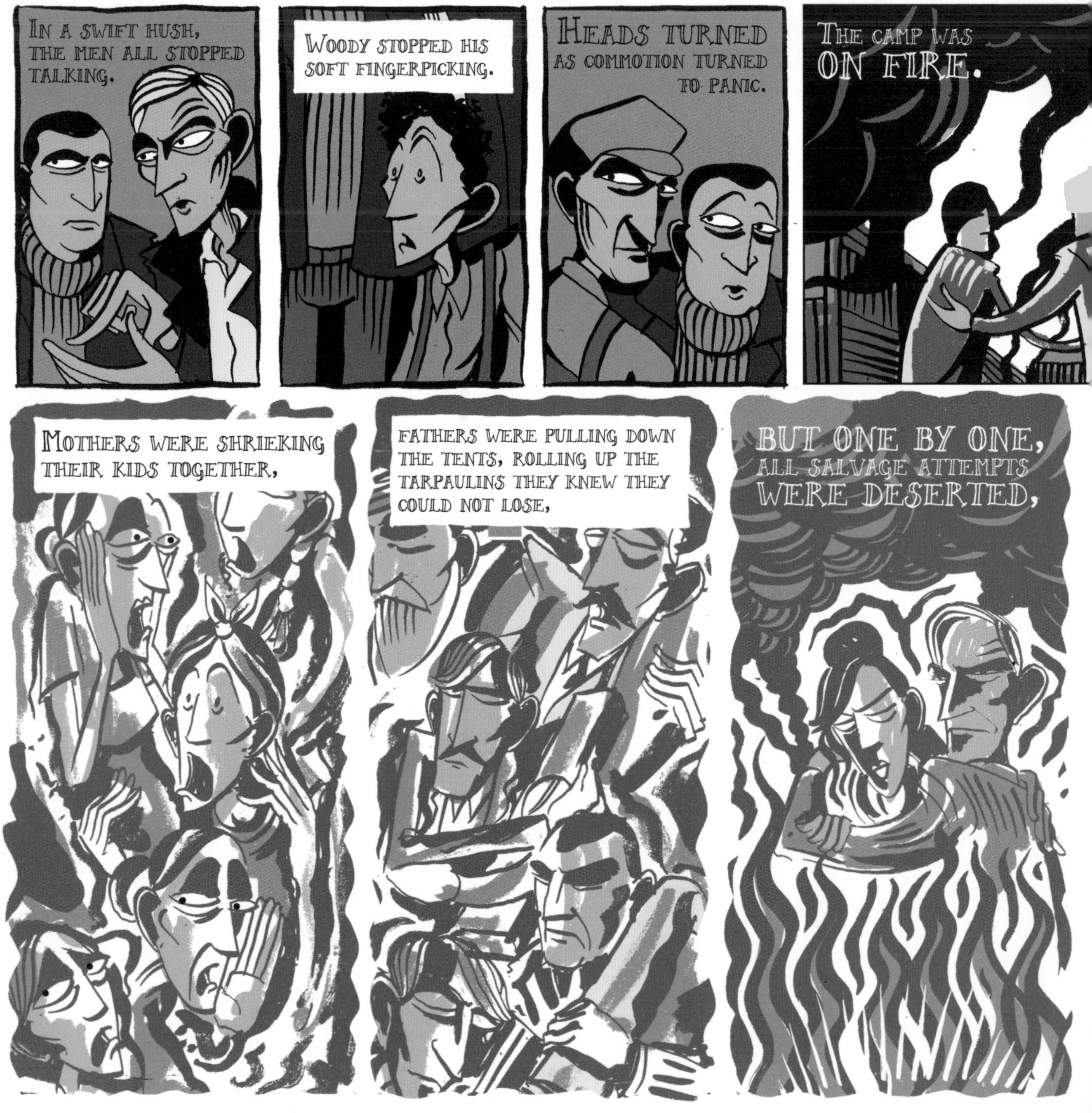
IN A SWIFT HUSH, THE MEN ALL STOPPED TALKING.
WOODY STOPPED HIS SOFT FINGERPICKING.
HEADS TURNED AS COMMOTION TURNED TO PANIC.
THE CAMP WAS ON FIRE.
MOTHERS WERE SHRIEKING THEIR KIDS TOGETHER,
FATHERS WERE PULLING DOWN THE TENTS, ROLLING UP THE TARPAULINS THEY KNEW THEY COULD NOT LOSE,
BUT ONE BY ONE, ALL SALVAGE ATTEMPTS WERE DESERTED,

AND EACH JOINED THE TERRIFIED EXODUS TO THE TOP OF THE HILL.

WITH THE WORLD SWIRLING AROUND HIM, WOODY WAS IN A DAZE.

Before he was born, a neighbor's oil stove had spilled on the lawn, and caught, and spread to that yellow house Charley had just built on a hill in Okemah. Seven rooms of new polished wood went up in smoke, and that, Charley reckoned, had been the start of it all with Nora.

They moved, Woody was born, and Nora's nerves had begun to shred.

Then one day, Clara had been kept home from school by her paranoid mother, and had poured coal oil over her dress, a form of masochistic defiance. Somehow, and to that day no one knew how, her dress had caught alight, and sent her screaming into the front yard.

NORA HAD STOOD, PETRIFIED IN
THE FRONT DOOR, AS CLARA WAS
ROLLED IN A CARPET BY ROY
AND TAKEN UPSTAIRS TO BED.
WHEN CHARLEY HAD RETURNED,
WHEN THE DOCTOR HAD LEFT,
WOODY WAS ALLOWED IN TO SEE
HIS SISTER. HER BLACKENED
FLESH HUNG OFF HER BONES
LIKE WET TISSUE, HER NERVES
SO SEARED THAT SHE COULDN'T
FEEL A THING.

SHE TOLD WOODY NOT TO CRY,
SHE PASSED AWAY, AND TO THIS
DAY HE KEPT HIS PROMISE.

FIRE HAD SCORCHED THROUGH THE
GUTHRIES' LIVES LIKE A VENGEFUL
CURSE, AND TO WOODY, NOTHING SPOKE
OF TOTAL UPHEAVAL, THE UPENDING OF
FATE, LIKE THE SWIFT CATCH OF FLAMES.

He had reached the crest of the hill, coughing soot from his lungs. The children around him were crying, the women holding on to them, and the men stood in tight-tendoned circles, spitting fury.

This weren't no accident.

Too right. We're sodden in rain, mud clings to yer boots, that's petrol that fueled them flames, and petrol ain't no accident.

It happens all through the valley.

You heard it, I heard it, and now it's happened to us.

But they brought us here in the first place.

If they don't have no use fer us, they don't care what happens to us. Cops'll move you on outta town till there ain't no more towns t' be in. Keep moving you on.

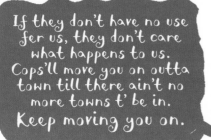

There ain't no place t' be.

If it rains tonight, I don't know what we'll do.

THE NEXT MORNING,

WOODY WOKE UP ABOUT TWENTY MILES FROM THE CAMP. FAMILIES HAD CURLED THEMSELVES INTO TIGHT BALLS, COVERING THEMSELVES WITH WHATEVER THEY HAD SALVAGED FROM THE DAMP, SMOKING EMBERS, AND THERE WAS NO PLACE FOR WOODY. HE HAD WALKED THROUGH THE NIGHT, THE HEADLIGHTS OF THE TRUCKS ZIPPING BY HIM LIKE BURNING ARROWS AND, FINALLY, AT DAWN, HE HAD CRAWLED UNDER A FENCE TO SLEEP IN AN ORCHARD, AWAY FROM THE WIND.

IT WAS A SUNNY DAY,

WITH A BRISK AND GENTLE BREEZE,

AND THE NIGHT BEFORE SEEMED AS DISTANT AS A DARK DREAM.

ORCHARDS OF ALMONDS SPREAD OUT BEFORE HIM, THEIR HEAVY BOUGHS SWAYING IN THE WIND, AND THE MOUNTAINS OF THE SIERRA NEVADA WERE GLEAMING ON THE HORIZON.

BUT THE ANGER FROM LAST NIGHT HAD NOT LEFT WOODY.

BECAUSE THIS WAS NOT THE CHISOS MOUNTAINS. SOMEONE HAD COME AND PUT FENCES AROUND THESE TREES, AROUND EVERY PLOT OF LAND IN AMERICA,

AND NOW THE ONLY PLACE HE COULD BE WAS ON THE ROAD.

AMERICA WAS AN ORCHARD OF PEACHY DREAMS BEHIND A GAUZED FENCE AND A SIGN THAT SAID...

NO TRESPASSING

FORGIVE US OUR TRESPASSES...

TRESPA

THIS LAND WAS HIS LAND AS MUCH AS THE NEXT MAN'S.

LIKE THE FOLK SONGS HE SANG, IT BELONGED TO EVERYONE, SO IT BELONGED TO NO ONE.

THE UNGODLY SIN WAS THE FENCE, NOT THE CROSSING OF IT.

AN OLD CARTER SONG CAME ON THE RADIO IN THE TRUCK'S CABIN.

This world is not my home, I'm just a-passing through,
My treasures and my hopes are all beyond the blue,
Where many friends and kindred have gone on before,
And I can't feel at home in this world anymore.

AS EVER, THAT OLD-TIME MELODY BROUGHT HIM INTO HIS MOTHER'S ARMS.

HE THOUGHT OF HER IN HER ASYLUM, THAT DAY HE HAD VISITED HER BEFORE HEADING TO PAMPA, THE SULLEN GLAZE ON HER EYES.

SHE HAD NOT SEEMED TO RECOGNIZE HIM.

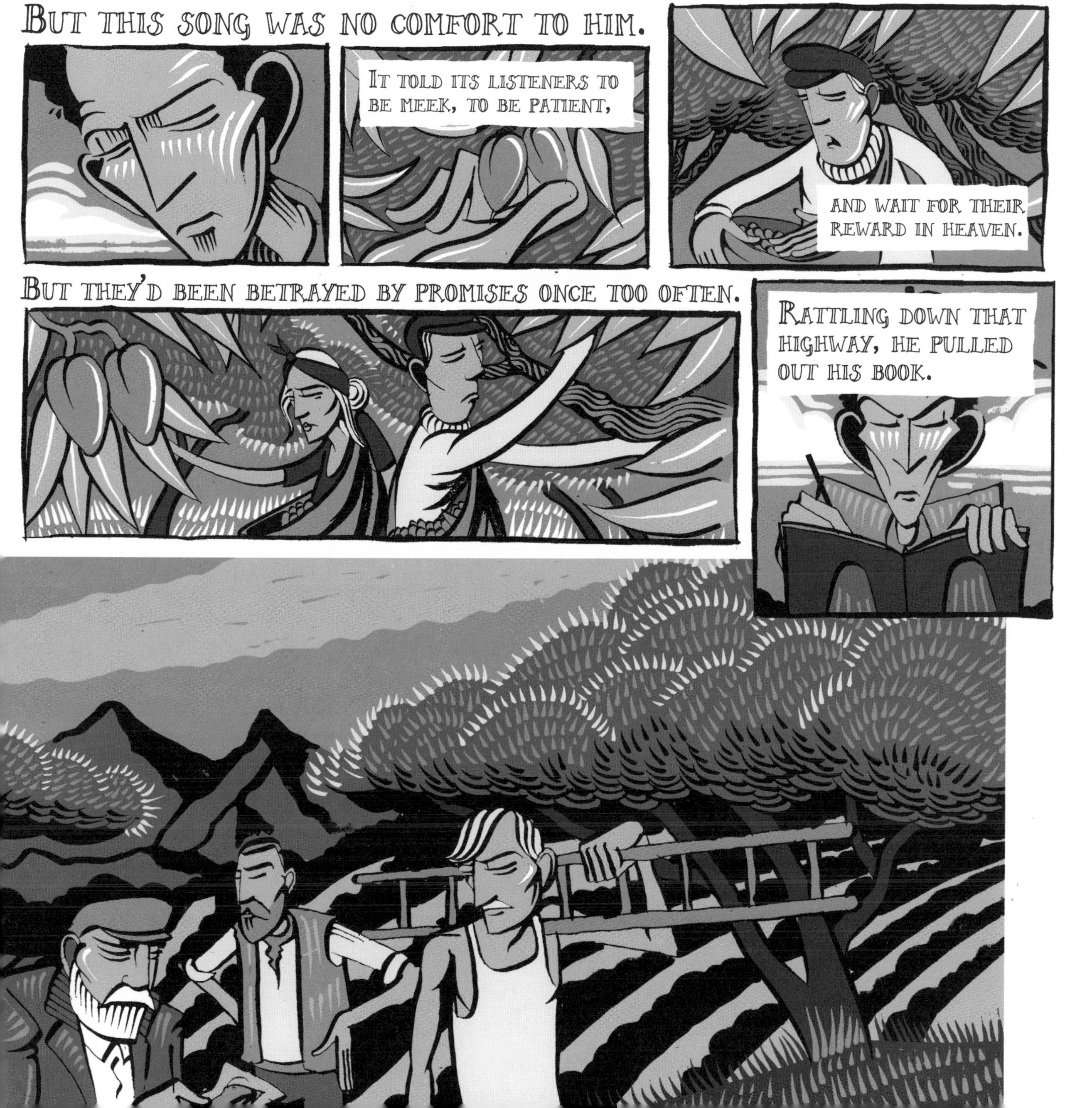

BUT THIS SONG WAS NO COMFORT TO HIM.
IT TOLD ITS LISTENERS TO BE MEEK, TO BE PATIENT,
AND WAIT FOR THEIR REWARD IN HEAVEN.
BUT THEY'D BEEN BETRAYED BY PROMISES ONCE TOO OFTEN.
RATTLING DOWN THAT HIGHWAY, HE PULLED OUT HIS BOOK.

HE WASN'T GOING TO WRITE A SONG OF PROMISE.

IF HIS SONG COULD DO ANYTHING, WOODY THOUGHT, IT COULD OPEN UP ITS LISTENERS TO THEIR VOLCANIC RAGE, AND RAISE THEM FROM THE DUST.

A SONG OF INSURRECTION.

A SONG OF RESURRECTION.

CHAPTER 10

WOODY WAS SOUND ASLEEP. SITTING ON THE STAGE, IN FRONT OF SIX HUNDRED FACES, HIS CHEST HEAVED GENTLY AS THE SNORES SLIPPED FROM HIS LIPS.

A MONTH OR TWO AFTER HE'D RETURNED FROM THE CAMPS, MARY HAD ANNOUNCED:

SHE WAS READY TO LEAVE.

CALIFORNIA HAD NOT OFFERED HER THE LIFE SHE HAD HOPED, SHE WAS LONELY, AND SHE MISSED HER HOME.

TOO EXHAUSTED TO ARGUE, WOODY HAD WATCHED HER DIS-APPEAR, UNAWARE OF THE CHILD GROWING IN HER BELLY.

His articles for "The Light" had been well received by the liberals of California,

And he had returned to a glittering array of socialist soirees and left-wing rallies, everyone eager to shake his hand.

He had met Ed Robbin, a union organizer,

And Will Geer, a statuesque actor who toured the South putting on dissident plays.

Both men were impressed by Woody's laconic drawl, his puckish demeanor, and both thought he could be a real asset in the rallies they organized...

Lending an Okie authenticity to their message.

So Woody had begun touring with Robbin and Geer.

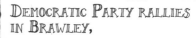
THEY WENT TO COMMUNIST PARTY MEETINGS IN MARYSVILLE,

WORKERS STRIKES IN REDDING,

DEMOCRATIC PARTY RALLIES IN BRAWLEY,

EACH FOLLOWING THE SAME PATTERN OF LONG MARXIST SPEECHES, AND DRAWN-OUT COMMUNITY DISCUSSION. NO MATTER HOW FRACTIOUS THE MEETING, NO MATTER HOW HOT THE TEMPERS FLARED UNDER THE BLANKET DRONE OF WORDS, THE EVENING ALWAYS ENDED IN A UNITED REVELRY.

BECAUSE TO SING TOGETHER WAS TO BAND TOGETHER.

My name's Woody Guthrie. I ain't a communist necessarily, but I bin in the red all my life!

And I'd like to sing you a song I wrote for y'all tonight, by the name of "Tom Joad"...

WHEN WOODY FOUND OUT THAT MARY WAS PREGNANT, HE KNEW HE HAD TO RETURN TO PAMPA.

THEY WERE ON THEIR LAST LEGS AS A COUPLE, BUT HE KNEW HIS MORAL DUTY LAY WITH HIS CHILDREN.

HE KNEW THAT'S WHAT CHARLEY WOULD SAY,

HE KNEW THAT'S WHAT THE CRISSMANS WOULD SAY,

AND HE KNEW IT IN HIS BONES.

SO WITH HEAVY FEET, HE TURNED BACK EAST, AND HITCHED TO PAMPA.

RUSTY SKELETONS OF CARS LINED THE HIGHWAY, SEATS STRIPPED OF THEIR LEATHER TO USE AS SHOES, HOODS TORN OFF FOR SHELTER.

THE SWATHES OF DESERT DUNES HAD GONE, BLOWN NORTH BY THE WINDS OF SEVERAL WINTERS, BUT WHEN WOODY FINALLY ARRIVED, THE TOWN WAS EMPTIER THAN EVER.

SEEGER and SON

HE PASSED SCORES OF EMPTY HOUSES,

DUST CRUSTED OVER CRACKED WINDOWS,

STRAY DOGS LOLLING ON THE PORCHES,

AND STOPPED TO READ THE LIST ON THE TOWN'S NEWSPAPER OFFICE, NOW BOARDED UP.

LISTS LIKE THIS HAD BEEN NAILED TO POSTS ALL OVER THE PANHANDLE; THEY WERE MEMBERSHIP REGISTERS FOR THE LAST MAN CLUBS, THE NAMES OF OLD SODBUSTERS WHO HAD ANGRILY VOWED TO PITCH DOWN IN TEXAS UNTIL THINGS GOT BETTER.

THE BIRTH OF THEIR CHILD IN OCTOBER DID NOTHING TO THAW THE FROSTY AIR OF THAT SHACK.

IN A TOWN SO BROKEN AND EMPTY, IT WAS IMPOSSIBLE TO MEND THE CRACKS IN THEIR RELATIONSHIP.

SIX YEARS INTO ROOSEVELT'S NEW DEAL, THE PLAINS HAD STILL NOT IMPROVED, AND MANY OF THE NAMES ON THE LIST WERE NOW GHOSTS TO THE TOWN, DEAD OR FORCED ON BY THE HUNGER OF THEIR CHILDREN.

AS WOODY OPENED THE DOOR TO THAT SAME SHOTGUN SHACK THAT HAD SEEN THEM THROUGH THE DUST STORMS, HE KNEW HE WOULDN'T STAY.

MARY'S REACTION WAS COLD.

AND SO, WHEN A LETTER ARRIVED FROM WILL GEER INVITING WOODY TO NEW YORK...

Woody Guthrie

THEY BOTH KNEW THIS WAS THE END.

You'll be off then...

MARY WAS WILLING WOODY TO LEAVE.

AND YEARNING FOR HIM TO STAY.

SHE WAS PUSHING AT HIS BACK...

AND AS HE WALKED DOWN THE HIGHWAY, HE PULLED OUT HIS HARMONICA AND SUCKED A LOW NOTE THROUGH ITS REEDS.

THAT LONESOME RAILWAY WHISTLE, THAT SOUND OF CHANGE, THAT BEND TO THE MINOR KEY.

NEW YORK WAS ALMOST TWO THOUSAND MILES AWAY. IN THE FEBRUARY RAIN, THIS WAS TO BE A LONG JOURNEY.

A SONG CAME ON THE RADIO THAT PRICKED HIS EARS.

KATE SMITH WAS A STOUT PATRIOT.

SHE SANG FOR REAL AMERICANS, WITH REAL VALUES, AMERICANS WITH JOBS AND A COLLEGE DEGREE, AMERICANS WHO BOUGHT TINNED APRICOTS AND NEW CARS.

EVERY WEEK, HER VOICE WOULD ENTER THE HOMES OF AMERICA LIKE A VISIT FROM A STATELY AUNT, AND REMIND AMERICANS OF THEIR ALLEGIANCES.

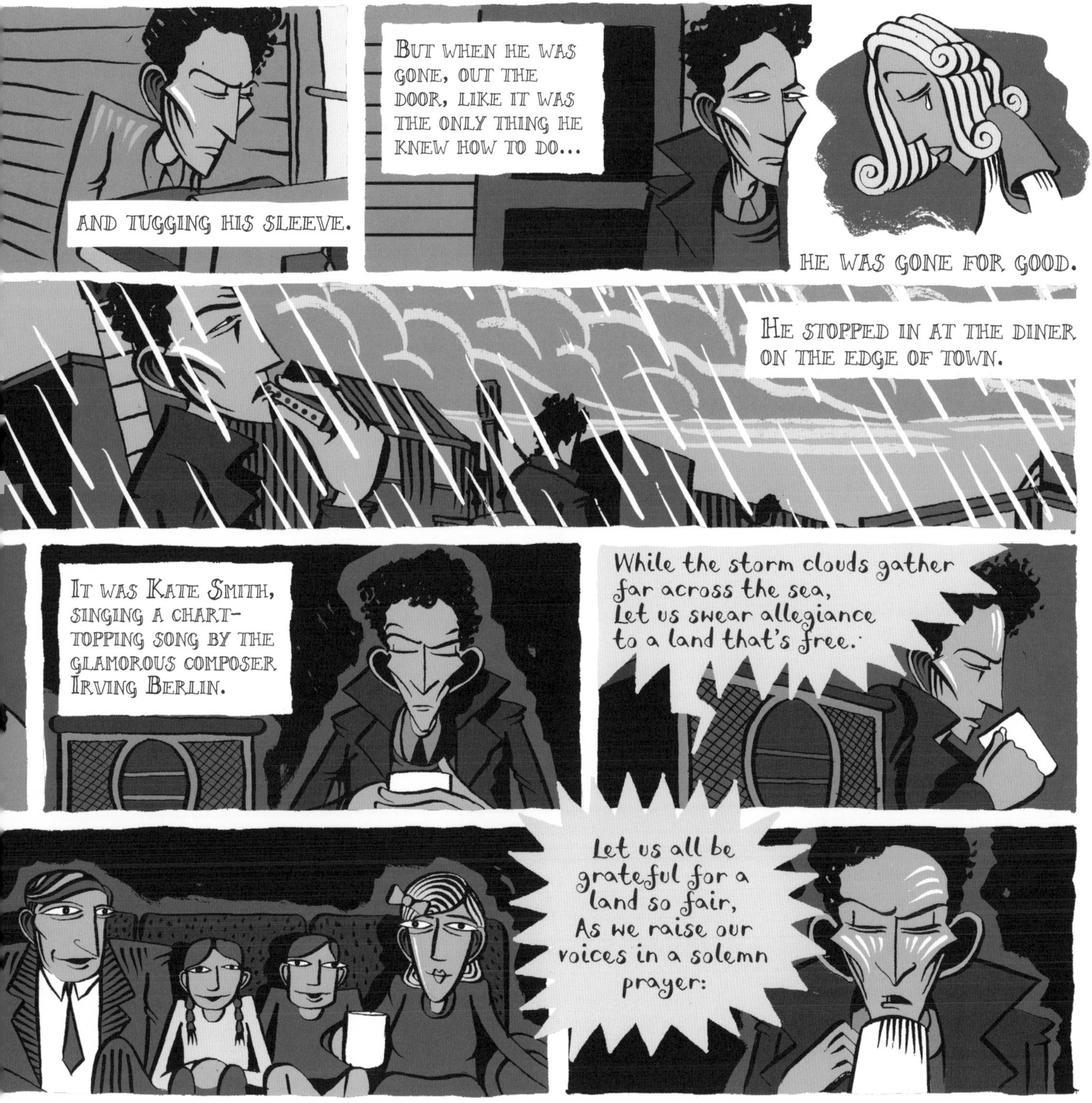
AND TUGGING HIS SLEEVE.
BUT WHEN HE WAS GONE, OUT THE DOOR, LIKE IT WAS THE ONLY THING HE KNEW HOW TO DO...
HE WAS GONE FOR GOOD.
HE STOPPED IN AT THE DINER ON THE EDGE OF TOWN.
IT WAS KATE SMITH, SINGING A CHART-TOPPING SONG BY THE GLAMOROUS COMPOSER IRVING BERLIN.
While the storm clouds gather far across the sea, Let us swear allegiance to a land that's free.
Let us all be grateful for a land so fair, As we raise our voices in a solemn prayer:

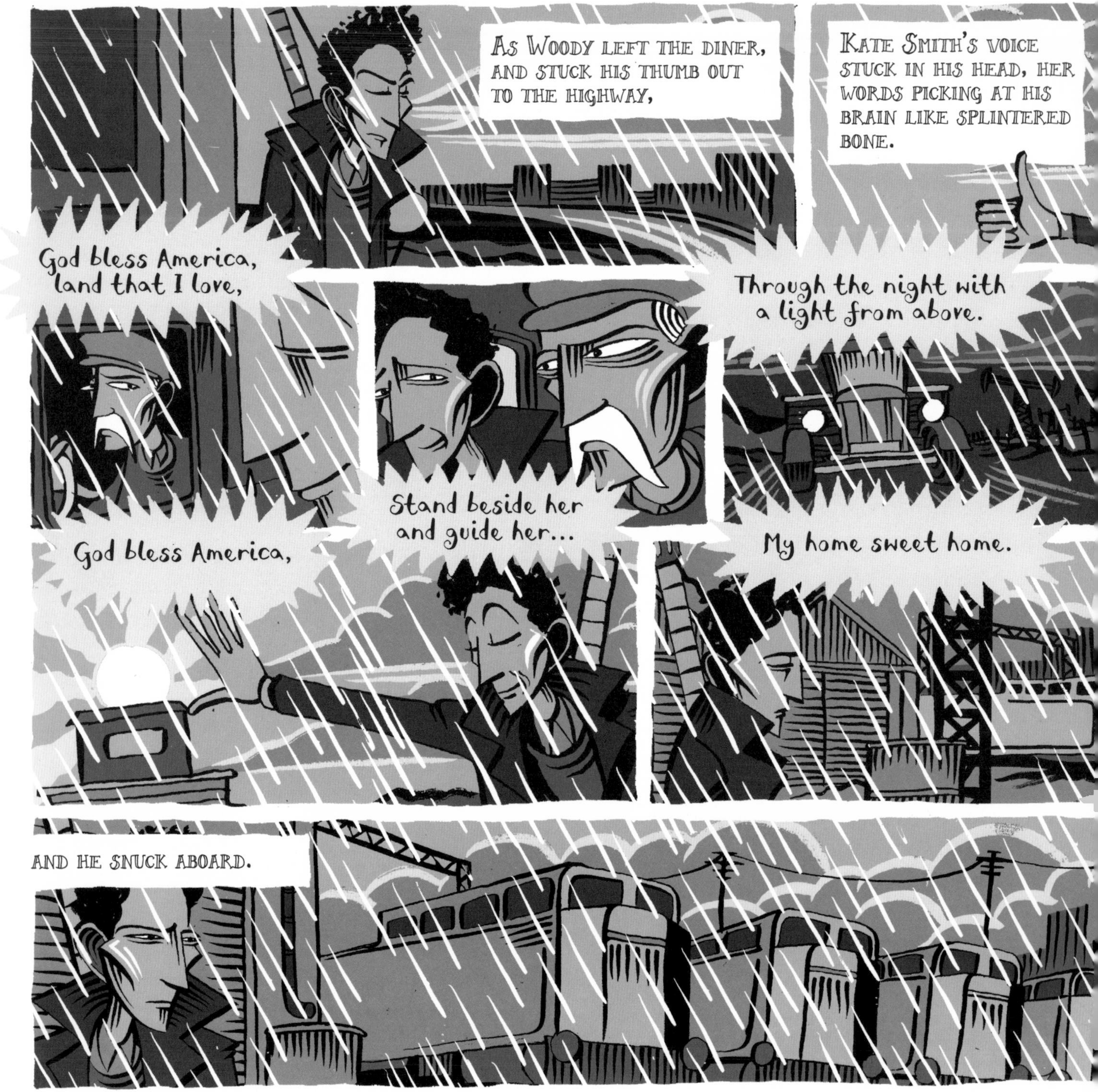
As Woody left the diner, and stuck his thumb out to the highway,
Kate Smith's voice stuck in his head, her words picking at his brain like splintered bone.
God bless America, land that I love,
Through the night with a light from above.
Stand beside her and guide her...
God bless America,
My home sweet home.
And he snuck aboard.

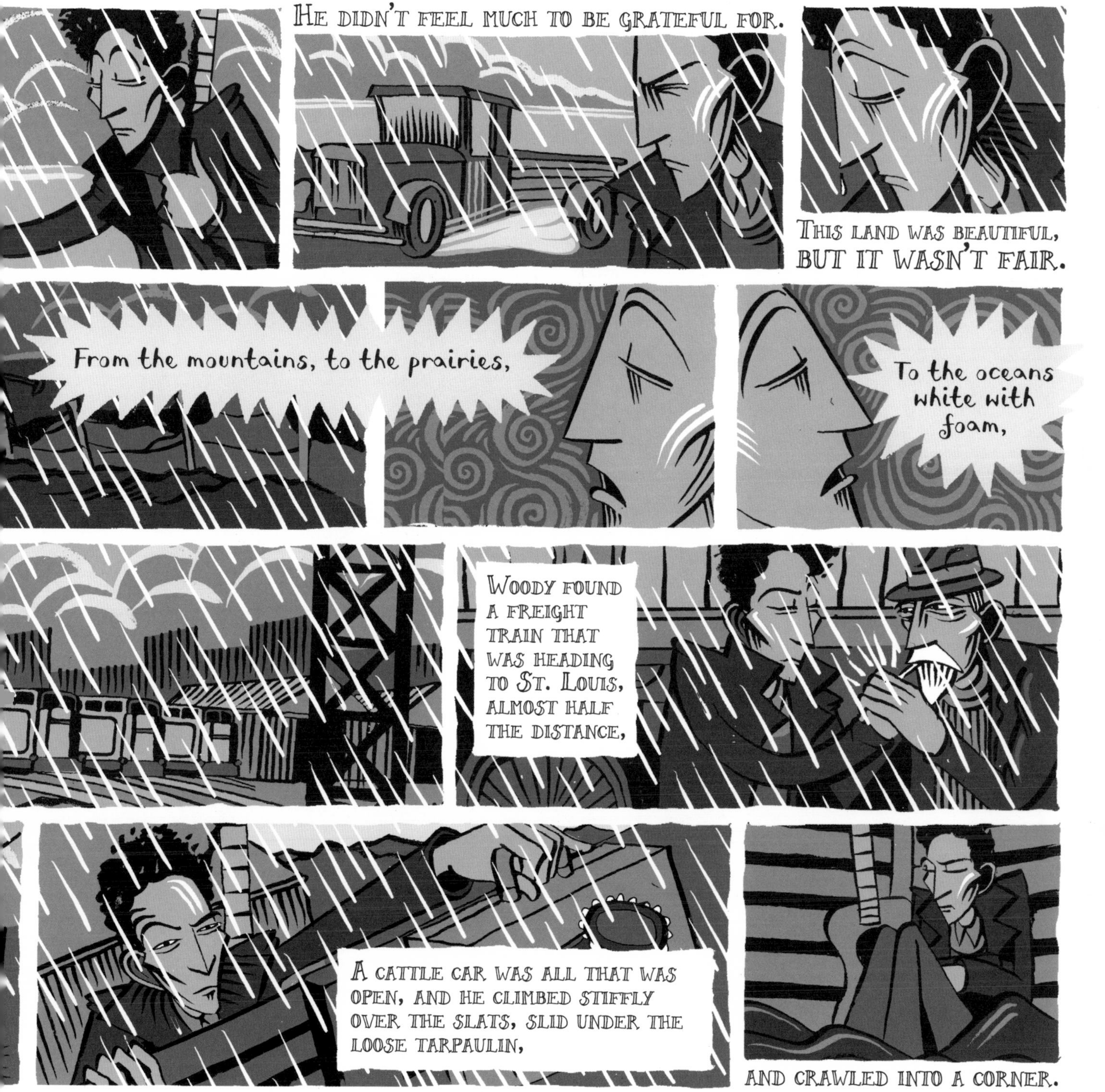
HE DIDN'T FEEL MUCH TO BE GRATEFUL FOR.
THIS LAND WAS BEAUTIFUL, BUT IT WASN'T FAIR.
From the mountains, to the prairies,
To the oceans white with foam,
WOODY FOUND A FREIGHT TRAIN THAT WAS HEADING TO ST. LOUIS, ALMOST HALF THE DISTANCE,
A CATTLE CAR WAS ALL THAT WAS OPEN, AND HE CLIMBED STIFFLY OVER THE SLATS, SLID UNDER THE LOOSE TARPAULIN,
AND CRAWLED INTO A CORNER.

A LITTLE WHILE LATER, AS THE TRAIN
PULLED AWAY, HE REARRANGED THE ROPES
AND PLASTIC SACKS INTO A MAKESHIFT BED.

HE TURNED ON HIS SIDE, PULLING THE
SHEETING OVER HIS SHOULDER, AND
CURLED HIMSELF INTO A TIGHT BALL.
HE SWITCHED HIMSELF OFF TO THE
RAIN AND WINDCHILL, AND BURROWED
DEEP INTO THE CAVERN OF HIS MIND.

AND SOMEWHERE ALONG THAT TRACK
TO ST. LOUIS, ROCKED BY THE RHYTHM
OF THE ROLLING WHEELS, HE DREAMED
OF THOSE CHISOS MOUNTAINS.

It was late spring when they had finally agreed to go. Jeff, Woody, Roy, and Charley, taking turns at the wheel, had covered the six hundred miles in a day and a half, driving through the night. And when Woody awoke to the fresh morning chill, he awoke to another world.

Gone was the thick smoke screen of the Texas oil fields. The sky was empty, a panoply of peace, and the sun so bright you couldn't see it.

GONE WAS THE THRUM AND GRIND OF THE TRAFFIC ALONG THE ROADS, THE PUMP AND THUMP OF THE PISTONS CIRCLING PAMPA.

GETTING OUT OF THE TRUCK, WOODY'S EARS ACCLIMATED TO THE SOUNDS IN THE SILENCE, THE SOFT SCURRIES AND SCRABBLES IN THE BRUSH, THE CALLS OF THE BIRDS SCREECHING OVERHEAD, THE SUBTLE SOUNDS OF MYRIAD CREATURES THAT LIVED BETWEEN HIM AND THE HORIZON.

WOODY WALKED FROM THE TRACK TO THE LOW-HANGING MESQUITE TREES BY THE SPRING.

THE BREEZE WAS AWASH WITH FLOATING SEEDS, A THICK PATINA OF POLLEN, AND FUZZED WITH THE BUZZ OF MATING INSECTS.

THERE WAS A HUMID FERTILITY IN THE AIR...

A PASSION ON THE EARTH AS HOT AS THE SUN.

WOODY BENT TO HIS KNEES ON THE SOFT DUFF OF THE TREES AND CUPPED THE WATER TO HIS FACE.

THREE YOUNG MEXICAN WOMEN WERE WASHING THEIR CLOTHES, LIMBS SLIPPING IN AND OUT OF THE WATER, DROPPING DRIPS INTO RIPPLES, BARE BACKS SHINING LIKE WET CLAY IN THE GLIMMERING LIGHT.

THEY NOTICED WOODY, BUT KEPT WITH THEIR SONG, UNABASHED.

HE STOOD, MESMERIZED AMONG THE MESQUITE BRUSH,

UNTIL JEFF HONKED THE HORN, AND BROKE THE SPELL.

Sam had known Gideon Guthrie, Charley's uncle, and herded cattle with Jerry some fifty years back.

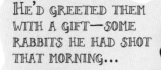

Though not native to these parts, his skin had weathered with the climate, and he was camouflaged against the soil of his farm.

He'd greeted them with a gift—some rabbits he had shot that morning...

And he drove with them the extra fifty miles to where they would be camping,

The ruins of Jerry's hand-built house, at the foot of Cathedral Mountain.

THE ROOF WAS DOWN, THE WINDMILL BLOWN TO BITS, BUT THE REST OF THE WALLS HAD DONE PRETTY WELL OVER THE HALF CENTURY.

THERE WERE CARVED WOODEN SPOONS STILL IN THE DRAWERS,

THE ODD RUSTED PAN,

AND THE DRONE OF BEES THAT HAD COLONIZED THE FRONT ROOM.

THEY SET OUT THEIR POSSESSIONS AND SHOWED SAM THE STASH OF ROCKS THEY HAD COLLECTED ALONG THE WAY.

THE PAST FIFTY MILES OF LAND HAD GLINTED WITH FALLEN CRYSTALS, AND THEY HAD NOT BEEN ABLE TO RESIST THIS BOUNTY, STOPPING INTERMITTENTLY TO STUFF THEIR POCKETS.

Not bad... you got obsidium, some quartzes—s'all over this country. You'll fetch a few dollars for them back in town...

but that ain't no gold mine.

SAM HAD STAYED WHILE THEY CUT UP THE RABBITS AND ROASTED THEM ON THE FIRE.

HE HAD STAYED WHILE ONE OF THE CORN LIQUOR JARS WAS EMPTIED,

AND SANG A FEW COWBOY TUNES WITH THE GUTHRIES WHILE THE SKY GLOWED INDIGO.

WHEN THE STARS CAME OUT, HE LEFT FOR HIS RANCH, AND LEFT THE GUTHRIES TO THEIR ANCESTRAL HEARTH.

THE OTHERS SOON WENT TO BED, BUT WOODY STAYED BY THE FIRE AND THOUGHT OF HIS GRANDFATHER WATCHING THE SAME MOON RISE FROM THOSE SAME SPIRES ON CATHEDRAL MOUNTAIN EVERY YEAR.

HE TRIED TO THINK OF A SONG JERRY WOULD HAVE SUNG WHILE HE SAT THERE, WOODY'S AGE, ALMOST A CENTURY AGO.

Well, he had not rode till the midnight moon,
I saw their campfire gleaming,
I heard the notes of the big guitar,
And the voice of the gypsies singing,
That song of the Gypsy Dave...

His ancient song rose in the air to join the wind of the mountains. Its tale of the outlawed gypsies seemed to suit the setting, and singing out there under the starlit sky, his song somehow sunk Woody into his surroundings: the chirrups of the grass-hoppers, the hoots of the owls, the rustle of the wind in the brush, rooting him to the moment.

That song of the Gypsy Dave.

He breathed in a gust of the smoking embers,

joined the others in the house,

curled up in his grandfather's bedroom,

And slept till morning.

JEFF HAD BEEN UP AT THE CRACK OF DAWN AND SHOT TWO MORE RABBITS,

WHICH HE WAS SKINNING WHEN WOODY AWOKE.

A quick bite, and then we find that goldymine!

THEY SPLIT UP TO SCOUR THE LAND.

JEFF AND ROY WENT SOUTH, TO THE CREEK, AND WOODY AND HIS FATHER, NORTH TO THE FOOT OF THE MOUNTAINS.

EACH HAD A COPY OF JERRY'S MAP, A SIMPLE PICTURE DRAWN IN PENCIL.

BUT OUT THERE IN THE FRACTAL EXPANSE OF PECOS COUNTY, EACH PENCIL LINE OF THE MAP WAS THE WIDTH OF A RAVINE. AND EACH RAVINE HAD A HUNDRED SMALL CREEKS, AND EACH CREEK HELD A HUNDRED MORE NOOKS AND CREVICES, ANY OF WHICH COULD STORE JERRY'S STONE.

BUT TO WOODY THERE WAS A KINSHIP HERE.

Waking in his grandfather's house, sipping coffee in his kitchen, and then heading out to wander the land, wide-eyed in wonder at the world, Woody felt as if he were his grandfather, following his own footsteps:

IN THIS OLD COUNTRY, THE PAST WAS PRESENT AT EVERY PACE.

Scrabbling up the sharp rocks of the mountain scree, they found it hard to keep their balance, and several times slipped and gashed their ankles.

Every few miles they came across another impenetrable thicket of stickers that spread across the gorge and meant another hour of walking in order to circumvent it.

THE SUN WAS BRASH, THE LAND WAS UNFORGIVING, AND WHEN CHARLEY SAT DOWN AND STRETCHED HIS ARM BENEATH A ROCK, HE PULLED IT BACK WITH TWO VENOMOUS HOLES OF A BABY-RATTLER BITE. THEY DECIDED IT WAS TIME TO HEAD FOR THE ADOBE HOUSE.

BY THE TIME THEY RETURNED, CHARLEY'S HAND HAD SWOLLEN TO TWICE ITS SIZE, AND EACH MAN TOOK TURNS SUCKING THE POISON FROM THE HOLES WHILE CHARLEY HELD HIS BURSTING HAND, TEARS IN HIS EYES.

This place is hard on a city man.

You just gotta learn its rules—mebbey don't put yer hand under rocks!

Yeh... mebbey

JEFF AND ROY HAD RETURNED WITH ABOUT FORTY MORE CRYSTALS, BUT NO SIGN OF THE MINE.

AS THEY WERE BUILDING THE CAMPFIRE, SAM NAIL TURNED UP AGAIN, THIS TIME WITH AN EVEN LARGER GIFT, A DEER HE HAD SHOT THAT DAY.

WOODY, SAM, AND ROY BUTCHERED THE DEER WHILE JEFF TUNED HIS FIDDLE. CHARLEY WAS QUIET, HAND THROBBING. THEY ATE IN SILENCE, EYES LOST IN THE STARS THAT PERFORATED THE VAST BLACKNESS.

IT WAS AS IF SPACE HAD STOOPED TO TOUCH THE GROUND.

THE NEXT DAY, UNCLE JEFF ATTACHED A LOCK TO THE DOOR, TO SAFE-KEEP THEIR CRYSTALS,

AND THEY SET OFF IN THE SAME PAIRS AS YESTERDAY.

CHARLEY'S HEAD WAS THROBBING FROM THE THUMPING PULSE IN HIS HAND,

AND AS THEY SAT FOR LUNCH,

WOODY PERSUADED HIM TO HEAD HOME.

AND SO THEY PARTED, AND WOODY HEADED UP THE MOUNTAIN.

HE STOPPED A COUPLE OF THOUSAND FEET UP IN THE AIR, DRAINED HIS CANTEEN, AND SURVEYED WHAT LAY BENEATH HIM.

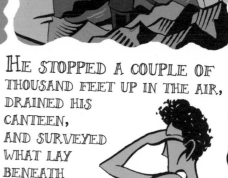

HE COULD SEE JERRY'S MUD HOUSE, HE COULD SEE THE TRACK THAT LED TO SAM'S RANCH, AND HE COULD SEE A GOOD FIFTY MILES INTO THE DISTANCE, TO WHERE THE SKY BURNED WHITE.

THE WINDS UP IN CATHEDRAL MOUNTAIN
WERE BILLOWING WITH CLOUDS OF MONARCH BUTTERFLIES,
JUST AWOKEN FROM THEIR COCOONS
AND HEADING FOR THE FIRST
MILKWEED BLOSSOMS IN TEXAS.
FOLLOWING THEM WERE THE BARN
SWALLOWS, THE HUMMINGBIRDS,
THE ORIOLES, AND THE RED-EYED
VIREOS, TRAVELING FOUR THOU-
SAND MILES FROM THEIR ROOSTING
SITES IN SOUTH AMERICA, FILLING
THE SKY WITH THEIR SOUNDS.

THE LAND AND AIR WERE ALIVE
WITH THE FOLK SONGS OF ITS CREATURES,
CALLS AND CRIES THAT ANNOUNCED THEIR
CONDITION TO THE WORLD AROUND THEM,
CONNECTING THEM IN SONG.

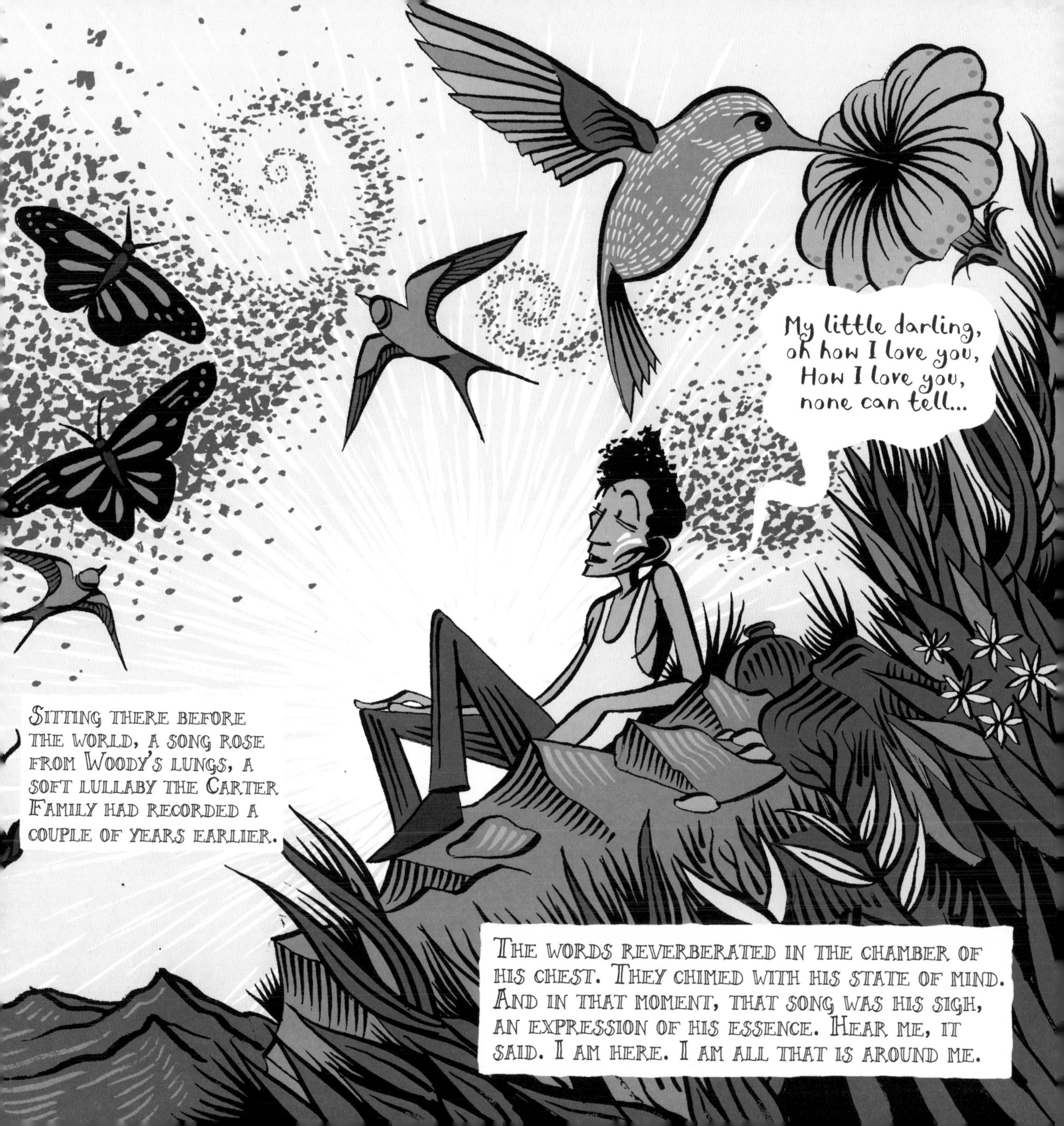
My little darling, oh how I love you, How I love you, none can tell...
SITTING THERE BEFORE THE WORLD, A SONG ROSE FROM WOODY'S LUNGS, A SOFT LULLABY THE CARTER FAMILY HAD RECORDED A COUPLE OF YEARS EARLIER.
THE WORDS REVERBERATED IN THE CHAMBER OF HIS CHEST. THEY CHIMED WITH HIS STATE OF MIND. AND IN THAT MOMENT, THAT SONG WAS HIS SIGH, AN EXPRESSION OF HIS ESSENCE. HEAR ME, IT SAID. I AM HERE. I AM ALL THAT IS AROUND ME.

RUSTLE

CHEEP-CHEEP CHEEP-CHE

TIKKKITIKKKI

Oh, little darling,

Chirrup how

RUS

AND WITH THE SOUND OF HIS SELF ON HIS BREATH, HIS SONG DIFFUSED INTO THE ASSONANCE OF THE LANDSCAPE, THAT PULSE OF NOISE AND MOTION, SONG AND DANCE ON THE MOUNTAIN.

KIKKA KIK

KIRRA

KIKKKAKIKIKIK

how I love you nor

RUSTLERUSTLE

RAWW
RAWW

BUZZZZZ

holla
holla
holla

SCRABBLORBBLOTABBLE

THERE WAS A HARMONY OUT HERE, AN ISONOMY BEFORE THE NATURAL LAW THAT CONJUGATED WOODY WITH THIS WORLD...

CHEEP

KA-KAWWWW
KA-KAWWWW

TIKKIT

BUZZZZ

Shush

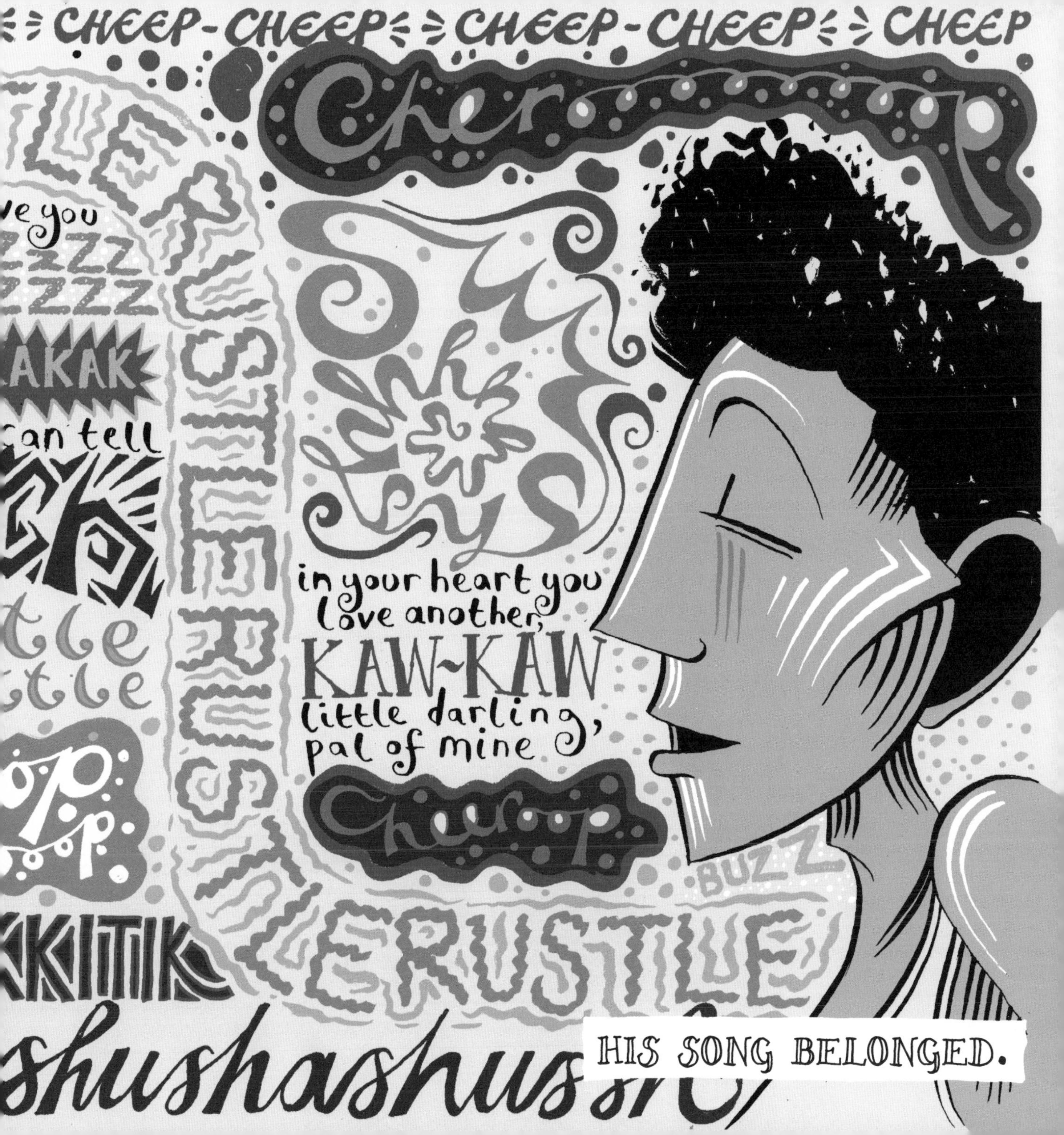
CHEEP-CHEEP CHEEP-CHEEP CHEEP
in your heart you love another,
KAW-KAW
little darling, pal of mine
BUZZ
RUSTLE

HIS SONG BELONGED.

As he climbed down the mountain, Woody saw a figure in the valley, stone still, arms outstretched to the sky.

The wind brought a soft chanting to Woody's ears.

Woody's mouth was sticky and his lips had cracked in the late-afternoon heat. He had heard tales from his pa about Indians who had escaped the clearances, or who broke from their reservations periodically to return to the lives they had lived for thousands of years before the whites had entered their land. Fenced into these reservations, cut off from the spring of their steps, their religions had withered, and their spirits had wilted. But some had escaped this fate, jumping the fence to live the life of their elders, hunting, and walking the land.

Woody approached the man and saw two rabbits skewered over a small fire.

The man reached into his pouch and pulled out a knife and a small barbed cactus barrel.

He cut a slice in it, and handed it to Woody.

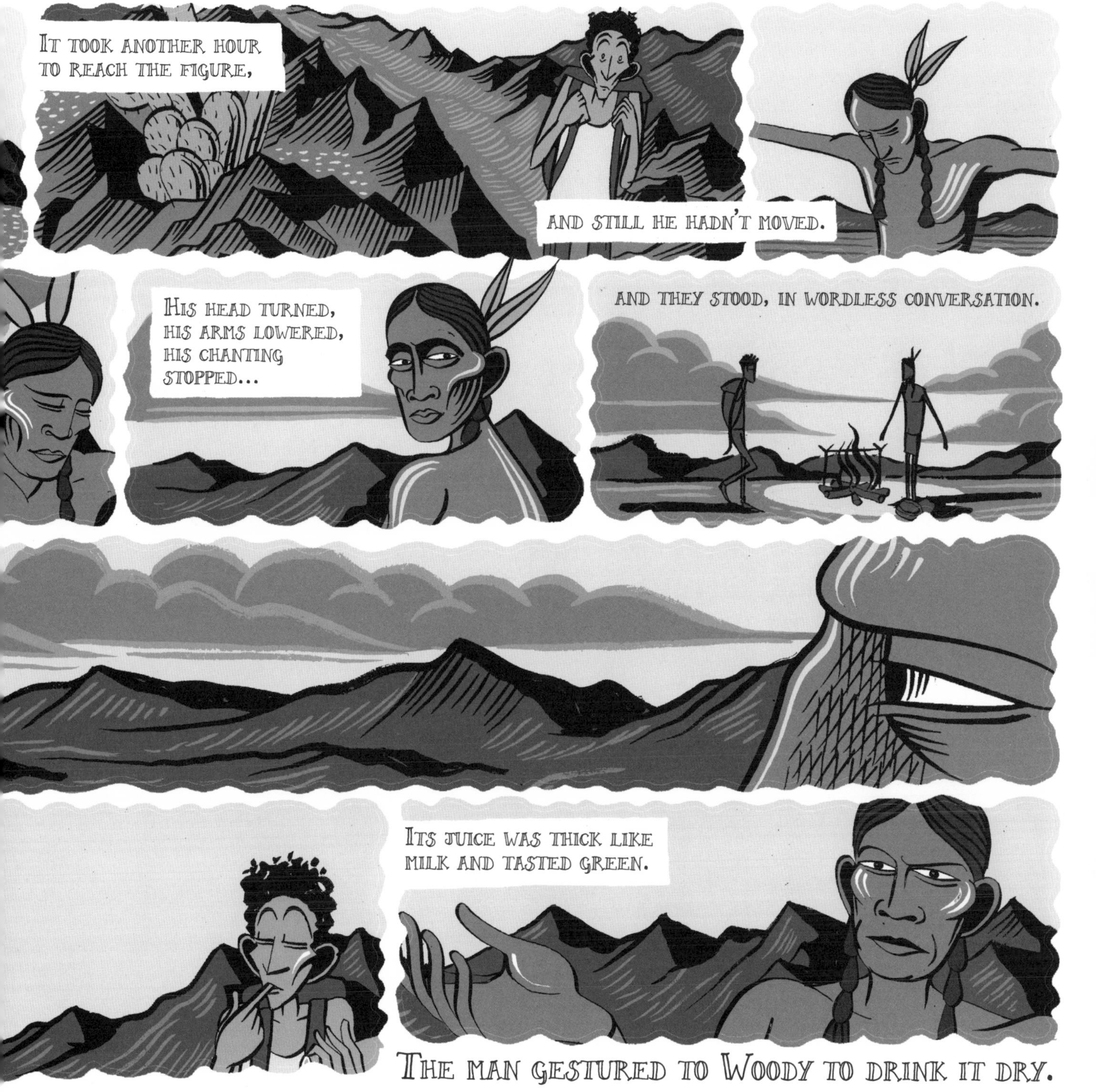

IT TOOK ANOTHER HOUR TO REACH THE FIGURE,
AND STILL HE HADN'T MOVED.
HIS HEAD TURNED, HIS ARMS LOWERED, HIS CHANTING STOPPED...
AND THEY STOOD, IN WORDLESS CONVERSATION.
ITS JUICE WAS THICK LIKE MILK AND TASTED GREEN.
THE MAN GESTURED TO WOODY TO DRINK IT DRY.

WHEN WOODY RETURNED, THE MOON WAS UP AND THE MEN WERE IN HOT DISCUSSION WITH SAM.

Where in the hellur you bin?

I saw an Injun...

Someone broke through our lock this morning.

He used the kitchen to chop his game, and left. Didn't touch the gems...

Them gems are worth a coupla dollars at best. And a dollar's 'bout as useful as a small piece of paper out here...

That's all very well—but he jest cain't walk in like he owns the place—Jerry P. owned this house, and you got the homestead rights, the grazing rights, the mineral rights, the oil and gas rights—that Injun ain't got no rights...

You're not in padlock country now, son.

I may own the pieces of paper, but it's a different world down here, ain't no lock 'n' key. It's the law of the Injuns, the Mexicans, the whites, of every damn color and creed and living creature in these canyons.

This place is too real for man-made laws.

Don't nobody own nothing down here?

Saywot?

You shoulda clocked him one 'round the jaw.

He had his arms stretched out to the sky—singing low in his throat—didn't move an inch...

Seeking counsel most likely—the spirits of his ancestors are all over these hills—bodies in the ground, souls in the endless skyway, ain't a place 'round here without a story or song attached to it...

Look at them bees. They don't ask for no paper permit.

If one of these folks here is hungry, or needs some place to shelter, there isn't a padlock or fence post in the world that's gunna stop them coming in.

Son, down here, we own the land like a hand owns its body. It don't belong to us. We belong to it. The land was here long before we came, and will be here long after we're gone.

All we can do is borrow it from our children.

SITTING THERE BENEATH THE STARS, IN THE SHADOW OF THE MOUNTAIN, THERE SEEMED LIKE NOTHING MORE TO SAY.

THEY DIDN'T LAST MUCH LONGER ON THAT CHISOS TRAIL.

JEFF WAS ITCHING TO RETURN TO ALLYNE, AND CHARLEY'S HAND, THOUGH NOT SERIOUS, NEEDED SOME MEDICAL ATTENTION.

AS THEY DROVE BACK, THEY WERE SILENT.

THE TRACK TURNED TO TARMAC,

THE ROADS GOT STRAIGHTER,

AND BUILDINGS STARTED TO APPEAR.

THEY WERE SOON INTO LAND THAT LOOKED JUST LIKE THEIRS IN PAMPA, A GOLD WASH OF WHEAT, CUT IN SQUARES INTO THE LAND.

AS THEY APPROACHED PAMPA, WOODY FELT THE CLOAK OF DUST AND SOOT CLOSE AROUND THEM, SHROUDING THAT MOMENT OF EQUANIMITY ON THE MOUNTAIN.

THE RIME OF THE MODERN MARINER

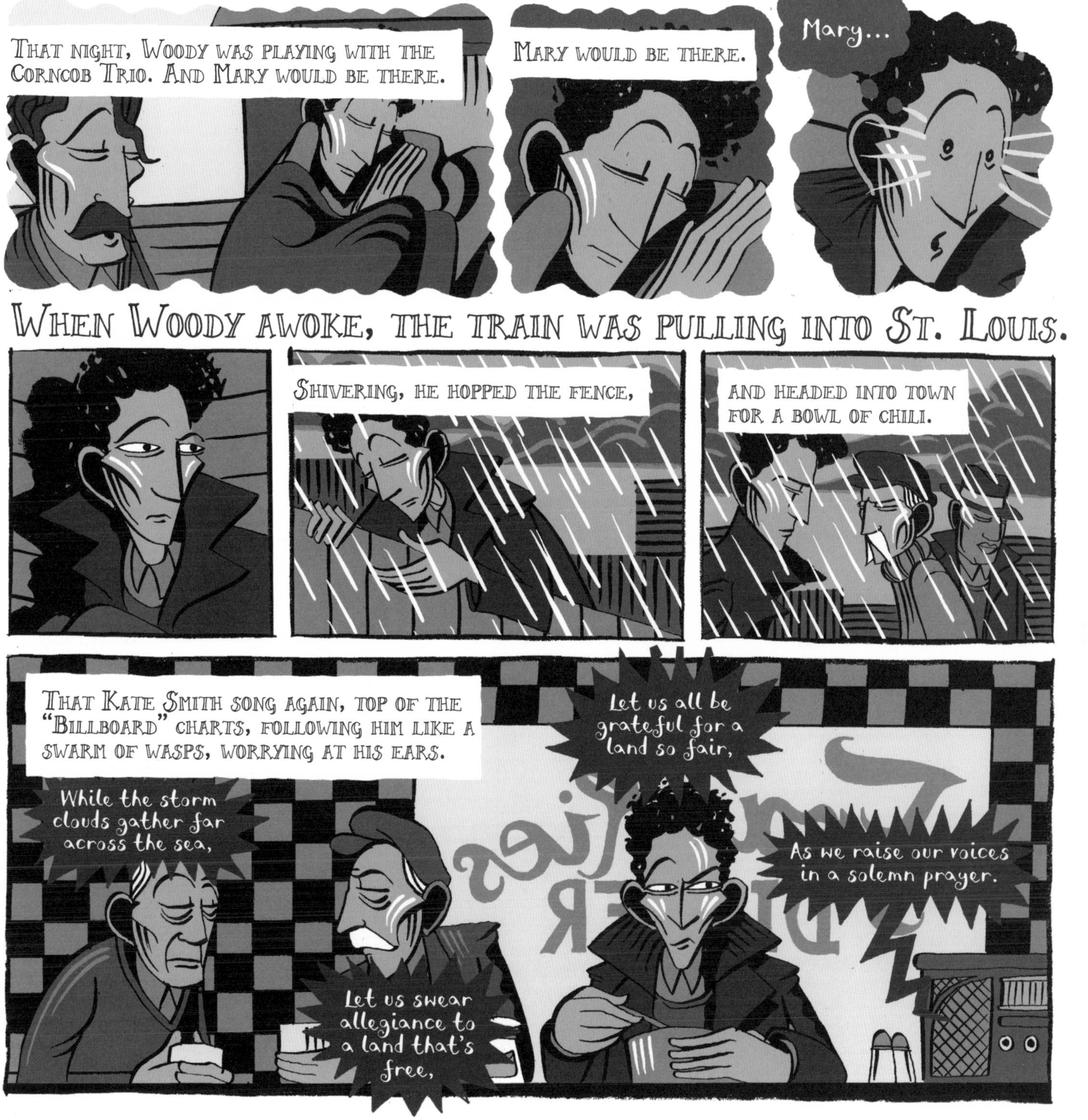

THAT NIGHT, WOODY WAS PLAYING WITH THE CORNCOB TRIO. AND MARY WOULD BE THERE.
MARY WOULD BE THERE.
Mary...
WHEN WOODY AWOKE, THE TRAIN WAS PULLING INTO ST. LOUIS.
SHIVERING, HE HOPPED THE FENCE,
AND HEADED INTO TOWN FOR A BOWL OF CHILI.
THAT KATE SMITH SONG AGAIN, TOP OF THE "BILLBOARD" CHARTS, FOLLOWING HIM LIKE A SWARM OF WASPS, WORRYING AT HIS EARS.
While the storm clouds gather far across the sea,
Let us swear allegiance to a land that's free,
Let us all be grateful for a land so fair,
As we raise our voices in a solemn prayer.

HE THOUGHT OF ALL THE PLACES HE HAD SUNG HIS SONGS.

ACROSS ALL THE HOEDOWNS, WORKERS RALLIES, PICKET LINES, CABBAGE PATCHES, BARBERSHOPS, AND MIGRANT CAMPS,

THERE WAS NOT ONE SINGLE PERSON IN THOSE CROWDS WHO WOULD JOIN THAT PRAYER.

IT WAS NOT FOR THEM.

THE WORDS WERE STIFF, AN OATH OF ALLEGIANCE, THAT BOXED ITS LISTENERS INTO ITS DOCTRINE. THE COUPLETS WERE TIGHT FENCE LINES THAT ROLLED OUT OVER THE AIRWAVES, AND RULED LINES AROUND THE MINDS THAT HEARD THEM.

THESE LINES WERE LIES, BOUGHT AND SOLD BY THE PEOPLE ON THE INSIDE.

The words came to Woody as he reached the highway.

Sticking out his thumb, humming that old Carter song that lingered from his dream, lost in the visions of Chisos, he sang:

He felt as bitter as the February rain, spitting the words in a spiteful parody of Kate Smith's chart-topping hit.

As the words rolled into Woody's head, carried on a two-four rhythm of footsteps, they seemed to cut through the barbed wire of Kate Smith's hit and trespass onto the hallowed space from which they came, that canon of capitalist creeds that governed America.

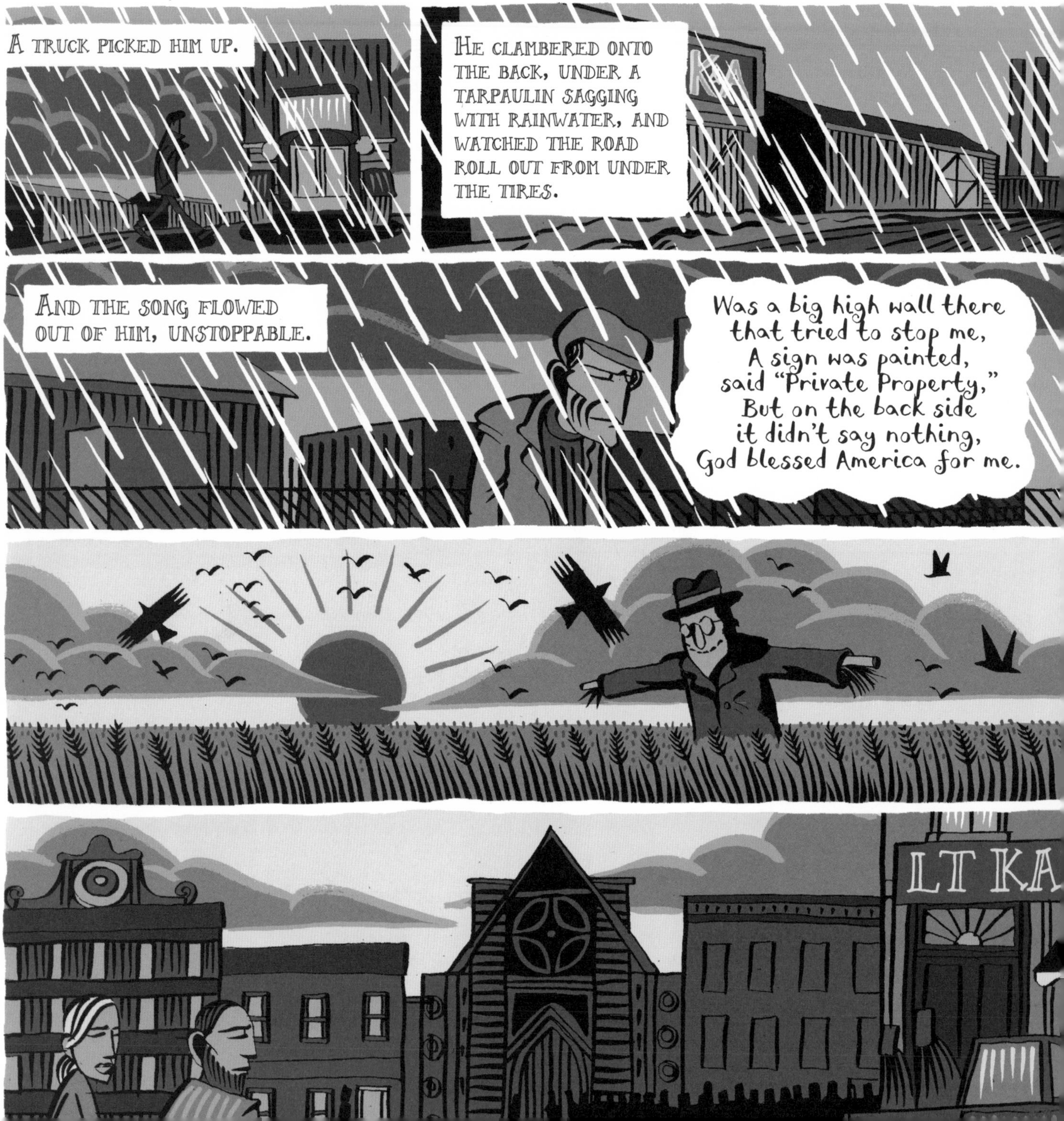
A TRUCK PICKED HIM UP.
HE CLAMBERED ONTO THE BACK, UNDER A TARPAULIN SAGGING WITH RAINWATER, AND WATCHED THE ROAD ROLL OUT FROM UNDER THE TIRES.
KA
AND THE SONG FLOWED OUT OF HIM, UNSTOPPABLE.
Was a big high wall there that tried to stop me, A sign was painted, said "Private Property," But on the back side it didn't say nothing, God blessed America for me.
LT KA

AND HE THOUGHT OF ALL THE PEOPLE HE HAD MET, STRETCHED ALONG THOSE HIGHWAYS, SPREAD IN DAMP CLODS ACROSS THIS VAST CONTINENT, NO ROOM FOR THEM, HOMELESS IN THEIR HOMELAND.

When the sun came shining,
    and I was strolling,
And the wheat fields waving
and the dust clouds rolling,
    A voice was chanting,
    As the fog was lifting,
God blessed America for me.

One bright sunny morning,
in the shadow of a steeple;
    By the relief office,
    I see my people.
As they stood there hungry,
    I stood there wondering,
If God blessed America for me.

When he got to New York, he checked in with Will Geer, who had arranged a room for him on South Street.

Will brought his wife's unused guitar and a bottle of whiskey.

They talked of future rallies, and a man from the Library of Congress who wanted Woody to put some of his songs down on record.

He might even make an album.

Things could really start to happen here.

As the traffic slowed beneath them, as day turned to night, they drank and they smoked and they sang and they toasted the future.

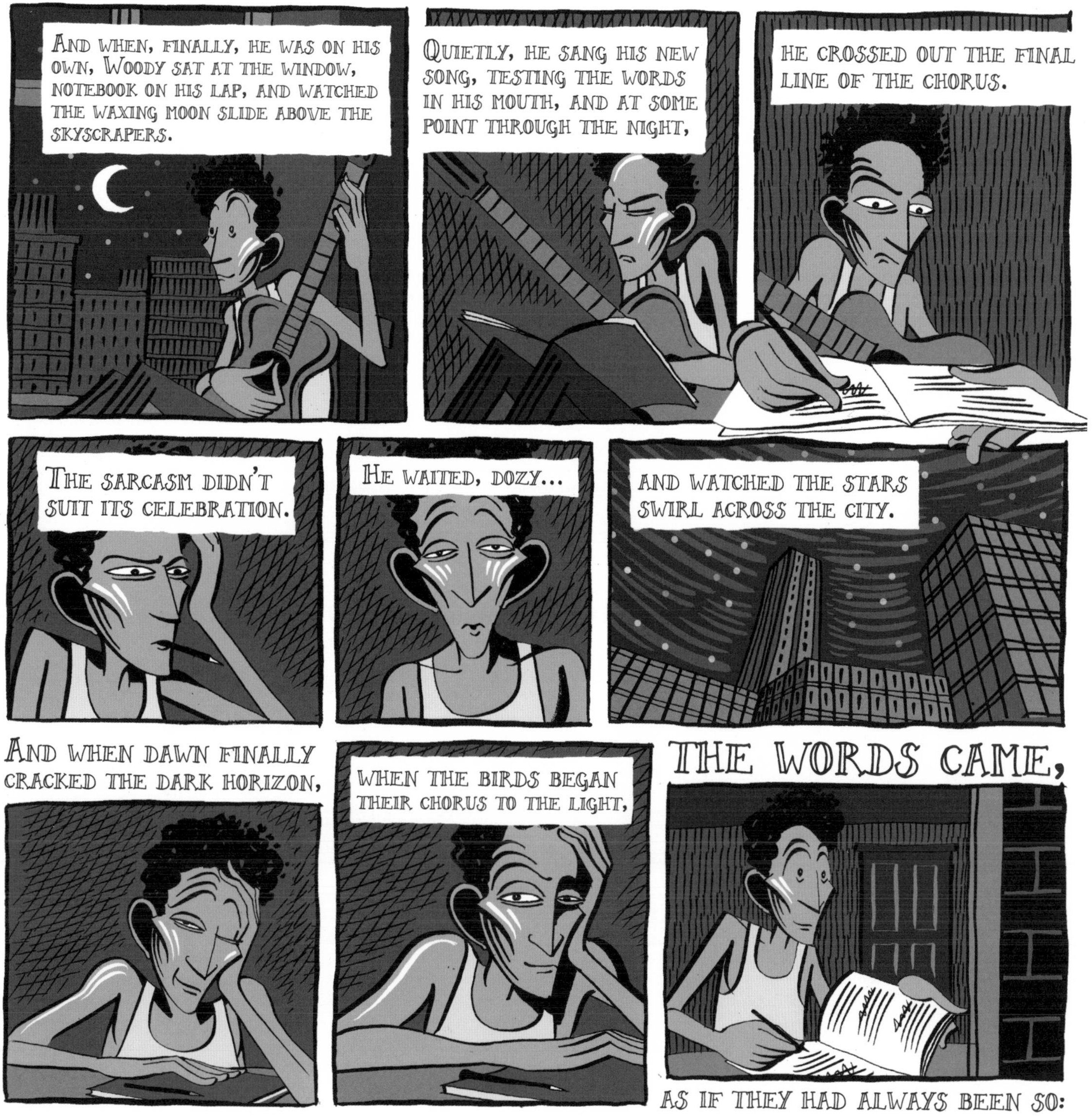
AND WHEN, FINALLY, HE WAS ON HIS OWN, WOODY SAT AT THE WINDOW, NOTEBOOK ON HIS LAP, AND WATCHED THE WAXING MOON SLIDE ABOVE THE SKYSCRAPERS.
QUIETLY, HE SANG HIS NEW SONG, TESTING THE WORDS IN HIS MOUTH, AND AT SOME POINT THROUGH THE NIGHT,
HE CROSSED OUT THE FINAL LINE OF THE CHORUS.
THE SARCASM DIDN'T SUIT ITS CELEBRATION.
HE WAITED, DOZY...
AND WATCHED THE STARS SWIRL ACROSS THE CITY.
AND WHEN DAWN FINALLY CRACKED THE DARK HORIZON,
WHEN THE BIRDS BEGAN THEIR CHORUS TO THE LIGHT,
THE WORDS CAME,
AS IF THEY HAD ALWAYS BEEN SO:

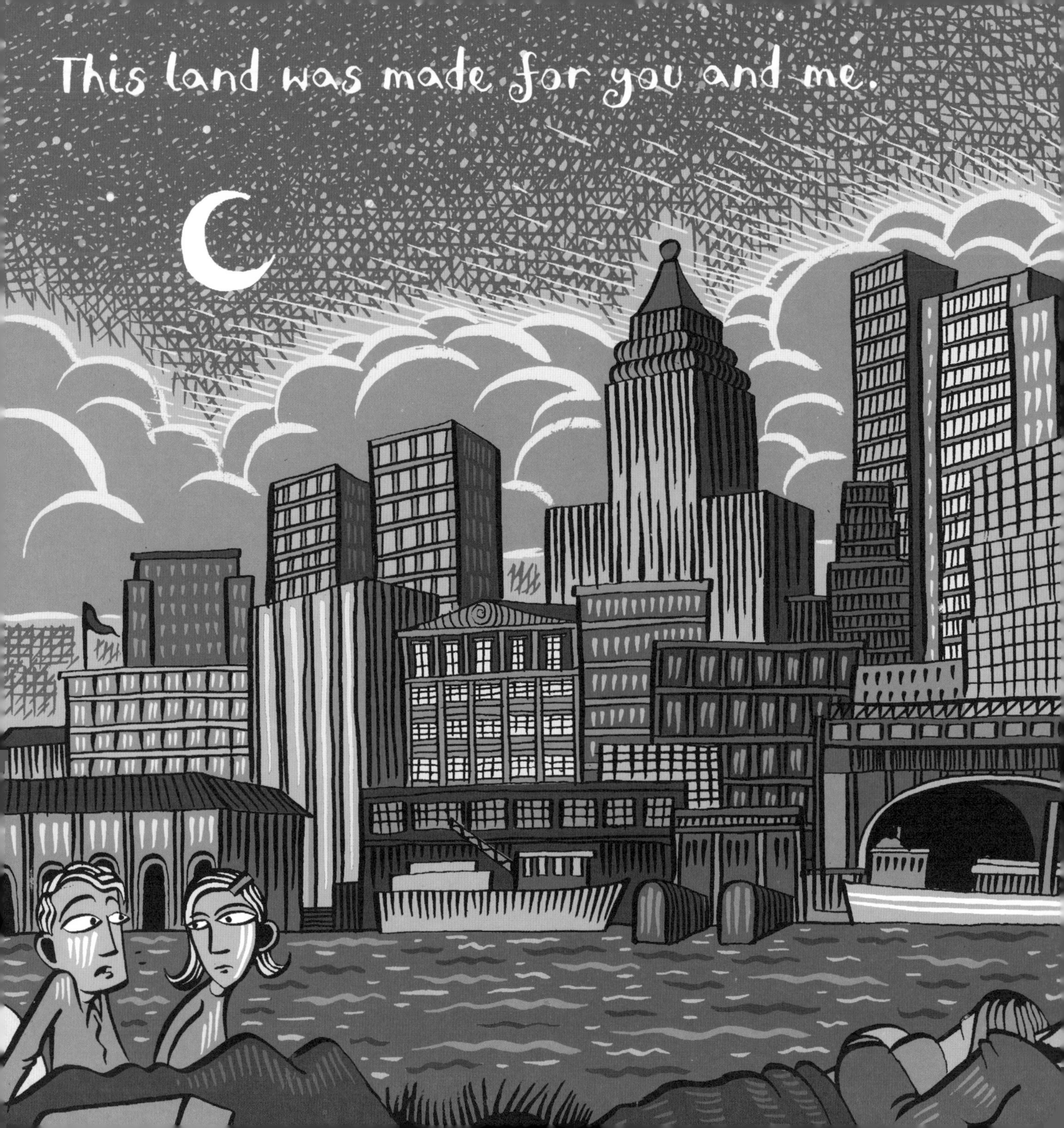
This land was made for you and me.

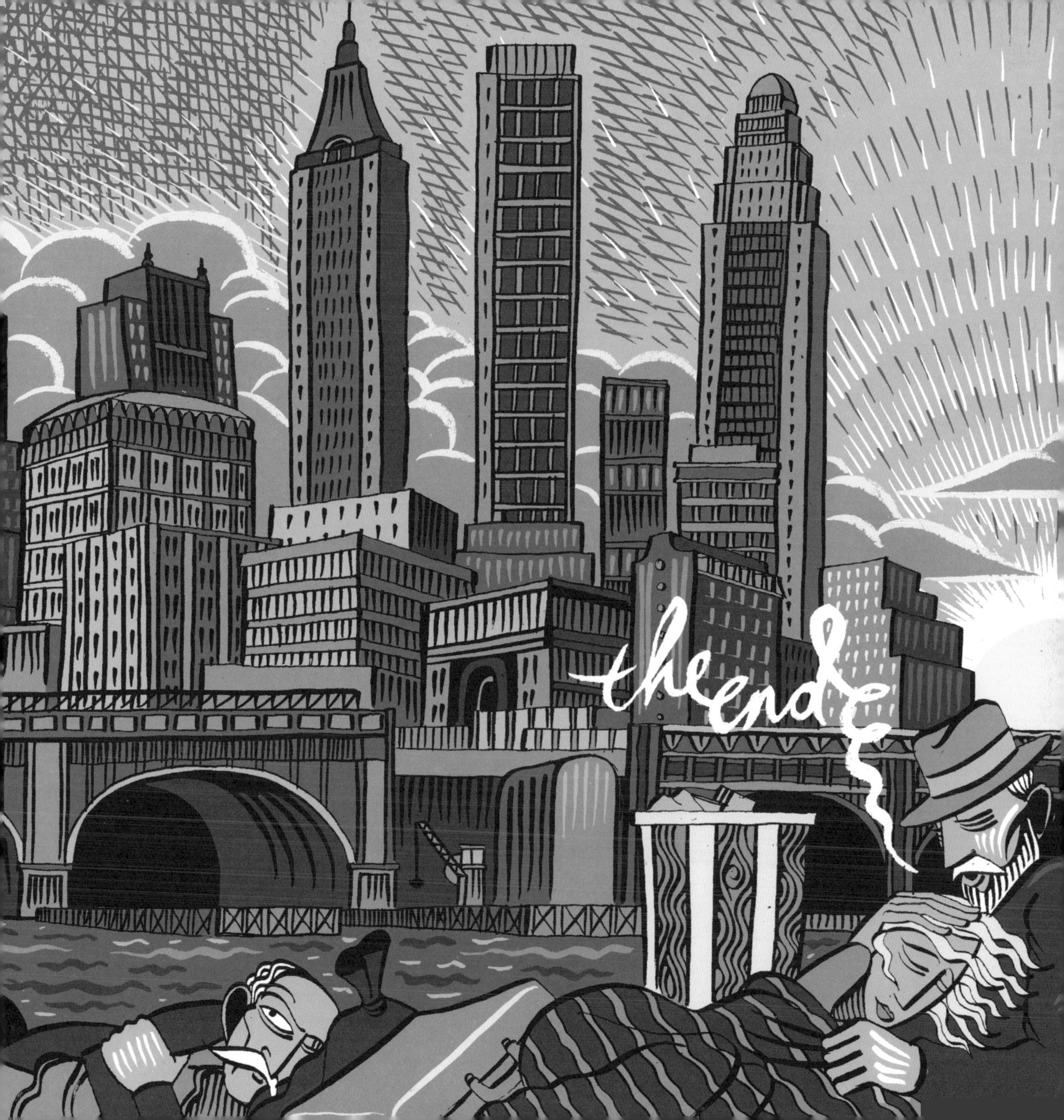
the end

Woody Guthrie wrote "This Land..." in February 1940 and stored it in his notes for four years, until Moses Asch put it onto record. It was later distributed as sheet music to schools, albeit with the fourth and sixth verses (the commie ones) redacted, and soon became America's unofficial national anthem.

Woody went on to record numerous albums, including several for children. He traveled the country with a host of musicians, including Pete Seeger, Sonny Terry, Cisco Houston, and Huddie Ledbetter, playing gigs and union meetings. Mary came to New York again, shortly after Woody wrote "This Land...," and followed him to Los Angeles and Washington. But when Woody decided it was time to uproot again, and head back to New York, Mary told him to go by himself. They divorced in 1943, and Woody later married Marjorie Mazia, a dancer and teacher who was part of the socialist arts scene in New York.

When Bob Dylan eventually met Woody, he was the in hospital, being treated for Huntington's disease. Woody eventually died of the disease in October 1967, leaving behind eight children, three ex-wives, and a mountain of songs, drawings, poems, books, and articles.

RIP.

Boxcars of Thanks

First and foremost, as ever, to my family: Mum, Dad,
Ben, and newest addition, Katherine.
To Elise and Harriet, the Warehouse tribe,
and everyone who helped with the Mariner launch party.

To my Austrian friends, for your beautiful town, your crystal air and
good living, but most of all for your kindness and generosity, which
turned my nightmare into a dream. To Georg, to Kathrin, to Lydia, Doris,
and Manfred, for helping me find my feet; to Rene, for your braces,
your wisdom, and your knightly deeds; to Lisa, for your chai tea, friend-
ship, and loud and lovely laugh; and to Julia, for the
sparkling lights from Schlossberg.

To Walter, for his incredible Miles Jazz Bar; to Francesco and his punk
fiddle for his accompaniment of the wayfaring stranger.

To Simon, the greatest gypsy guitarist in all of Europe (except for one
fellow, I believe, in Paris); to Werner, Mattias, Michael, Robert, and all
the musicians who play so brilliantly underneath Mariahilferplatz.
And most of all, to Frau Wunderlich, my great aunt, who is magnificent.

To Simon of Actant and to Alex of Jonathan Cape, for his very great
generosity of time and patience. To Rob Macfarlane, for the old ways.
To Titus, Jasmin, Electra, Anouk, and old hairy-big-balls himself,
for their hospitality.

And special musical dedications to
Pokey la Farge and the South City Three, Meschiya Lake and the Little
Big Horns, Tuba Skinny, Jesse Carolina and the Hot Mess, Johnny Flynn,
the Manuel Warner Caravan band, Rob Heron and the Teapad Orchestra,
the Carolina Chocolate Drops, Nic Jones,

Natchez on Fire, the Hokum High Rollers, the Cable Street Rag Band, Yes
Ma'am, and Mister Gunn and the Pistol Packin' Mamas
for playing the music that accompanied the drawing of this book.

And, of course, to Woody.

SO LONG IT'S BEEN GOOD TO KNOW YUH

DO RE MI

DUST STORM DISASTER

GYPSY DAVY

TALKING DUST BOWL BLUES

Words and Music by Woody Guthrie
WGP/TRO-© Copyright 1960 (Renewed), 1961 (Renewed Woody Guthrie Publications, Inc. & Ludlow
administered by Ludlow Music, Inc.
Music, Inc., New York, NY
Used by Permission

THIS LAND IS YOUR LAND

WGP/TRO-© Copyright 1956, 1958, 1970 and 1972 (copyrights renewed) Woody Guthrie
Words and Music by Woody Guthrie
Publications, Inc. & Ludlow Music, Inc., New York, NY
administered by Ludlow Music, Inc.
Used by Permission

CAN'T FEEL AT HOME

Words & Music by A.P. Carter
©1931 Peer International Corporation, USA

LITTLE DARLING PAL OF MINE

Words & Music by A.P. Carter
©1935 Peer International Corporation, USA

PRETTY BOY FLOYD

written by Woody Guthrie,
Published by Harmony Music Limited on
behalf of Sanga Music Inc.

GOD BLESS AMERICA

NOBODY KNOWS YOU WHEN YOU'RE DOWN AND OUT

Nick Hayes is the author of
"The Rime of the Modern Mariner,"
an updating of Coleridge's
famous poem and among the most highly regarded
of recent British graphic novels.
A cartoonist for "The Guardian"
and "New Statesman," he works in a crow's nest
towering above a flower market in London.

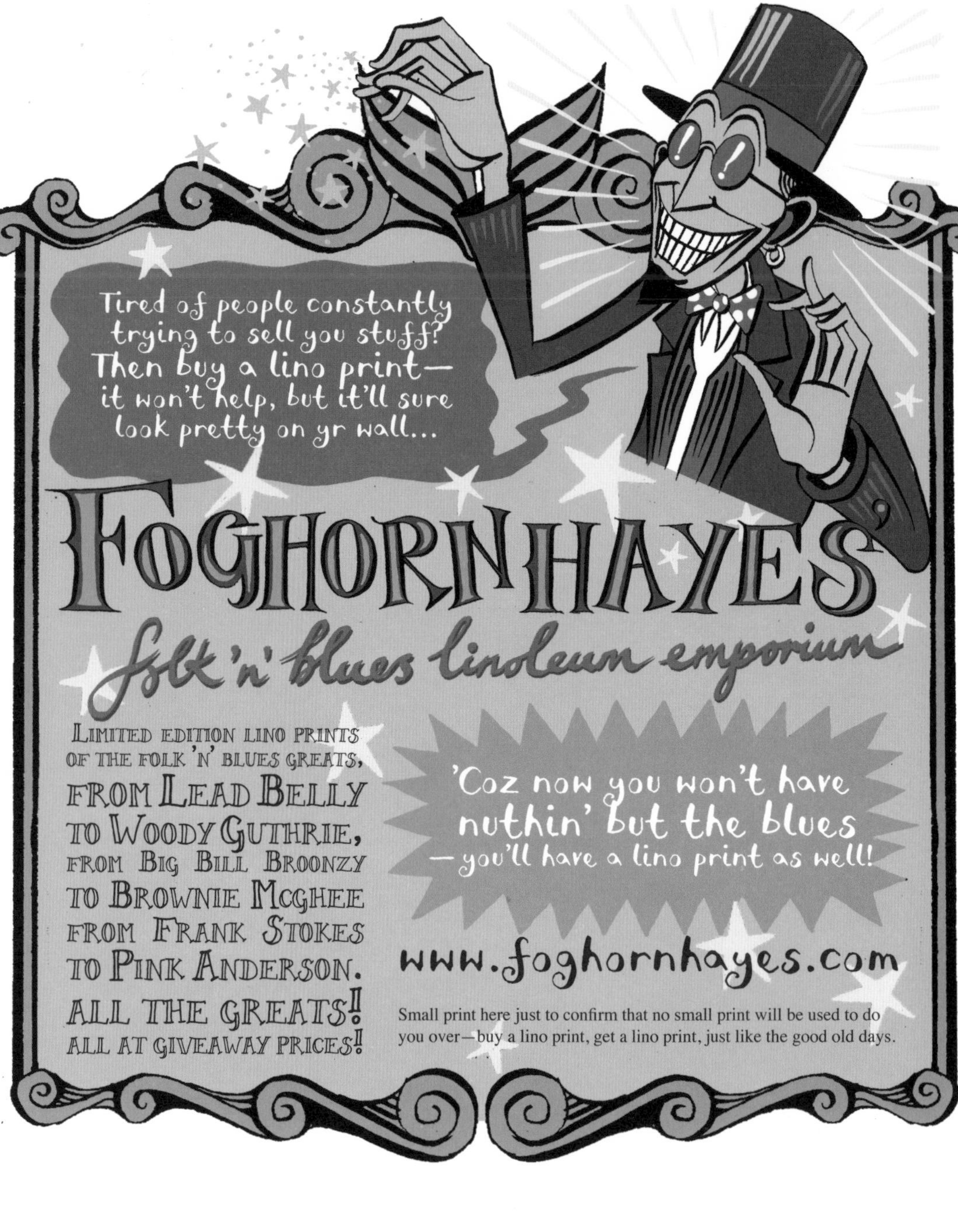
Tired of people constantly trying to sell you stuff? Then buy a lino print— it won't help, but it'll sure look pretty on yr wall...
FOGHORN HAYES'
folk 'n' blues linoleum emporium
LIMITED EDITION LINO PRINTS OF THE FOLK 'N' BLUES GREATS, FROM LEAD BELLY TO WOODY GUTHRIE, FROM BIG BILL BROONZY TO BROWNIE MCGHEE FROM FRANK STOKES TO PINK ANDERSON.
ALL THE GREATS! ALL AT GIVEAWAY PRICES!
'Coz now you won't have nuthin' but the blues —you'll have a lino print as well!
www.foghornhayes.com
Small print here just to confirm that no small print will be used to do you over—buy a lino print, get a lino print, just like the good old days.

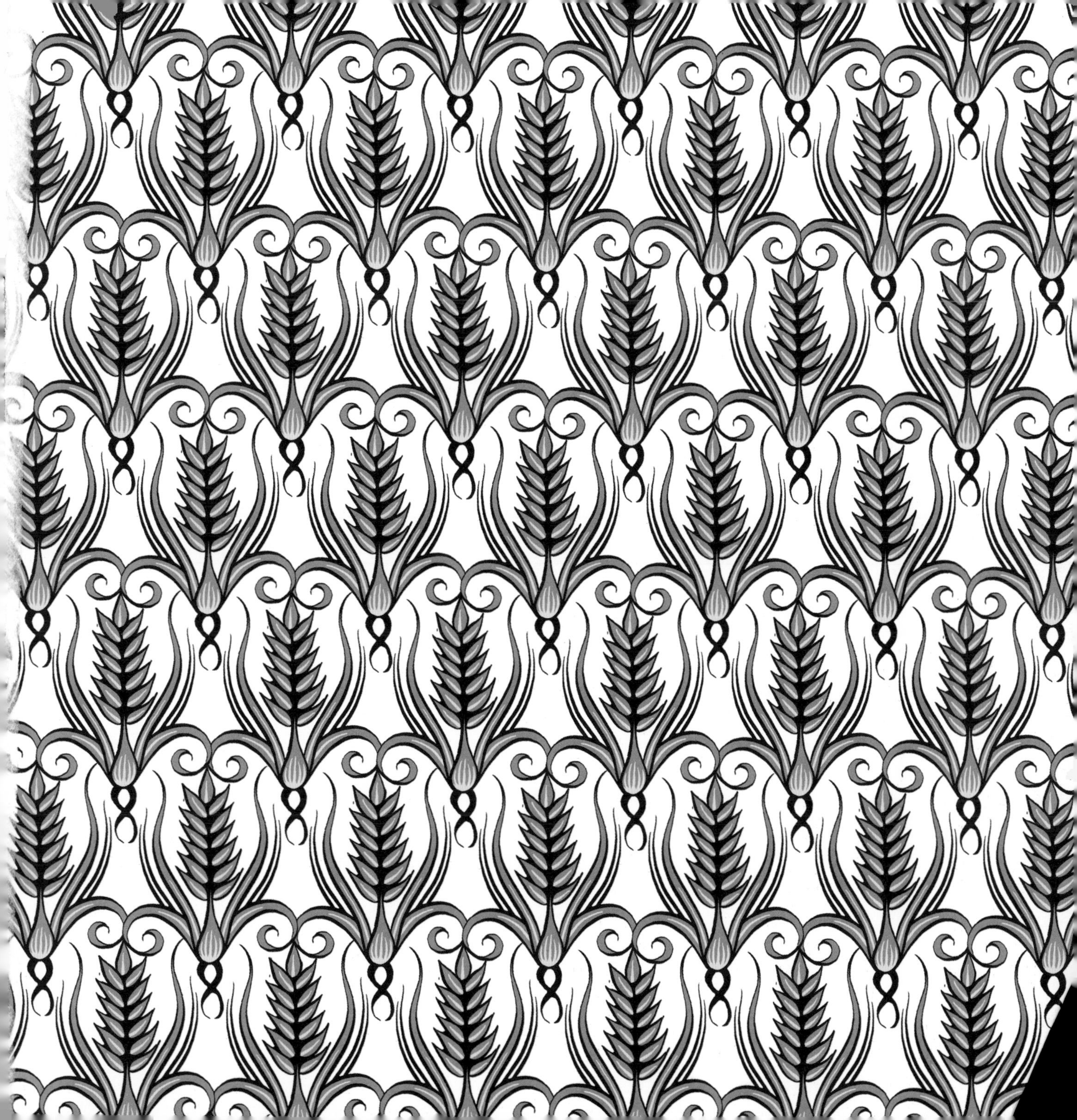

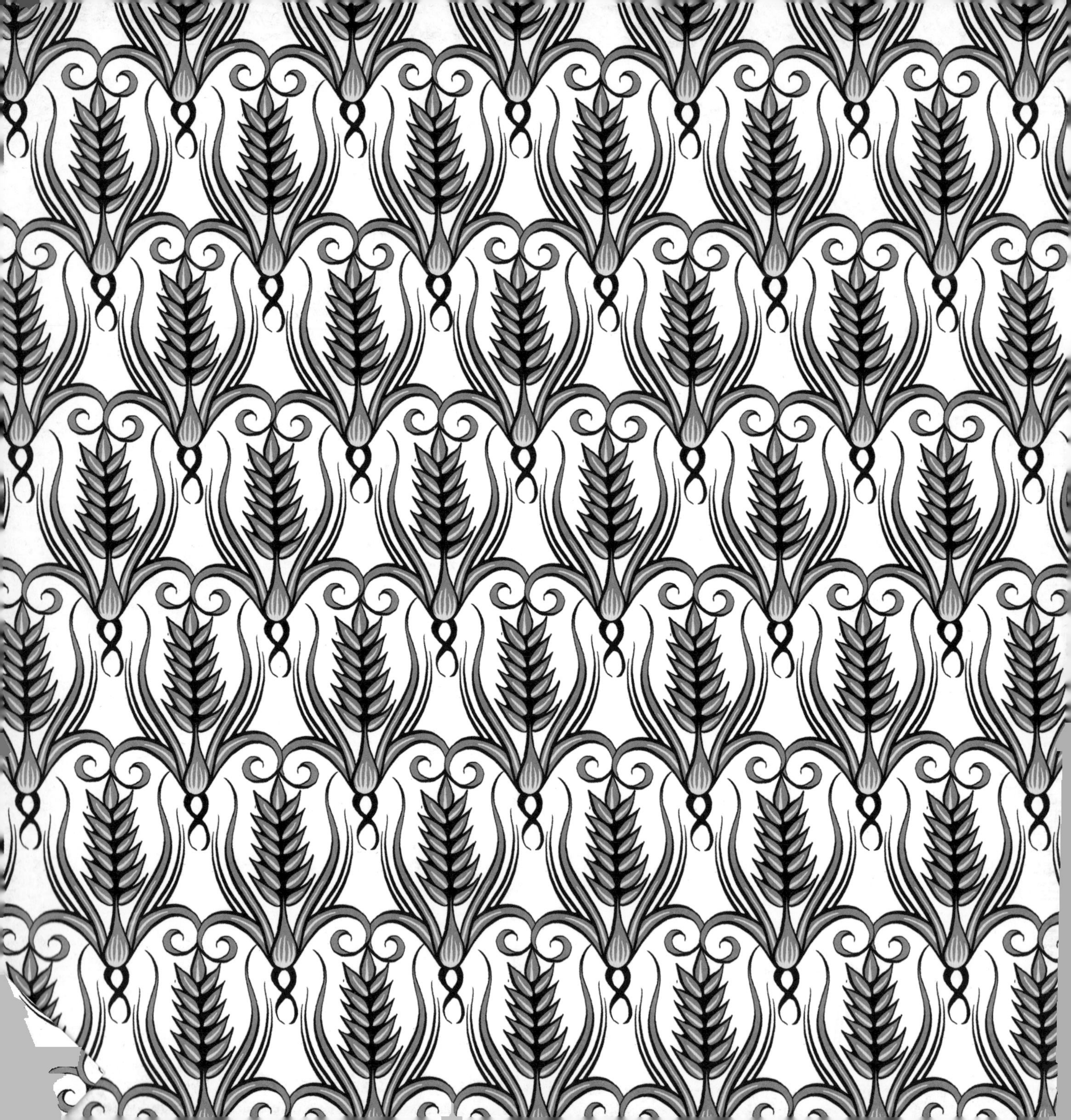